THE BEST OF NEWSPAPER DESIGN

7

1985
1986

SEVENTH EDITION CHAIRPERSON: ROB COVEY

BOOK DESIGN: JIM CHRISTIE
PRODUCTION: ELLEN ELFERING, JUDY STANLEY
COVER PHOTOGRAPHY: REX RYSTEDT
COMPETITION PHOTOGRAPHY: ALAN BERNER, TOM REESE
TOY NEWSBOY COURTESY OF DEAN LYMAN—A TRAIN HOUSE, SEATTLE, WA.

© 1986 THE SOCIETY OF NEWSPAPER DESIGN
LIBRARY OF CONGRESS CATALOG CARD NUMBER: 86-72316
ISBN: 0-89730-187-0

CONTENTS

THE COMPETITION 4

1
REGULARLY APPEARING NEWS SECTION 8

2
NEWS PAGE DESIGN 23

3
BREAKING NEWS 31

4
SPECIAL NEWS TOPICS 50

5
REGULARLY APPEARING FEATURES SECTION 61

6
FEATURES PAGE DESIGN 70

7
SINGLE SUBJECT 88

8
NEWSPAPER SPECIAL SECTIONS 95

9
NEWSPAPER MAGAZINE REPRINTS 110

10
NEWSPAPER OVERALL DESIGN 112

11
MAGAZINE OVERALL DESIGN 117

12
MAGAZINE SPECIAL SECTIONS 122

13
MAGAZINE COVER DESIGN 127

14
MAGAZINE PAGE DESIGN 130

15
ART AND ILLUSTRATION 139

16
PHOTOGRAPHY AND PHOTOJOURNALISM 156

17
INFORMATIONAL GRAPHICS 182

18
TYPOGRAPHY IN DESIGN 198

19
MISCELLANEOUS 199

INDEX 207

1985
1986

7
THE COMPETITION

Louis Silverstein, Design Consultant, *The New York Times*.

Marshall Arisman, Chairman, Visual Journalism, School of Visual Arts, New York.

What you'll find in the following pages is the best work submitted from 300 newspapers from eight nations participating in the Seventh Annual Design Competition sponsored by the Society of Newspaper Design.

Twelve tough-minded judges spent two long days in Seattle in early June sorting through more than 9,600 entries. They selected the top 5 percent of the entries as worthy of 398 Awards of Excellence, 48 Silver Awards and two Gold Awards. Without a doubt, this was a demanding jury. But it was also a jury well qualified to be that way.

One Gold Award went to John Cayea of *The New York Times* for his art direction of the Week in Review section. Judges were impressed by the clear and consistent format that incorporates good typography, photographs and graphics into a vigorous, newsy, yet well-ordered presentation.

Photographer David Leeson of *The Dallas Morning News* earned the only other Gold for a stunning portrayal of the troubles in South Africa. Judges were impressed that every image in this 22-page special section contributed something new and significant. Under difficult circumstances, Leeson captured a whole range of emotions that offers the reader new insights and empathy for a country at war with itself.

What else did the judges like?

Novedades for one. The judges found this Mexico City newspaper refreshingly different, something new in a sea of sameness. Lou Silverstein, design consultant to *The New York Times*, observed that the roots of its unique appearance come from its different journalistic approach.

"It's as though all the rest of us were using the same big building blocks

Ronn Campisi, Design Director, *The Boston Globe*.

Richard A. Curtis, Managing Editor/Graphics and Photography, *USA Today*.

4 The Best of Newspaper Design

Michael Keegan, Assistant Managing Editor/News Art, *The Washington Post*.

and they decided to use little mosaics," he said. The result was a Silver Award to Roger Black, Mario Garcia, and Claudio Rodriguez for overall design, one of only two medal awards given for newspapers in the overall design category.

The other Silver in overall design went to *The Washington Times*. This is the second time this newspaper has garnered a Silver from a panel of Society judges for its overall design and the fourth year in a row that it has won in this category. Judges find it to be a paper in which everything works together.

Though not represented in the overall design category, a clear favorite was *The Wall Street Journal*. The *Journal* picked up four Silver Awards and six Awards of Excellence. Three of the Silvers came from special-section entries

Rob Covey, Design Director, *The Seattle Times*.

Johnny Maupin, Art Director, *The Courier-Journal* and *The Louisville Times*.

where the judges gave special plaudits to the typographic sophistication. The typography style maintained a clear link with the daily newspaper but reordered the emphasis to create a new and distinctive voice. Additionally, three *Journal* artists won Awards of Excellence for their illustration portfolios.

But the competition's big winner for the seventh year in a row was *The New York Times*, gathering one Gold, two Silvers and 43 Awards of Excellence. Other leading award-winners were *The Boston Globe* with three Silvers and 30 Awards of Excellence, and *The Seattle Times* with two Silvers and 26 Awards of Excellence.

Among the foreign entries, judges awarded a Silver to *Dagens Nyheter* for its coverage of the assassination of Prime Minister Olof Palme.

Throughout all categories, the jury responded favorably to greater use of white space—between stories and headlines, around photos and between lines of type. Judges favored

April Silver, free-lance designer, former Art Director of *Esquire* magazine.

Jack W. Dykinga, free-lance photographer.

"designs that didn't use a hundred rules to separate everything."

As Silverstein put it during the wrap-up discussion, "As my strength began to ebb, I became disgusted with newsprint. The goddamned type is so dirty. I kept changing my glasses in the hope that things would improve. The one thing I'm going to do in my next design is get some space in and around the characters. More lead!"

What did the judges find lacking? How can newspapers improve most?

Start with typography. Judges were uniformly critical of our collective pro-

Seventh Edition 5

Phil Nesbitt, Assistant Managing Editor/Graphics, *The Record*, Bergen, N.J.

gress in basic typographic sophistication. Hayward Blake, president of Hayward Blake Co., who judged SND's First Edition seven years ago, noted that while the general level of newspaper design has risen in that period of time, it still has not come as far as one would hope or expect. "Considering the point that they are redone each day, you'd think in this many years you could do it better. But the typography is so loaded, jammed, with no air and handled so heavy-handedly."

Judges complained about the uncontrolled, unrestrained use of color. Johnny Maupin, Art Director of *The Courier-Journal* and *The Louisville Times*, observed, "It's gotten to the point where it's really overdone. It's not even legible anymore. You can't even read the type."

verstein postulated that "three-fourths of them are going in a totally wrong direction. They are more confusing than they are clarifying."

Richard Curtis, Assistant Managing Editor/Graphics and Photography at *USA Today*, expressed disappointment at how few maps were entered in the competition. "The map should just be a basic part of reporting, like a headline."

Another concern: lookalikes. "Everybody is imitating everybody else at this point. You either look like *The Seattle Times*, *USA Today*, *The Washington Times* or two or three other papers," lamented Dick Cheverton, Assistant Managing Editor/Features at *The Orange County Register*.

Cheverton, Curtis and others discussed the need for a major conference to

Hayward R. Blake, President, Hayward Blake and Co., a Chicago design firm.

And our distinguished crew was not much impressed with the run of informational graphics, either. Phil Nesbitt, Assistant Managing Editor/Graphics for *The* (Bergen, N.J.) *Record*, called them "forced." Sil-

Richard E. Cheverton, Assistant Managing Editor/Features, *The Orange County Register*.

explore where we go from here. Sandra Eisert, Photo Editor of *The San Jose Mercury News* cautioned, "To get from where we're at to the kind of change that needs to be made requires a heck of a lot more cooperation, interest and support — a completely different league of support and backing and effort."

Once again, Lou Silverstein tossed the clincher: "It's not a design problem; it's a journalist problem."

And so it is.

I'd like to express my deep appreciation to the hard-working judges who gave the best of their minds and bodies. Their energy and intelligence gave us this exceptional group of winners.

My thanks also goes to the scores of volunteers who helped orchestrate this competition from the opening call for entries through proofing the last bluelines.

Rob Covey
Design Director,
The Seattle Times

Sandra Eisert, Photo Editor, *San Jose Mercury News*.

7
AWARD WINNERS

1985
1986

1

REGULARLY
APPEARING
NEWS SECTION

Entries consisted of three complete sections, from three different dates, representing either national, local, business or sports news.

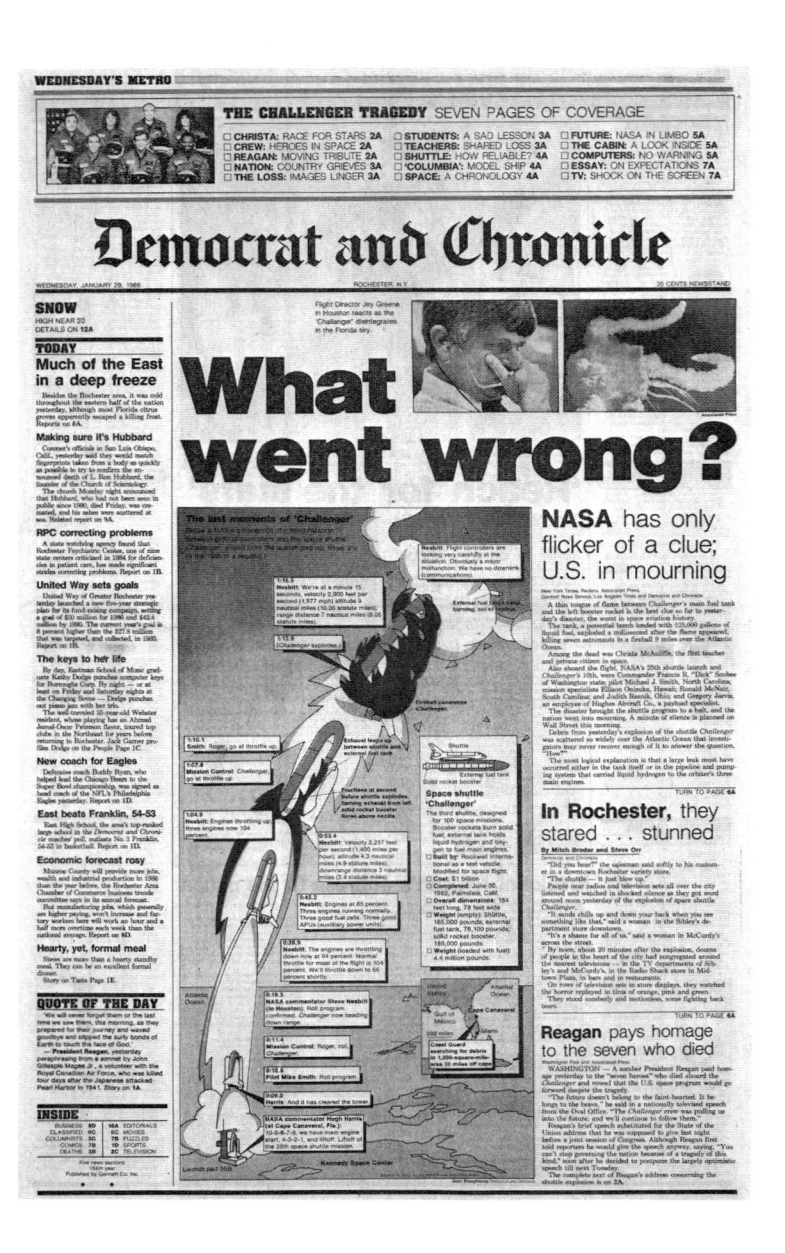

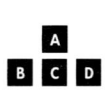

SILVER AWARD

A-D DEMOCRAT AND CHRONICLE
Dale Peskin, Dierck Casselman, Matt Dudek, Mark Wert, Joette Riehle, Christy Bradford, Bill Hawken

SILVER AWARD

A-E THE ORANGE COUNTY REGISTER
Staff

1
MAIN NEWS SECTION

A–E USA TODAY
Richard Curtis

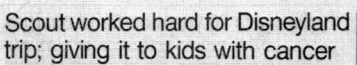

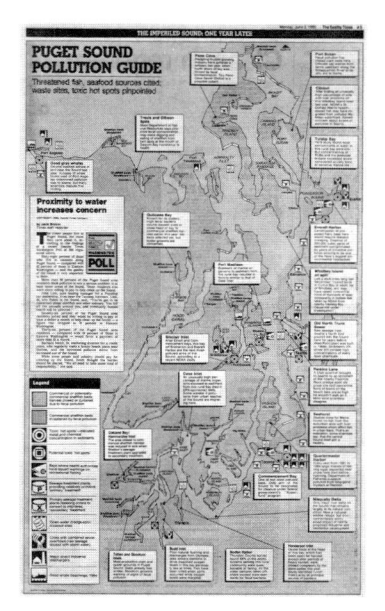

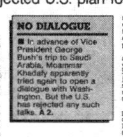

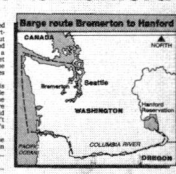

A-E THE SEATTLE TIMES
Staff

1
MAIN NEWS SECTION

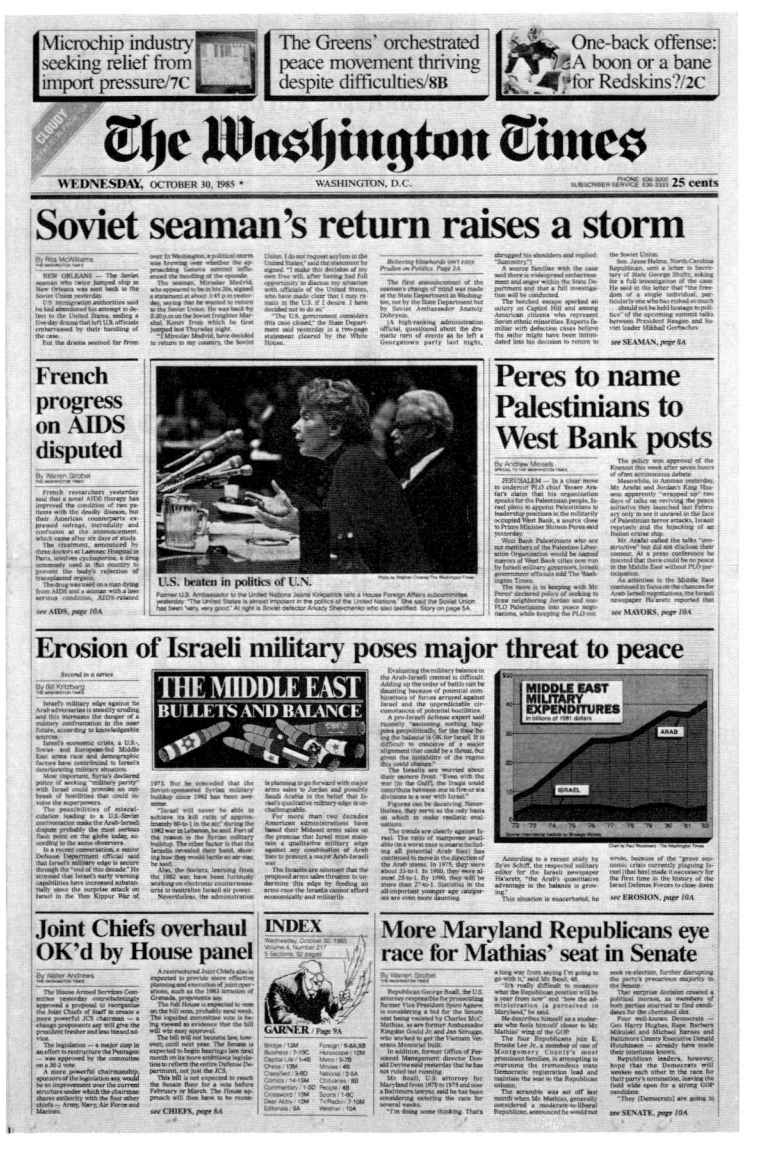

A-D THE WASHINGTON TIMES
Staff

12 The Best of Newspaper Design

A-E MONTGOMERY JOURNAL
Lisa M. Griffis

1
MAIN NEWS SECTION

A,B THE ORLANDO SENTINEL
Staff

C-E TIMES-UNION
Ray Stanczak

14   The Best of Newspaper Design

LOCAL NEWS SECTION

A,C,D THE WASHINGTON TIMES
Henry Christopher

B,E THE SEATTLE TIMES
Staff

1
SPORTS SECTION

A-C THE HARTFORD COURANT
Staff

D-F USA TODAY
Richard Curtis

16 The Best of Newspaper Design

A-D THE ORANGE COUNTY REGISTER
Jim Colonna, Staff

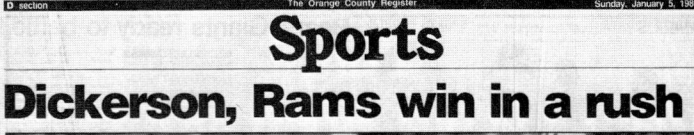

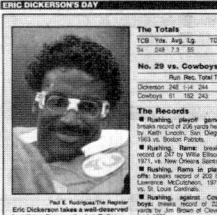

1

BUSINESS SECTION

SILVER AWARD
A-E USA TODAY
Richard Curtis

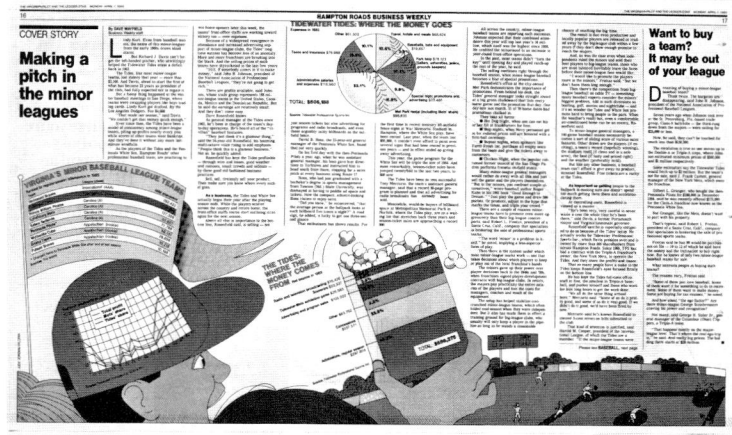

SILVER AWARD

A-F THE VIRGINIAN-PILOT/
LEDGER-STAR
Sam Hundley, Judy Jordan-Valoria,
Chris Kouba, Alan Jacobson

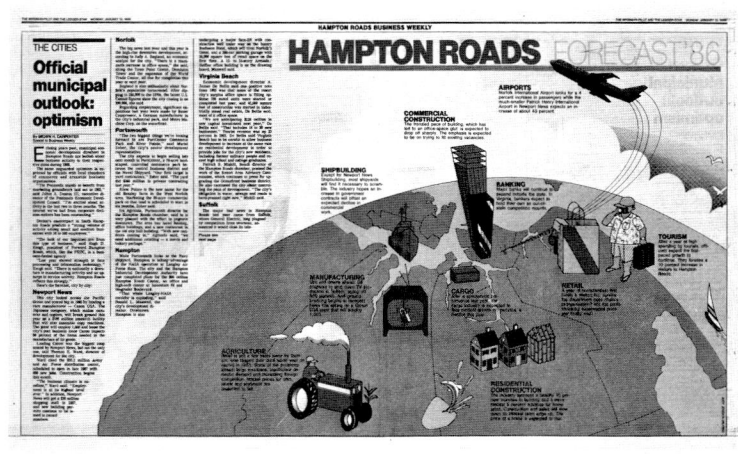

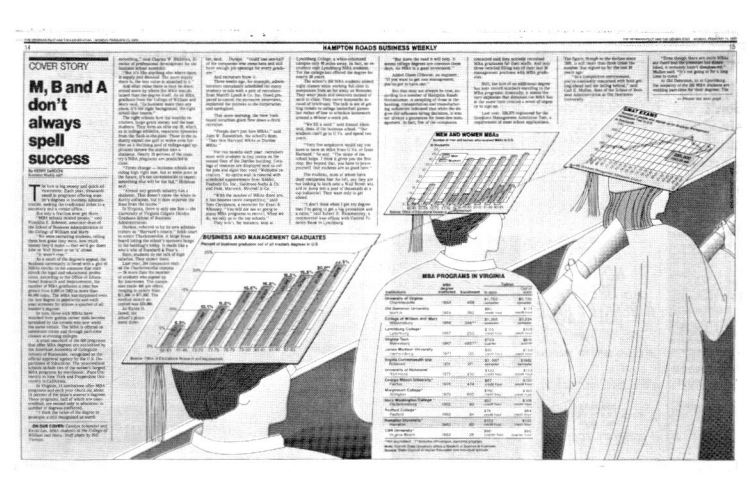

1

BUSINESS SECTION

A B C
D E F

A-C THE MIAMI HERALD
Matt Walsh, Bob Barkin, Ana Lense, Randy Stano

D-F THE SEATTLE TIMES
Staff

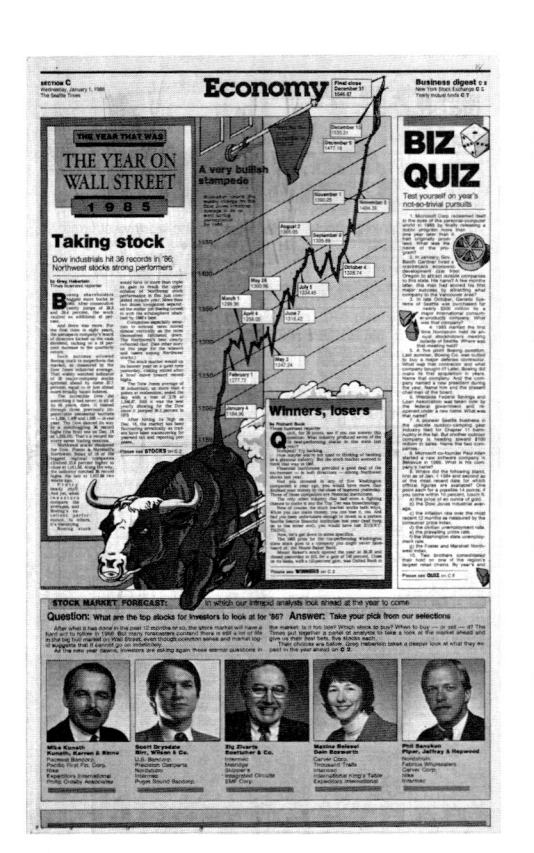

20 The Best of Newspaper Design

A-F DALLAS TIMES HERALD
Chris Butler, John Green

Seventh Edition 21

1

OTHER NEWS SECTION

GOLD AWARD

A-F THE NEW YORK TIMES
John Cayea, Art Director

22   The Best of Newspaper Design

2

NEWS PAGE DESIGN

Entries consisted of full pages taken from the national, local, business or sports sections.

A B
C D

A MONTGOMERY JOURNAL
Lisa M. Griffis

B RESTON TIMES
William Castronuovo

C THE LEDGER
David Farnham

D THE FINANCIAL POST
Jackie Young, Paul Stulberg, Neville Nankivell

Seventh Edition 23

2
FRONT PAGE DESIGN

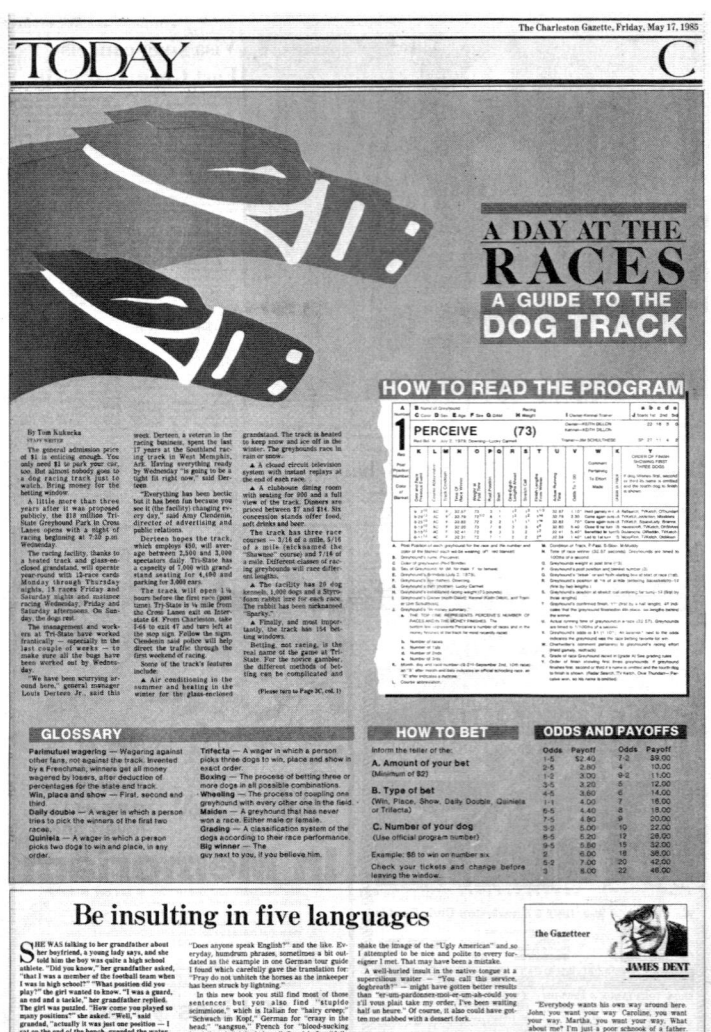

2
LOCAL NEWS FRONT

A MONTGOMERY JOURNAL
Les Brindley

B THE CHARLESTON GAZETTE
Tim Cochran, Brenda Pinnell

C ANCHORAGE DAILY NEWS
Dwight Boyles, Don Byron

24   The Best of Newspaper Design

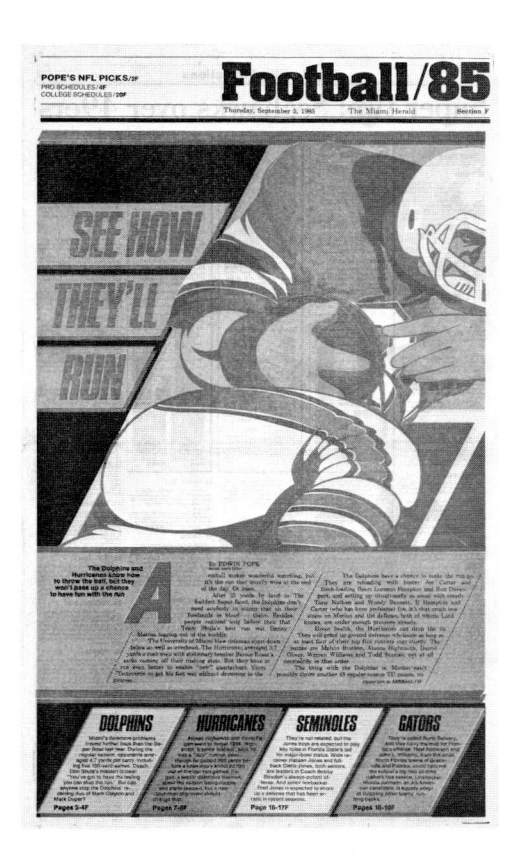

A THE NEW YORK TIMES
Ron Couture, Art Director
John MacLeod, Designer

B THE MIAMI HERALD
Kent Barton

C THE HARTFORD COURANT
Randy Cox, Peter Hoey

D LOS ANGELES TIMES
Chuck Nigash

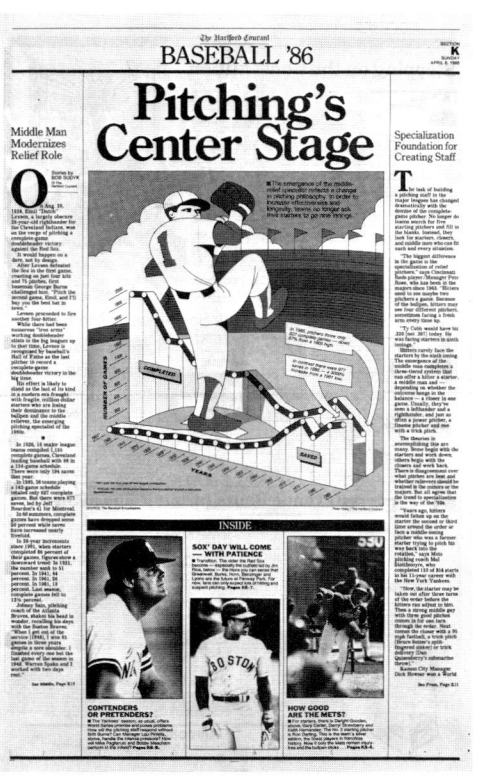

Seventh Edition 25

2

BUSINESS FRONT

SILVER AWARD

A THE COLUMBUS DISPATCH
Mary Knueven

B SAN JOSE MERCURY NEWS
Chuck Waltmire, Brad Zucroff,
Mark Scwanhaisser

C THE NEW YORK TIMES
Greg Ryan, Art Director

D THE NEW YORK TIMES
Greg Ryan, Art Director

26 The Best of Newspaper Design

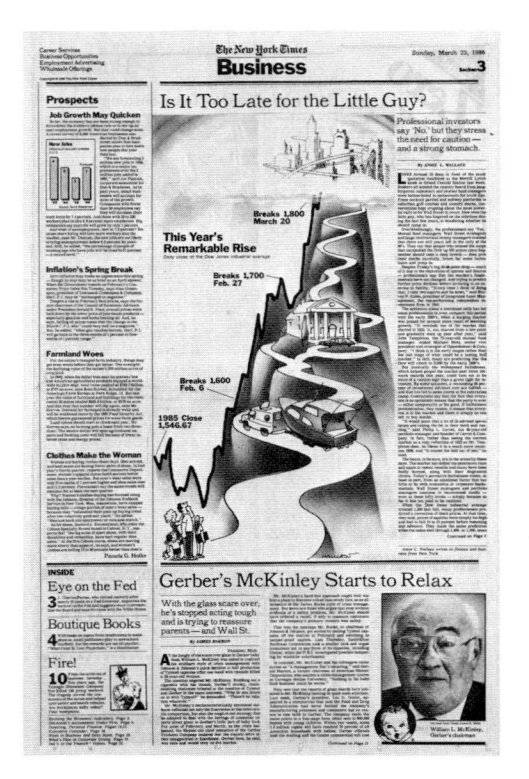

A USA TODAY
Richard Curtis

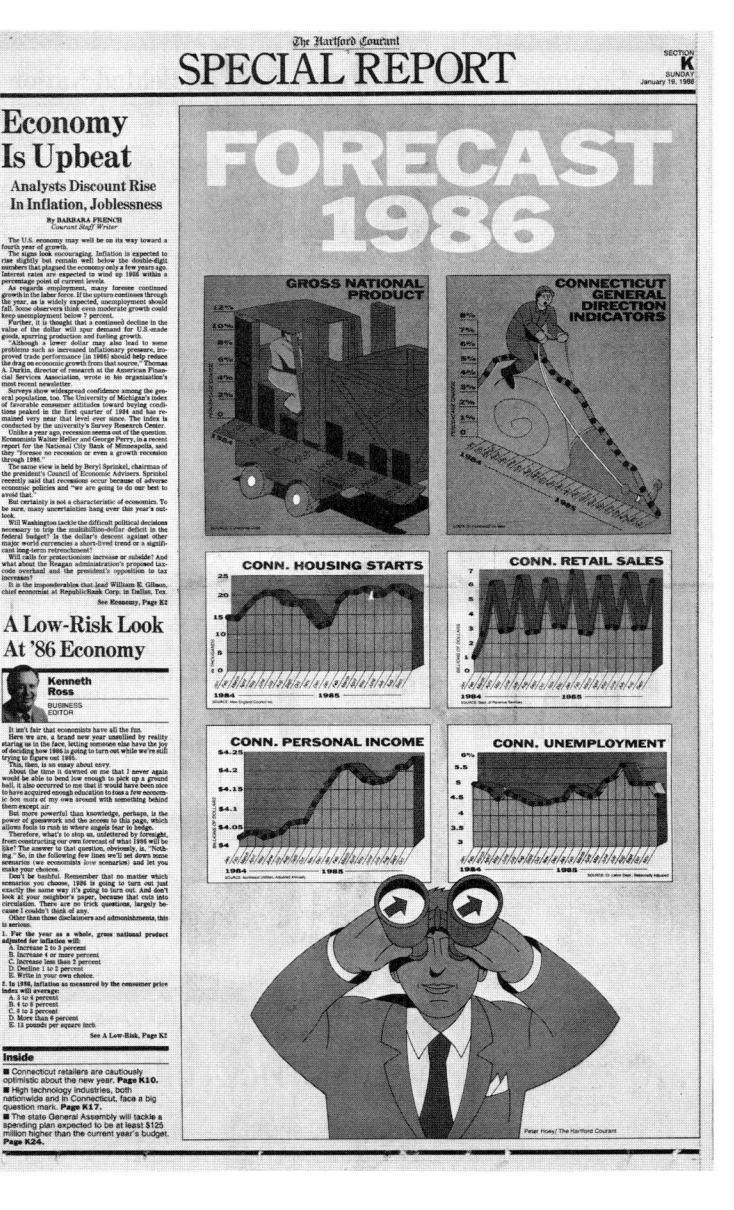

B THE CHICAGO TRIBUNE
Kevin P. Fewell, Art Director

C USA TODAY
Richard Curtis

D THE HARTFORD COURANT
Peter Hoey

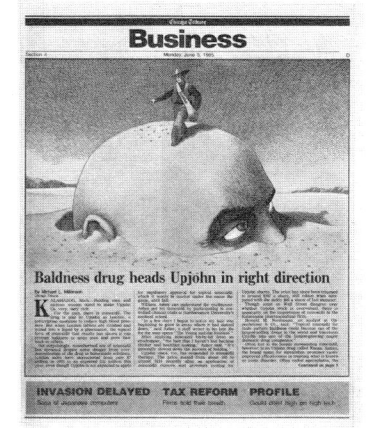

2
BUSINESS FRONT

Seventh Edition 27

2
OTHER NEWS FRONT

A THE CHICAGO TRIBUNE
Earl Toledo, Art Director

B SAN JOSE MERCURY NEWS
Karen Karlsson, Brad Zucroff, Paul Engstrom

C THE FINANCIAL POST
Paul Stulberg

D THE WALL STREET JOURNAL
Jerry Litofsky, Karl Hartig, Randy Price

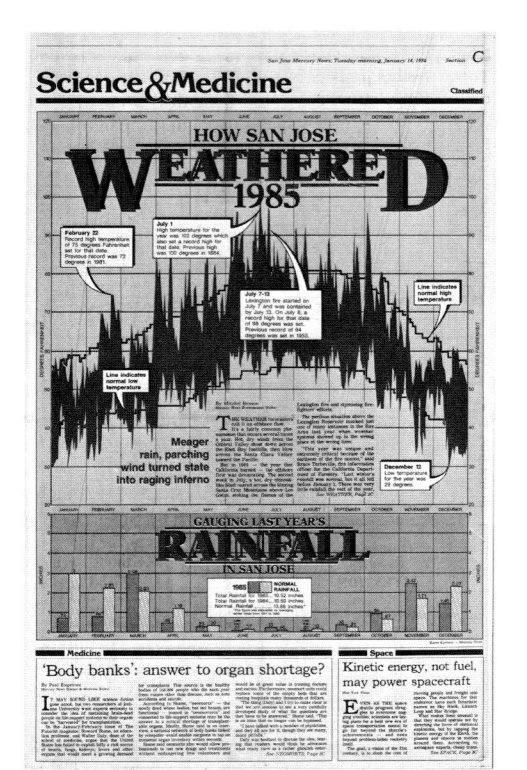

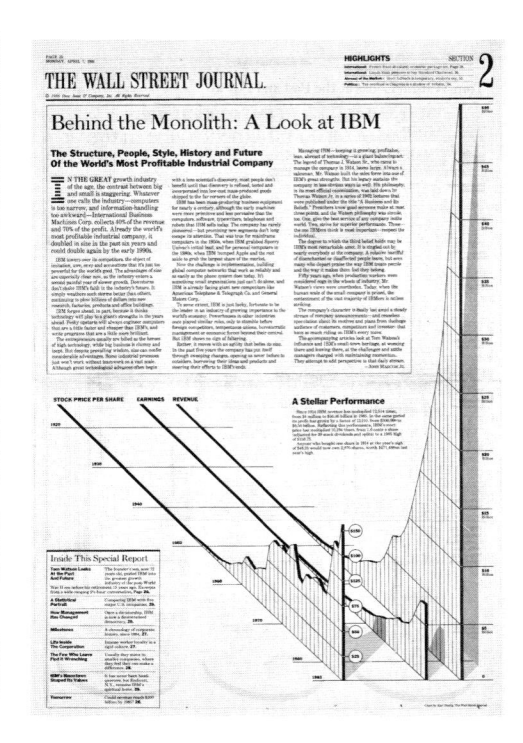

28   The Best of Newspaper Design

2
INSIDE NEWS PAGES

A THE DALLAS MORNING NEWS
George Benge

B THE MESA TRIBUNE
Marcy Manley, Dave Seibert

C USA TODAY
David Miller, Bob Laird

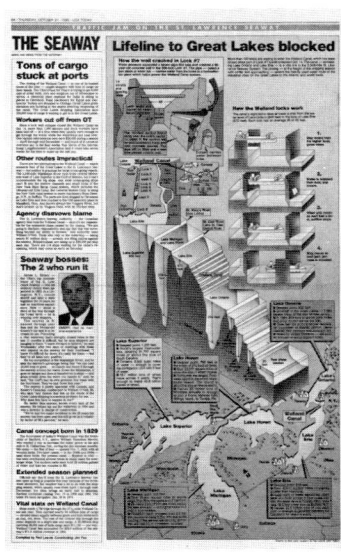

Seventh Edition 29

2
INSIDE NEWS PAGES

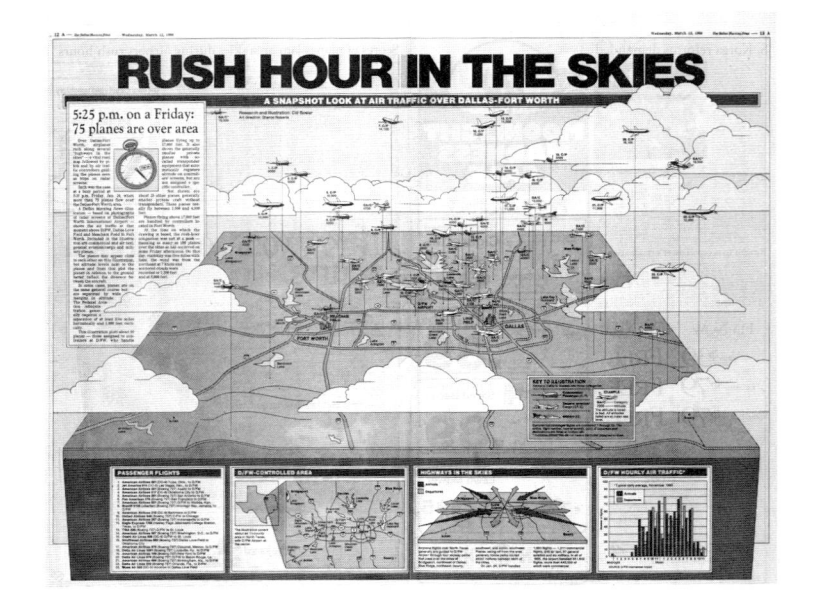

A THE DALLAS MORNING NEWS
Clif Bosler, Sharon Roberts

B THE SAN DIEGO UNION
Ray Downey-Laskowitz, Chris Ross

C THE NEW YORK TIMES
Tom Bodkin, Art Director; Nancy Lee, Graphic

D THE SAN FRANCISCO EXAMINER
Roman Lyskowski

30 The Best of Newspaper Design

3
BREAKING NEWS

Entries consisted of full pages from the nearest complete news cycle reporting the Mexican earthquake, Colombian volcano, space shuttle disaster or other major news event.

A-E THE DALLAS MORNING NEWS
Staff

3
MEXICAN
EARTHQUAKE

A–D THE SAN FRANCISCO
EXAMINER
Staff

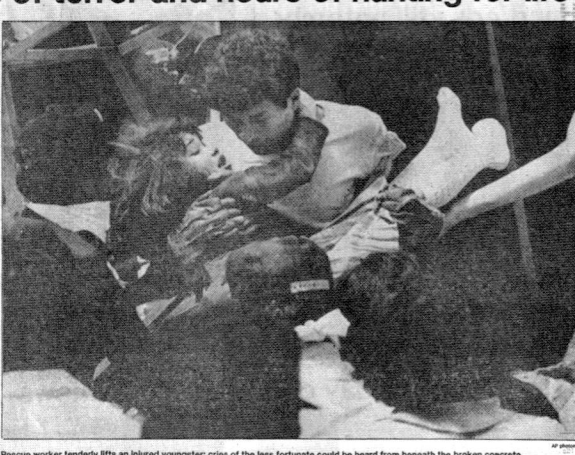

32   The Best of Newspaper Design

SILVER AWARD

A-D THE SEATTLE TIMES
Rob Covey, Chuck Taylor, Liz Nielsen

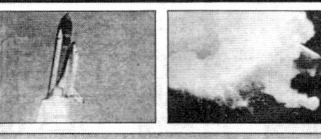

3

SHUTTLE DISASTER

SILVER AWARD

A-D ANCHORAGE DAILY NEWS
Jim Mackinicki, Mike Campbell, Tom Setzer

SILVER AWARD

A-D THE ORLANDO SENTINEL
Staff

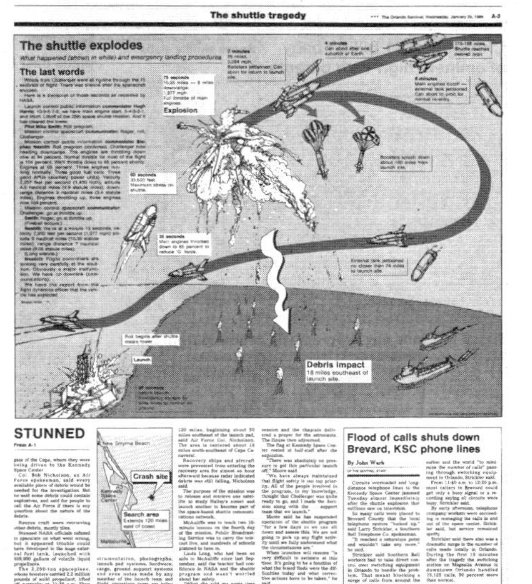

SHUTTLE DISASTER

SILVER AWARD

A-D DEMOCRAT AND CHRONICLE

Christy Bradford, Joette Riehle, Dale Peskin, Dierck Casselman, Janet Shaughnessy, Allen Dise, Andrea Kundin, Matt Dudek, David Cowles

Shuttle explodes; crew of seven dies

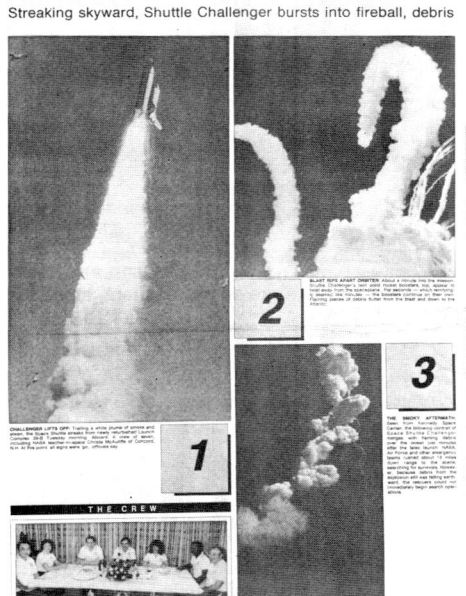

SHUTTLE DISASTER

The Shuttle Tragedy: Nine Full Pages of Coverage

- The astronauts had no way to escape ... 10A
- Cheers, then horror at McAuliffe's school ... 11A
- Reagan says space program must go on ... 11A
- Christa McAuliffe: A place in history ... 13A
- Accomplishments, disasters in space ... 14A
- How the Bay Area's kids reacted ... 1E

Wednesday morning, January 29, 1986

San Jose Mercury News

Serving Northern California Since 1851

25 cents — Morning Final

A nation mourns its 7 space heroes

NASA starts hunt for cause of worst space-program disaster

The space shuttle Challenger, carrying a crew of seven, explodes 10 miles above the Atlantic Ocean just 72 seconds after a spectacular launch

Fuel-tank leak is focus of speculation on blast

Faith in technology to make dreams come true shattered

Inside
NFL players union to fight Pats' testing — Sports

The Weather
Rain today. High near 65.

A-D SAN JOSE MERCURY NEWS
David Yarnold, Marty Gradel, Jeff Thomas, Dale Cockerill, Graham David Frazier

Valley's blind faith in technology is shattered

Day of celebration becomes day of catastrophe at JPL

Living

The shuttle disaster was especially tough for children, who had cheered on the first teacher in space

Students try to cope

School kids express sorrow

Anchors seek explanations amid shock

One tragic jolt back to reality

Cheers at launch site turn to grim silence

What they said about the tragedy

A-D THE HOUSTON POST
Staff

3
SHUTTLE DISASTER

A-D SAN ANTONIO LIGHT
Ted Warmbold and staff

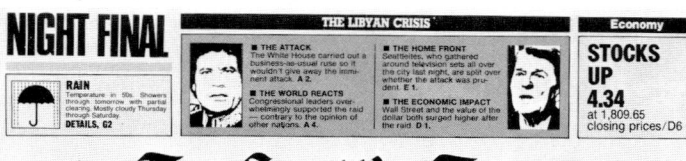

3
DESIGNER'S CHOICE
NATIONAL

A B
C D

SILVER AWARD
A-D THE SEATTLE TIMES
Rob Covey, Chuck Taylor

Seventh Edition 41

SILVER AWARD

A-F DAGENS NYHETER
Staff

MORDET PÅ PALME

Eleven efterträdde läromästaren. Under extatisk stämning valdes Olof Palme till ny partiledare den 1 oktober 1969. Palmes tacktal till Tage Erlander var en lysande oratorisk prestation.

Han gjorde politiken spännande

Av SVEN SVENSSON

Olof Palme hade stor lidelse för demokrati och frihet. De små staternas oberoende såg han som ett omistligt inslag i kampen för freden. Inställningen gjorde Olof Palme till en av världens mest respekterade politiska ledare.

Från studentpolitiker till statsminister

MORDET PÅ PALME

Skjuten bakifrån på mycket nära håll

MORDET PÅ PALME

"Vi respekterade Palmes önskan"

Kontrollen på Arlanda skärptes

Svårt att bevaka gränser i söder

MORDET PÅ PALME

Ingvar Carlsson ny statsminister

Expeditionsministär regerar tills vidare

Palmes problemknäckare

Vi har valt den vi anser bäst skickad

Öppenheten får inte minska

MORDET PÅ PALME

Över tiotusen människor samlades på Sergels torg för att hedra Olof Palmes minne. Hundratals facklor lyste i den kalla natten.

Tiotusen hedrade Palme

Av MATS CARLBOM och BO WESTMAR

Över 10 000 människor samlades på Sergels torg i Stockholm på lördagskvällen för att hedra den bortgångne Olof Palme. Tysta, sammanbitna, allvarliga stod de där medan många hundra facklor lyste upp den mörka vinterkvällen.

Högmässans bön

En speciell bön med anledning av mordet på statsminister Olof Palme kommer att läsas i kyrkor vid söndagens högmässa. Det är biskopen i Stockholm, Krister Stendahl, som rekommenderat att följande bön används:

O Gud, du som i Jesus Kristus kommer till oss
vapenlös men starkare än all världens makt
I vår bestörtning och vanmakt söker vi oss till Dig
Bryt våldets meningslöshet såsom du allena kan
I dina händer överlämnar vi Olof Palme
Hans liv och hans verk
Låt oss inte sörja som hade vi inget hopp
Beskydda Sveriges land och folk dessa dagar
I Jesu namn
Amen

"Hur kan någon vara så ond?"

Av INGEMAR LÖFGREN

3

DESIGNER'S CHOICE
LOCAL

SILVER AWARD

A-K THE COURIER JOURNAL
Johnny Maupin, Jerry Ryan

44   The Best of Newspaper Design

Seventh Edition 45

3

DESIGNER'S CHOICE
LOCAL

A B C D

A-D DALLAS TIMES HERALD
Staff

46   The Best of Newspaper Design

A-D ANCHORAGE DAILY NEWS
Jim Mackinicki, Tom Setzer, Mike Campbell

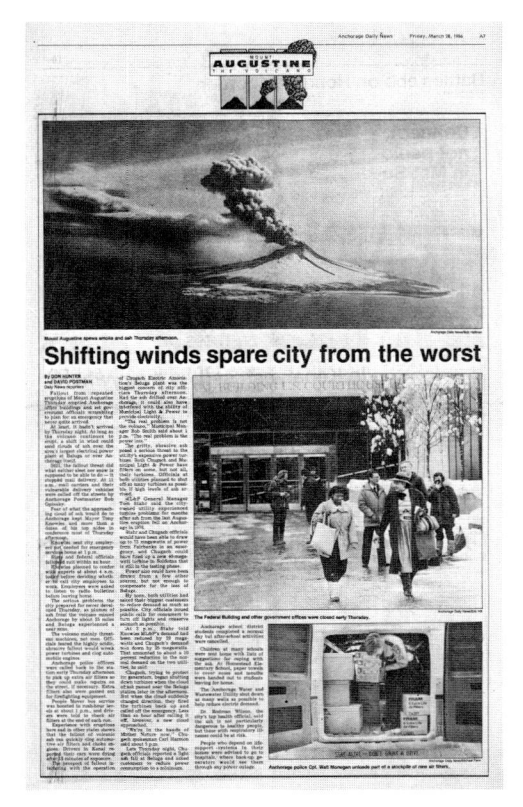

3

DESIGNER'S CHOICE
LOCAL

A-D THE PRESS DEMOCRAT
Randy Wright, Randy Seelye,
Jime Fremgen

3

DESIGNER'S CHOICE
LOCAL

A-E THE DALLAS MORNING NEWS
Staff

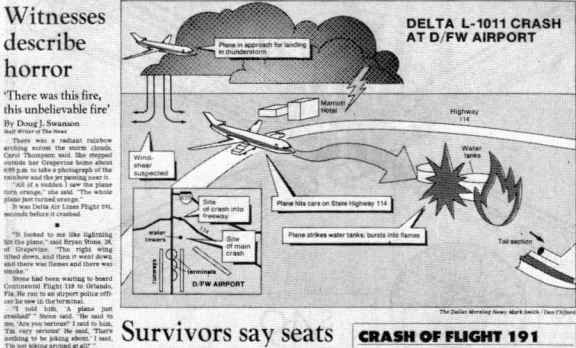

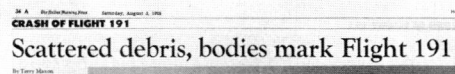

4

SPECIAL

NEWS TOPICS

Entries consisted of no more than five days of coverage of these themes: The Budget Deficit • A Year of Helping • The Fall of Marcos • other major national or local stories.

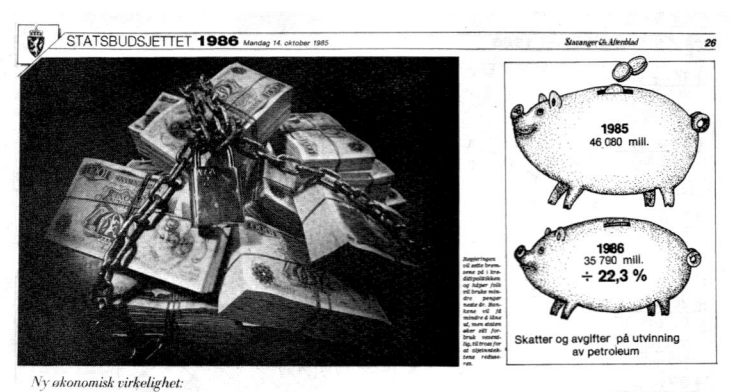

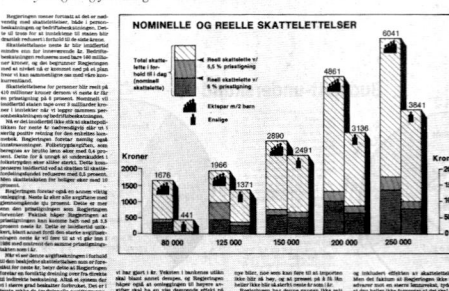

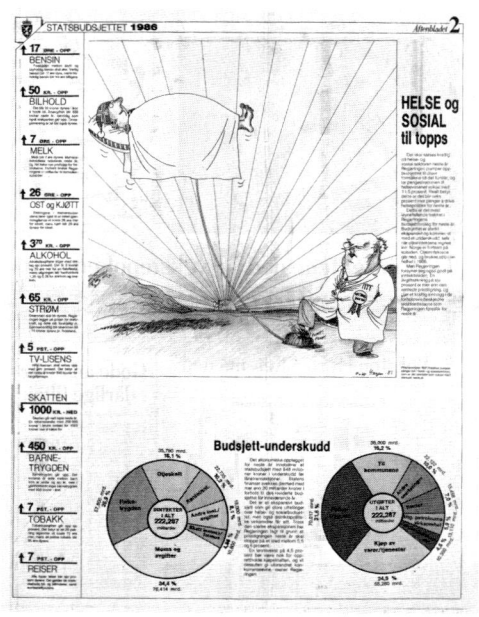

A-E STAVANGER AFTENBLAD
Staff

4

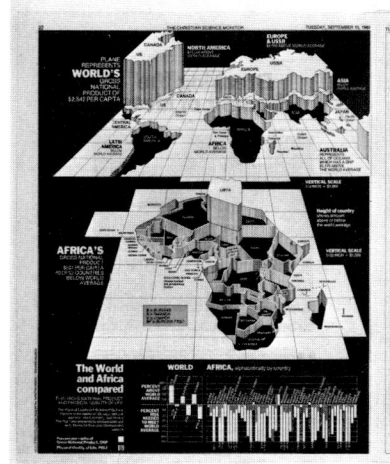

A YEAR OF HELPING

A,B THE HARTFORD COURANT
Randy Cox, Phil Lohman

C-F THE CHRISTIAN SCIENCE MONITOR
Robin Jareaux

Seventh Edition 51

4
THE FALL OF MARCOS

A-E SAN JOSE MERCURY NEWS
David Yarnold, Brad Zucroff

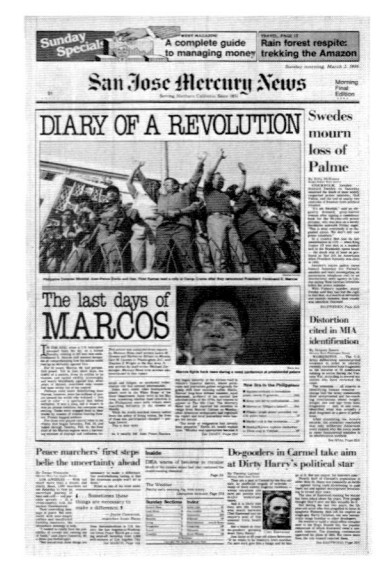

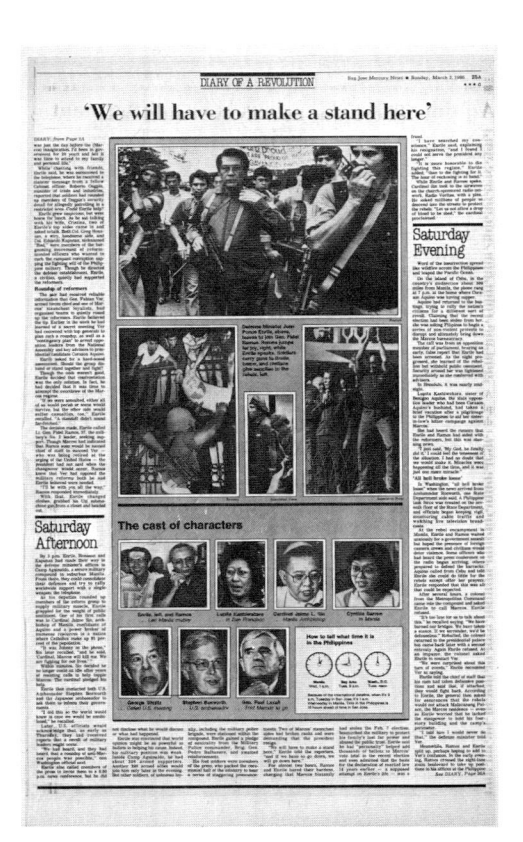

52 The Best of Newspaper Design

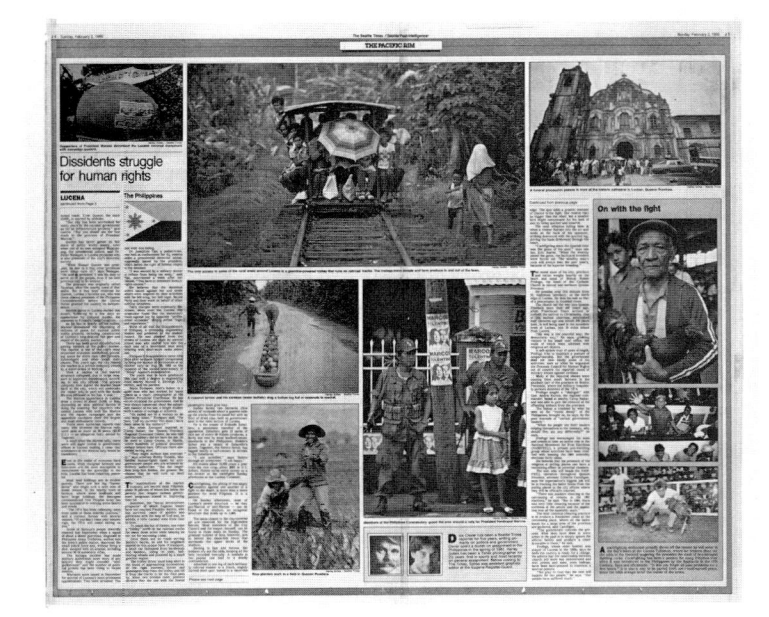

4

THE FALL OF MARCOS

A-D THE SEATTLE TIMES
Robert Massa, Chuck Taylor, Fred Nelson; Photos by Harley Soltes

Seventh Edition 53

4

DESIGNER'S CHOICE
NATIONAL

A B
C D

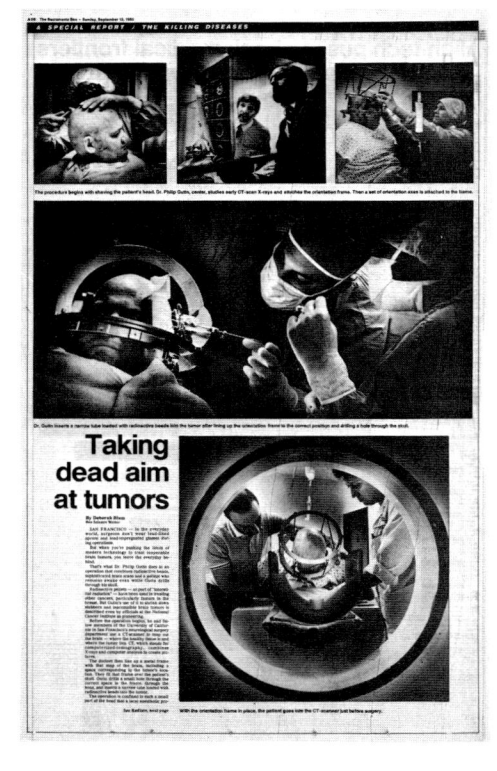

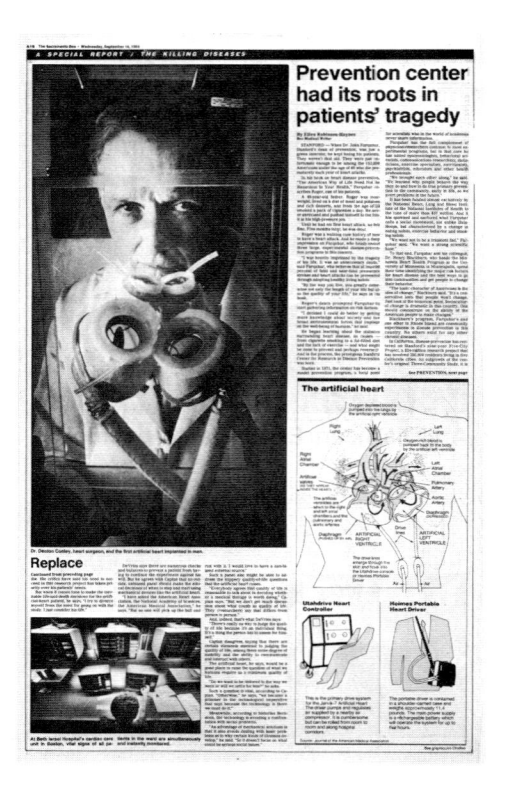

A-D THE SACRAMENTO BEE
Ed Canale

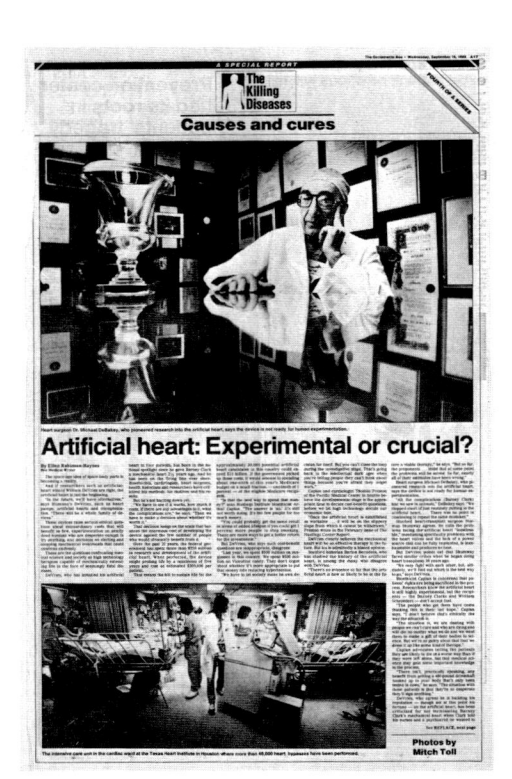

4

DESIGNER'S CHOICE
NATIONAL

A B
C D
E
F

A-F THE CHRISTIAN SCIENCE
MONITOR
Robin Jareaux

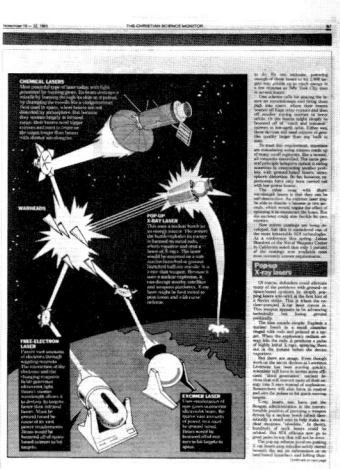

Seventh Edition 55

4

DESIGNER'S CHOICE
NATIONAL

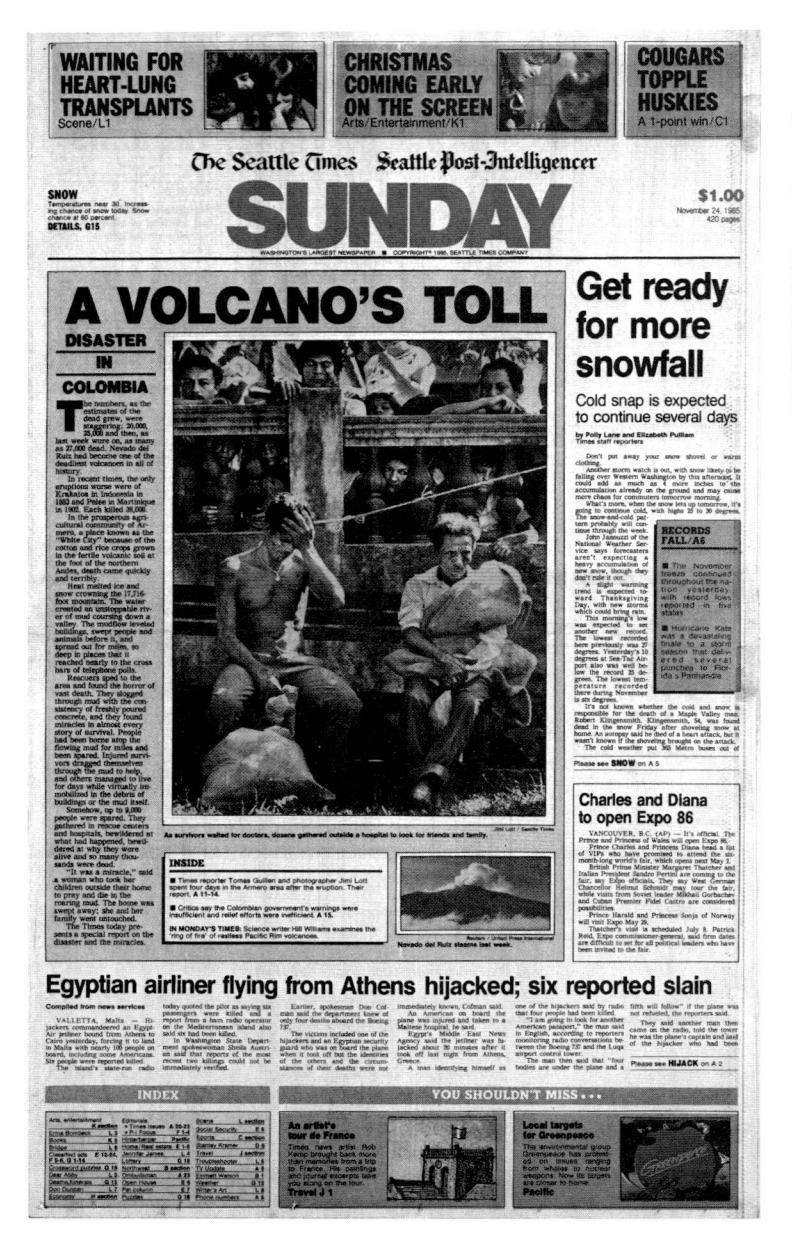

A,B THE SEATTLE TIMES
Rob Covey, Chuck Taylor, Liz Nielsen

C,D THE SEATTLE TIMES
Fred Nelson, Chuck Taylor

56 The Best of Newspaper Design

4

DESIGNER'S CHOICE
NATIONAL

A
B
C

A-C THE SEATTLE TIMES
Steve McKinstry, Chuck Taylor

Seventh Edition 57

4

DESIGNER'S CHOICE
NATIONAL

A-K SAN JOSE MERCURY NEWS
David Yarnold, Marty Gradel, Mike Healy, News Desk

58 The Best of Newspaper Design

4
DESIGNER'S CHOICE
NATIONAL

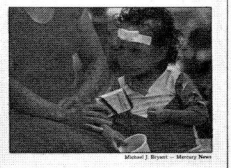

F G H I J K

4
DESIGNER'S CHOICE
NATIONAL

A B C D E

A-E THE SEATTLE TIMES
Rob Covey, Chuck Taylor

5

REGULARLY
APPEARING
FEATURES SECTION

Entries consisted of three complete sections from three different dates from • Opinion • Lifestyle • Entertainment • Food • Fashion • Home and Travel sections.

SILVER AWARD
A-C LOS ANGELES TIMES
Tom Trapnell

5
LIFESTYLE FEATURES

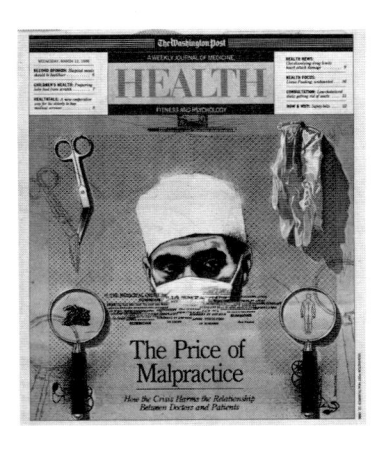

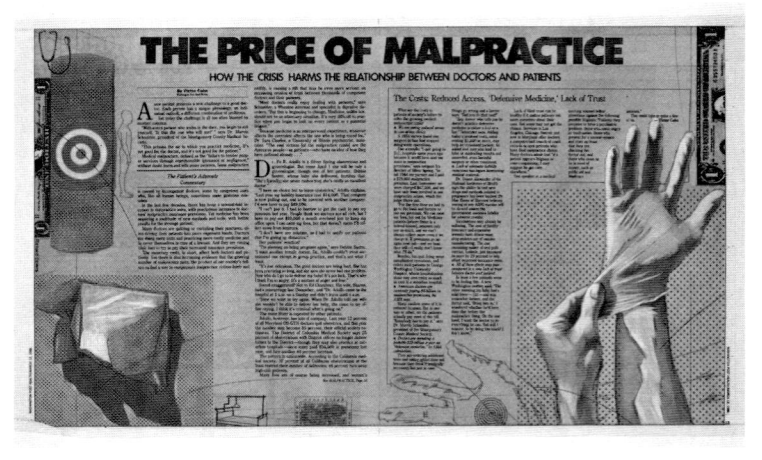

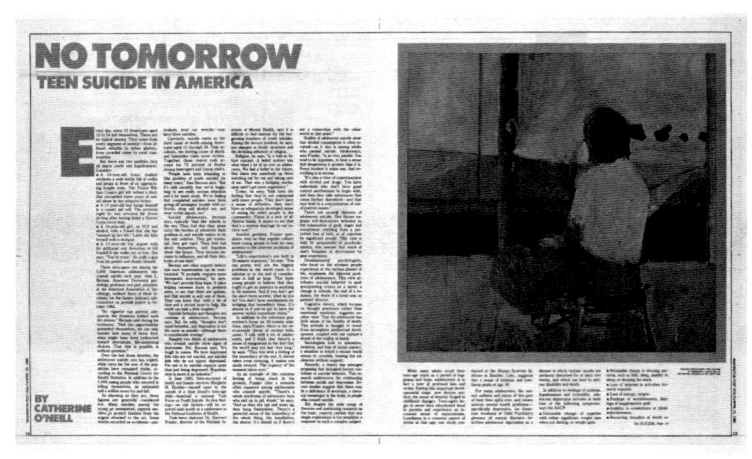

A-F THE WASHINGTON POST
Peggy Robertson

G-I THE NEW YORK TIMES
Steve Heller: Art Director

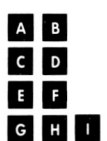

62   The Best of Newspaper Design

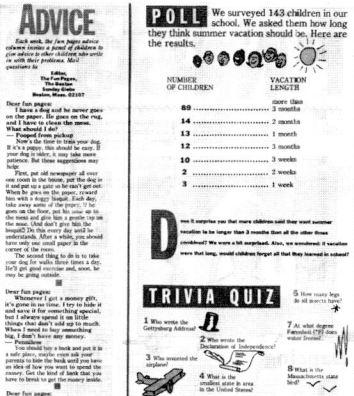

SILVER AWARD

A-F THE BOSTON GLOBE
Ronn Campisi, Judy Loda: Art Directors; Judy Loda: Designer

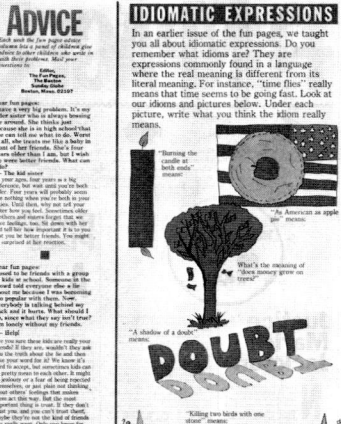

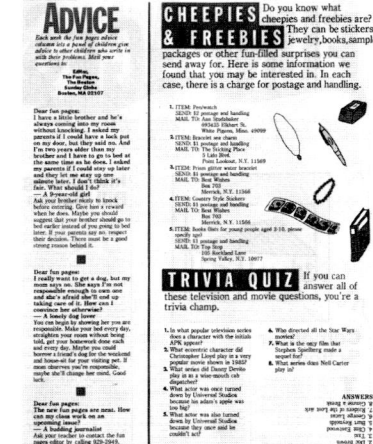

5
LIFESTYLE FEATURES

A,B THE CHICAGO TRIBUNE
Mare Earley, Art Director

C-E THE HARTFORD COURANT
Peter Hoey, Randy Cox

64 The Best of Newspaper Design

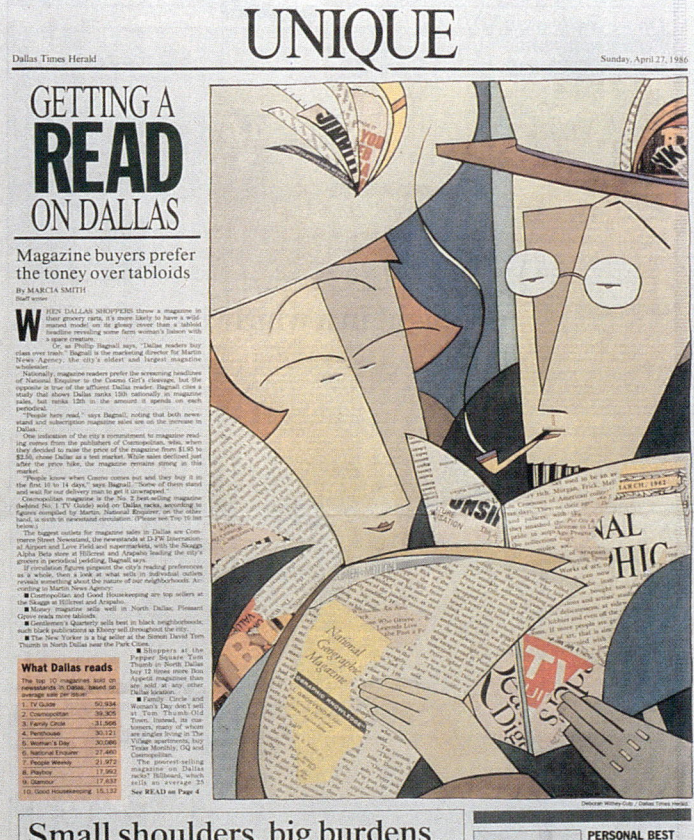

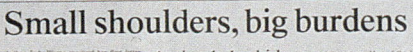

A,C DALLAS TIMES HERALD
Deborah Withey-Culp, Features and Art Staff

B BERKELEYAN
John Hickey, Design Director;
Linda Currie, Designer

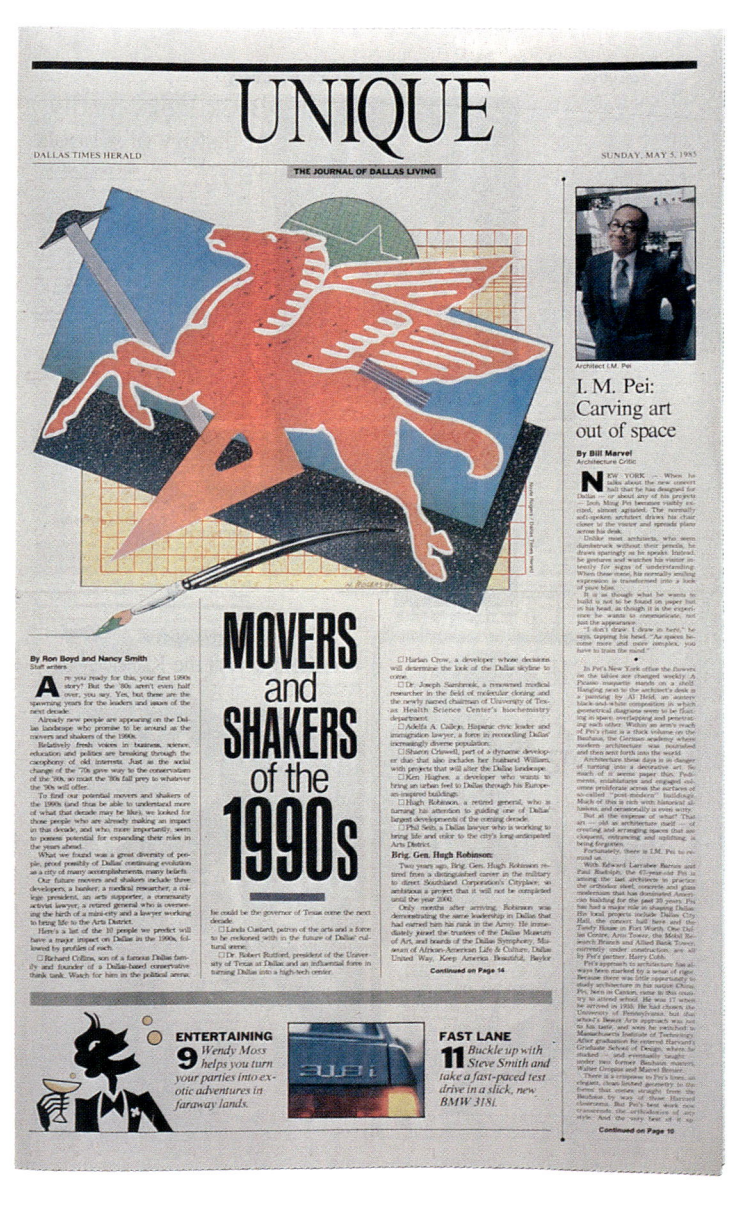

5
TRAVEL SECTIONS

A
B
C

A-C THE NEW YORK TIMES
Linda Brewer: Art Director

66   The Best of Newspaper Design

A
B C D

A-C THE CHRISTIAN SCIENCE MONITOR
Susan Ballenger Tyner, Robin Jareaux

D EL NUEVO DIA
Jose L. Diaz de Villegas, Rica Alos

5
TRAVEL SECTIONS

Seventh Edition 67

5
FOOD SECTIONS

A,B THE CHICAGO TRIBUNE
Nancy Donohue

C,D THE DALLAS MORNING NEWS
Kathleen Vincent, Dottie Griffith

68 The Best of Newspaper Design

A-D THE BALTIMORE SUN
Donna Albano

6
FEATURES PAGE DESIGN

Entries consisted of single pages from Opinion • Lifestyle • Entertainment • Food • Fashion • Home and Travel sections.

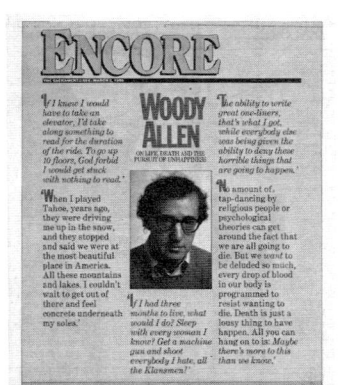

A THE WASHINGTON POST
Richard P. Whiting, Jeff Dever

SILVER AWARD
B DALLAS TIMES HERALD
Edna Jamandre

C THE SACRAMENTO BEE
James Carr, Designer; Howard Shintaku, Art Director

D NEWSDAY
Gary Rogers

E GANNETT WESTCHESTER NEWSPAPERS
Laura Schwed, Ray Vella

F THE GLOBE AND MAIL
Frank Teskey

G THE CHRISTIAN SCIENCE MONITOR
Robin Jareaux

70 The Best of Newspaper Design

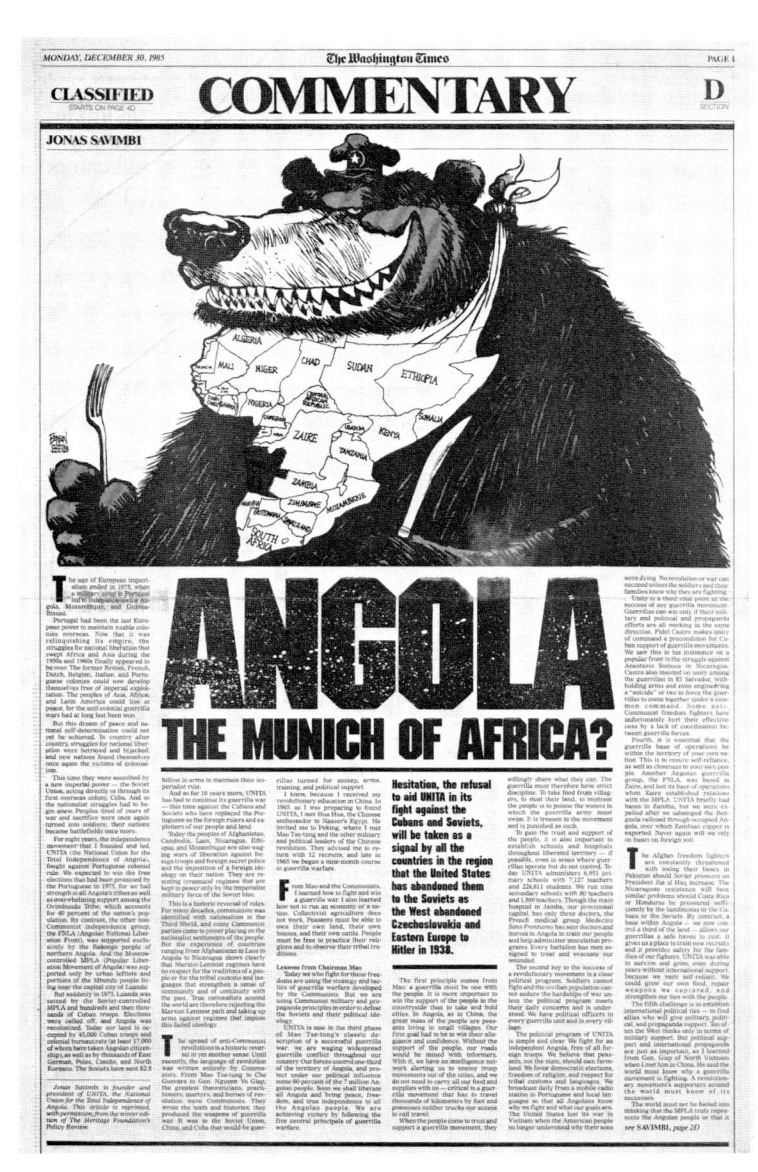

A THE WASHINGTON TIMES
Alex Hunter

B LOS ANGELES TIMES
Tom Trapnell

C LOS ANGELES TIMES
Tom Trapnell

D LOS ANGELES TIMES
Tom Trapnell

E THE ORANGE COUNTY REGISTER
Bob Reynolds

6

FASHION PAGES

A THE CHICAGO TRIBUNE
Mare Earley, Art Director

B DALLAS TIMES HERALD
John Goecke

C THE GAZETTE
Lucy Lacava

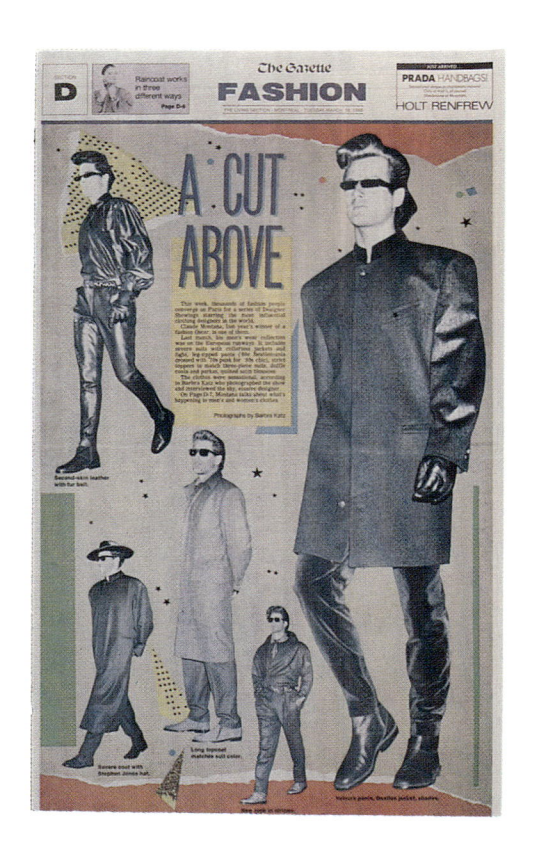

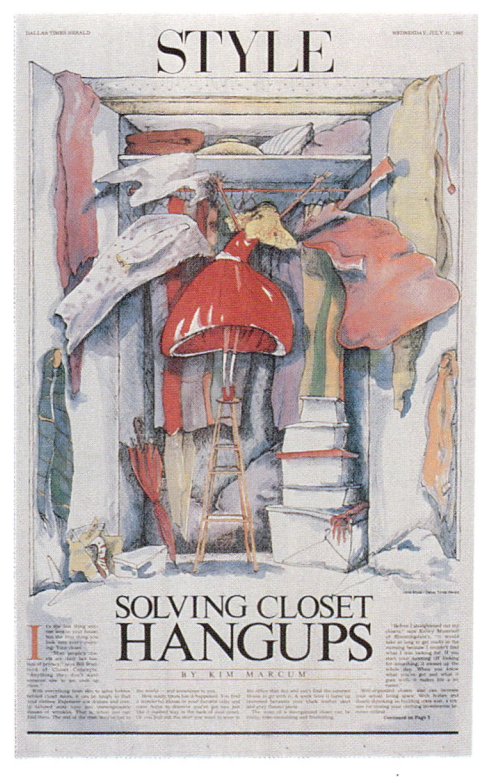

D DALLAS TIMES HERALD
Janis Bryza

SILVER AWARD
E NOVEDADES
Francis X. Garcia F., Designer;
Claudio Rodriguez, Art Director

FASHION PAGES

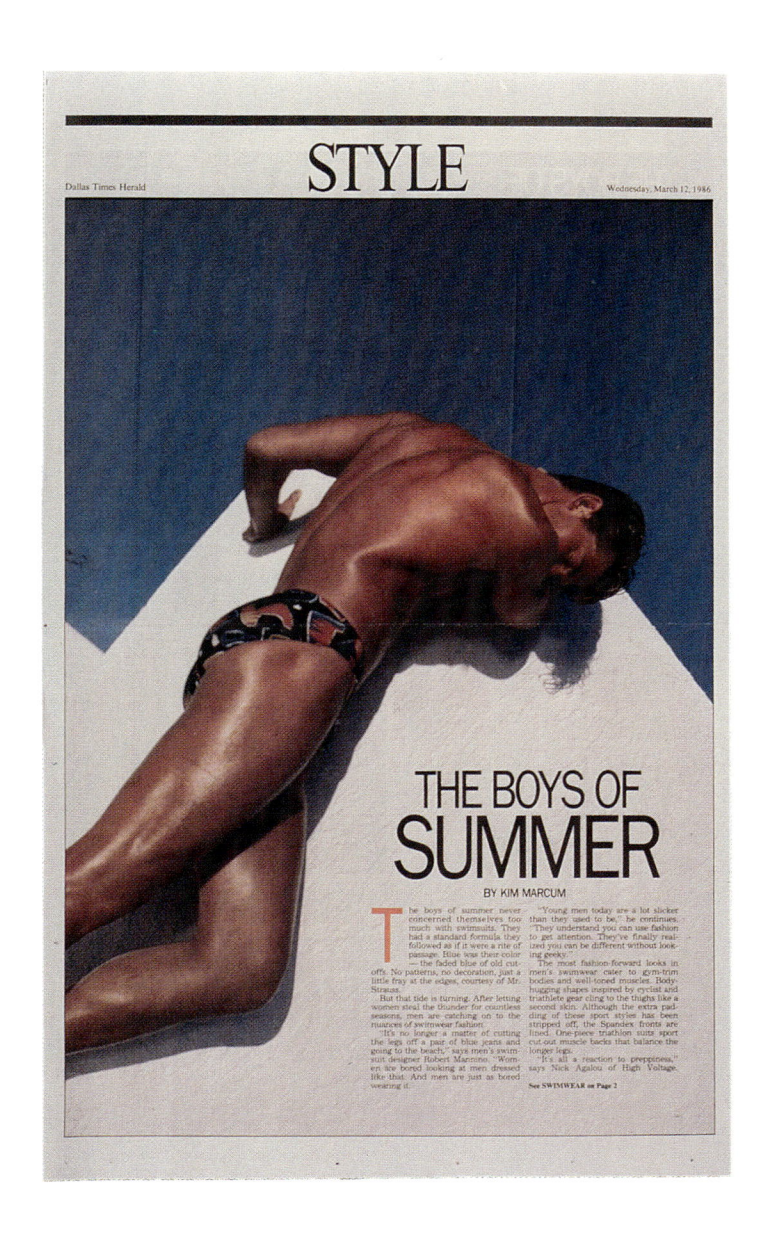

A DALLAS TIMES HERALD
Janis Bryza

B THE CHICAGO TRIBUNE
Mare Earley, Art Director

C DALLAS TIMES HERALD
Stan Hulen, Jane Corbellini

D LOS ANGELES TIMES
Donald Burgess

E THE DALLAS MORNING NEWS
G.W. Babb

6
FOOD PAGES

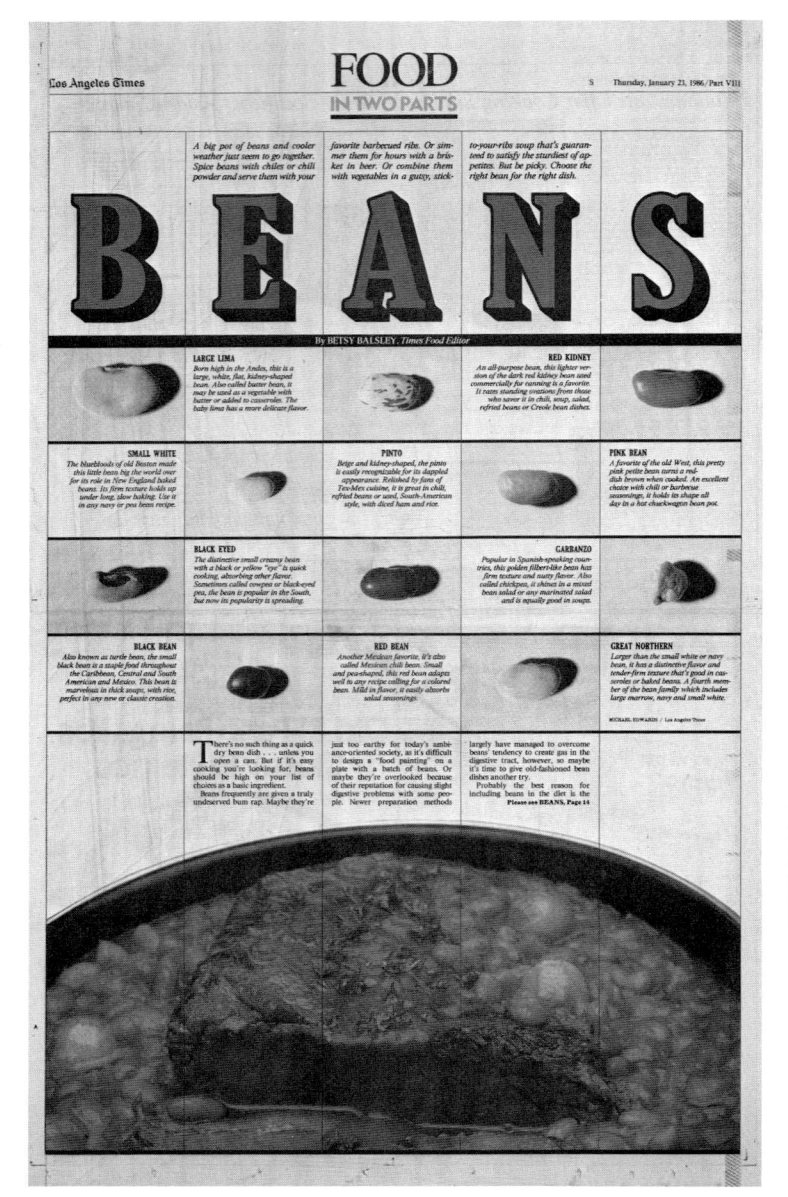

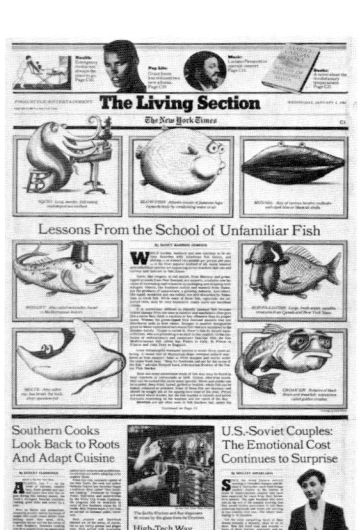

A THE BOSTON GLOBE
Catherine Aldrich

B THE HARTFORD COURANT
Randy Cox
SILVER AWARD

C LOS ANGELES TIMES
Terry Redknapp

D THE NEW YORK TIMES
Nancy Sterngold, Art Director

A,B EL NUEVO DIA
Jose L. Diaz de Villegas

C THE DALLAS MORNING NEWS
Kathleen Vincent

D THE BALTIMORE SUN
Donna Albano

E THE CHICAGO TRIBUNE
Earl Toledo, Art Director

F LOS ANGELES TIMES
Terry Redknapp

Seventh Edition   75

A THE WASHINGTON POST
Steve McCracken,
Linda L. Halsey

B LOS ANGELES TIMES
Donald Burgess

SILVER AWARD

C EL NUEVO DIA
Jose L. Diaz de Villegas

D THE BOSTON GLOBE
Lucy Bartholomay

E THE NEW YORK TIMES
Linda Brewer, Art Director

6
TRAVEL PAGES

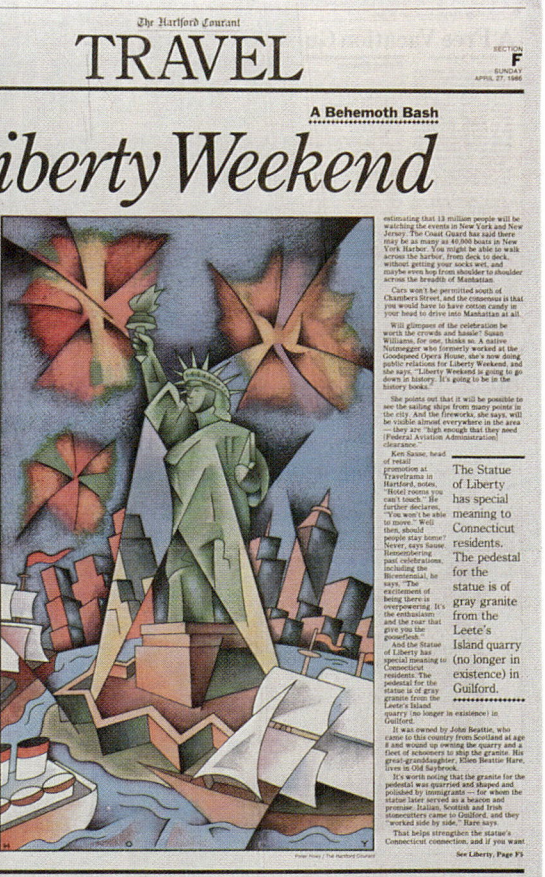

A B C
D E F

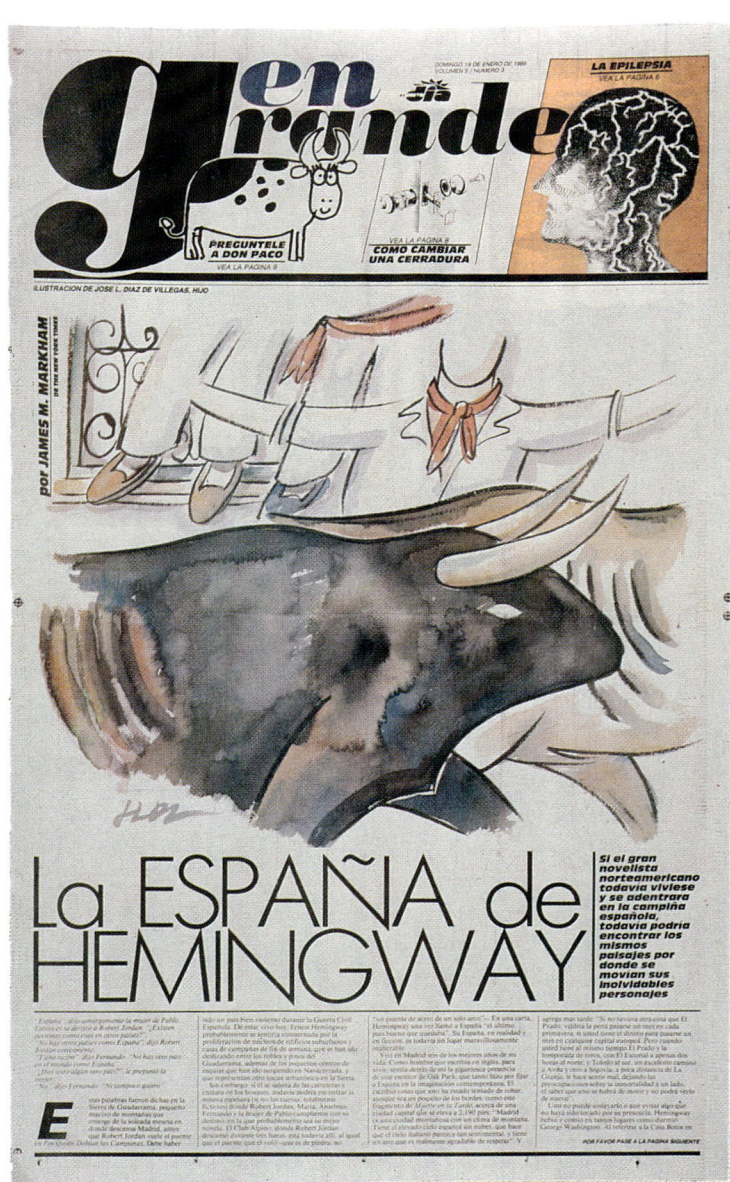

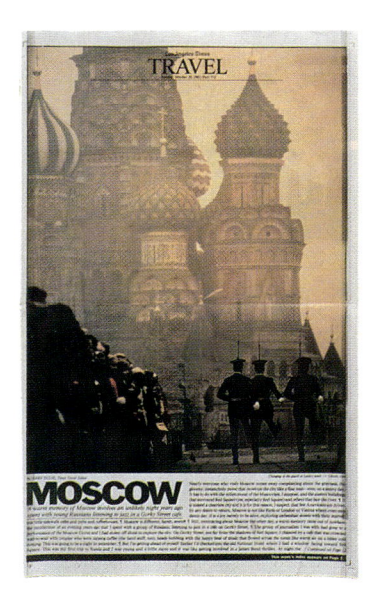

A THE HARTFORD COURANT
Rene Smith, Peter Hoey

B LOS ANGELES TIMES
Donald Burgess

C THE BOSTON GLOBE
Lucy Bartholomay

D, E LOS ANGELES TIMES
Donald Burgess

F EL NUEVO DIA
Jose L. Diaz de Villegas

Seventh Edition 77

6
TRAVEL PAGES

A B C
D E F

A THE NEW YORK TIMES
Linda Brewer, Art Director

B LOS ANGELES TIMES
Donald Burgess

C THE BOSTON GLOBE
Lucy Bartholomay

SILVER AWARD

D THE BOSTON GLOBE
Lucy Bartholomay

E, F EL NUEVO DIA
Jose L. Diaz de Villegas

78   The Best of Newspaper Design

A THE NEW YORK TIMES
Elizabeth Williams, Art Director

B,C,D THE BOSTON GLOBE
Aldona Charlton

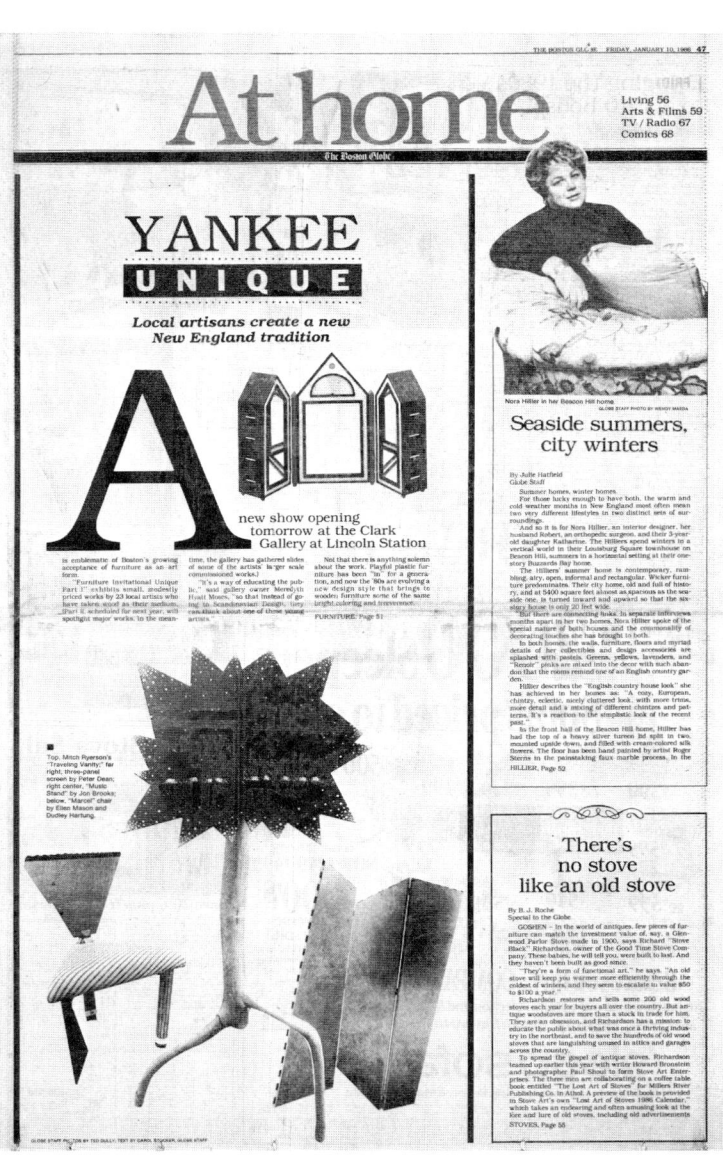

6

HOME · REAL ESTATE

Seventh Edition 79

A THE ORANGE COUNTY REGISTER
Gwendolyn Wong; Marty Braun, Illustrator

B THE CHICAGO TRIBUNE
Nancy Donohue

C THE SEATTLE TIMES
Robert Massa

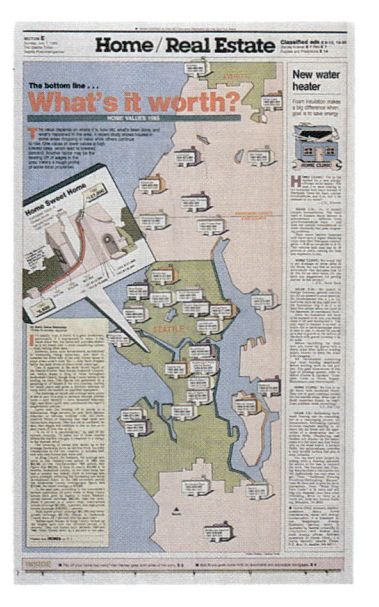

A THE BOSTON GLOBE
Aldona Charlton

B THE NEW YORK TIMES
Nancy Kent, Art Director

C THE BOSTON GLOBE
Aldona Charlton

6
LIFESTYLE FEATURES

A B C D

SILVER AWARD
A THE BOSTON GLOBE
Judy Loda

SILVER AWARD
B THE COURIER JOURNAL
Johnny Maupin

SILVER AWARD
C THE HARTFORD COURANT
David Griffin

SILVER AWARD
D DALLAS TIMES HERALD
Deborah Withey-Culp

82   The Best of Newspaper Design

6
LIFESTYLE FEATURES

A THE HARTFORD COURANT
David Griffin

B THE BOSTON GLOBE
Richard M. Baker

C THE WASHINGTON TIMES
Sheri Taylor

D THE HARTFORD COURANT
David Griffin

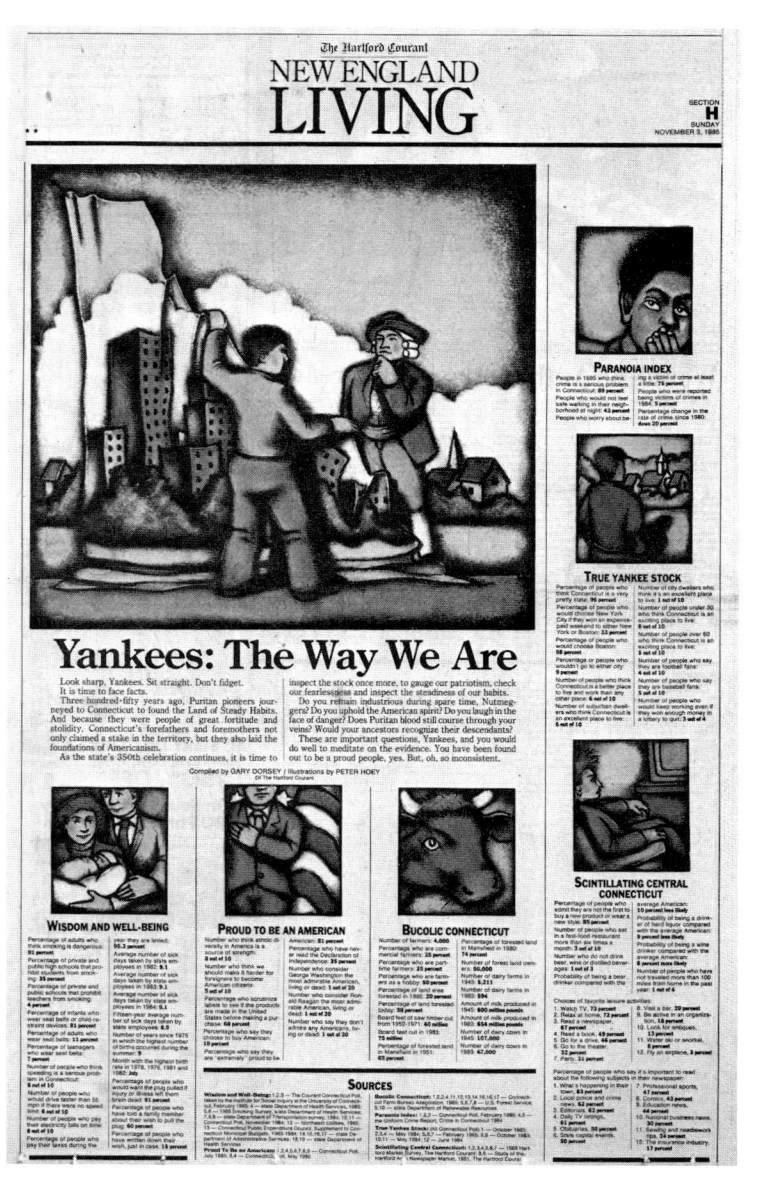

Seventh Edition 83

6

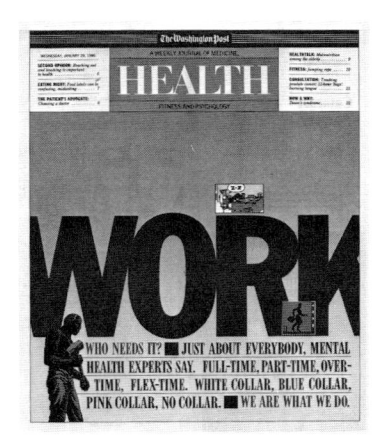

LIFESTYLE FEATURES

A THE WASHINGTON POST
Carol Porter, Mike Keegan

B THE BALTIMORE SUN
Donna Albano

C DALLAS TIMES HERALD
Deborah Withey-Culp

D THE WASHINGTON POST
Peggy Robertson, Art Director;
Mark Penberthy, Illustrator

84   The Best of Newspaper Design

6
LIFESTYLE FEATURES

A B
C D

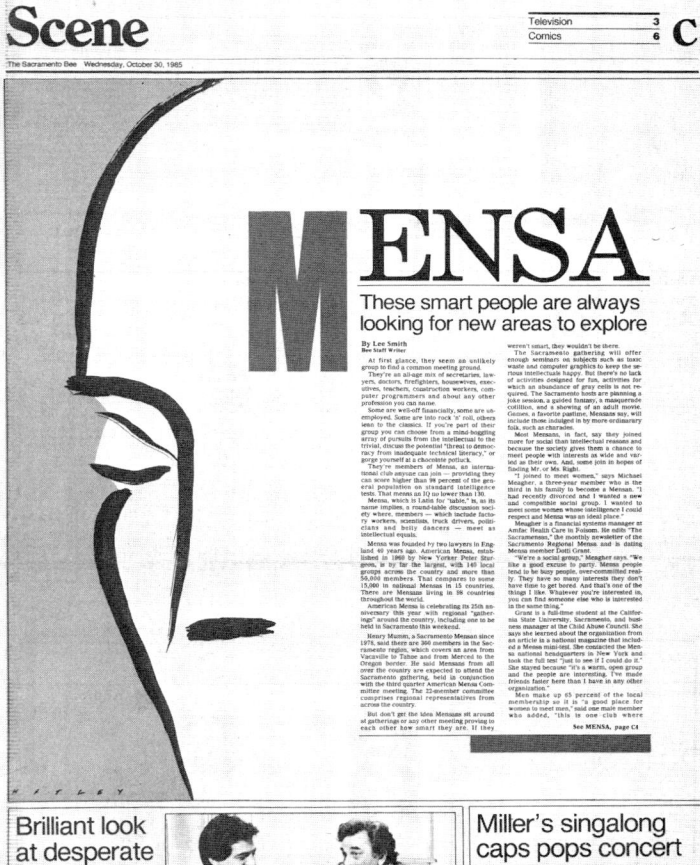

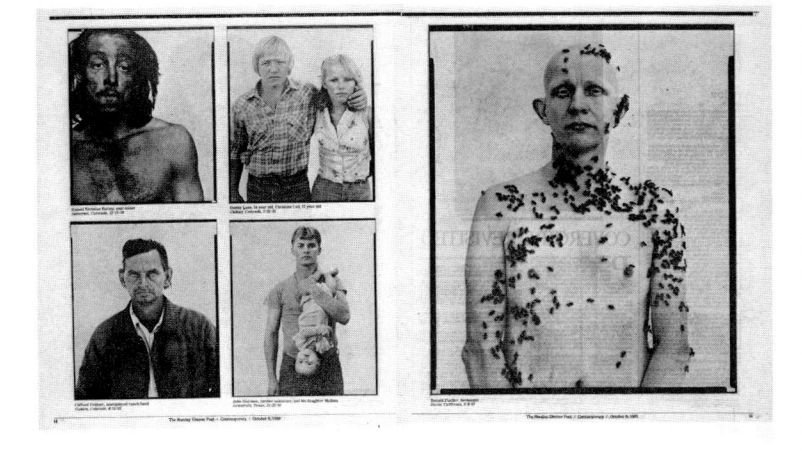

A THE BOSTON GLOBE
Richard M. Baker

B,C THE DENVER POST
Gayle Sims, Editor

D THE SACRAMENTO BEE
Hatley Norton Mason III, Howard
Shintaku, Art Director

Seventh Edition   85

6
LIFESTYLE FEATURES

A STAVANGER AFTENBLAD
Layout Department

B THE DENVER POST
Randy Miller, Maureen Scance,
Paul Keebler

C THE BOSTON GLOBE
Ronn Campisi

D THE BOSTON GLOBE
Richard M. Baker

86   The Best of Newspaper Design

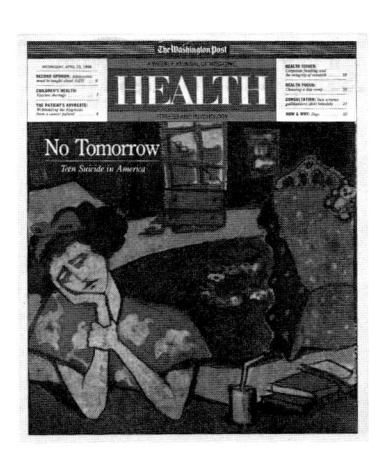

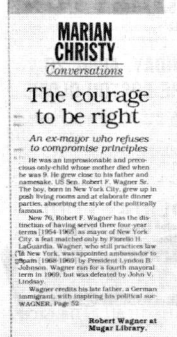

6
LIFESTYLE FEATURES

A
B
C

A THE BOSTON GLOBE
Judy Loda

B THE WASHINGTON POST
Peggy Robertson, Art Director;
Beth Rubin, Illustrator

C THE BOSTON GLOBE
Judy Loda

7

SINGLE SUBJECT

Entries consisted of either news or feature stories published on at least three consecutive dates.

A-C THE CHRISTIAN SCIENCE MONITOR
Robin Jareaux

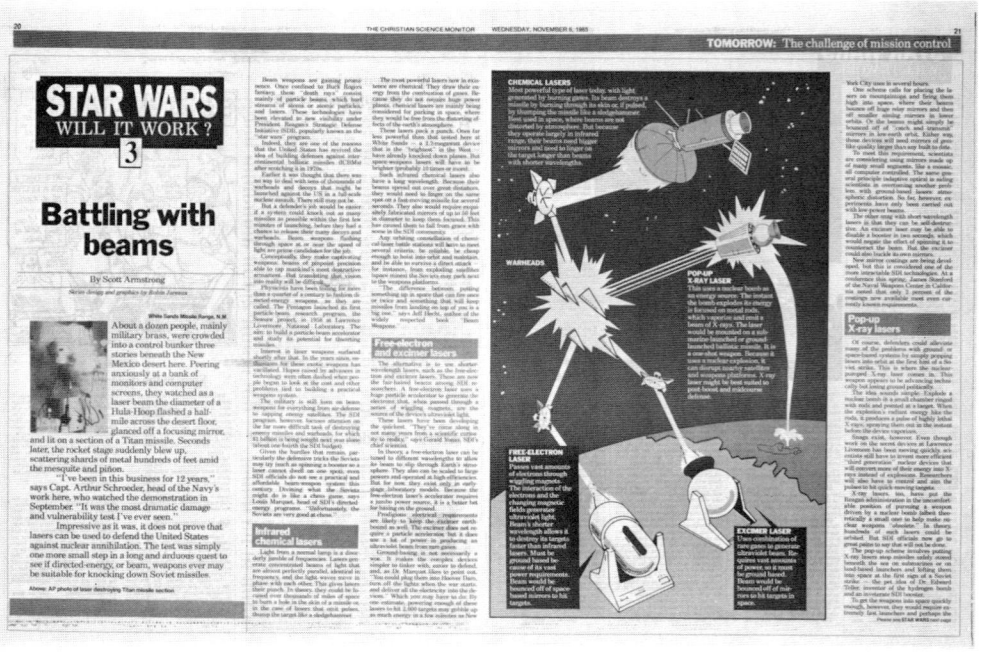

88 The Best of Newspaper Design

7

SINGLE SUBJECT

A–D THE CHRISTIAN SCIENCE MONITOR
Robin Jareaux

7
SINGLE SUBJECT

A-F THE SEATTLE TIMES
Steve McKinstry

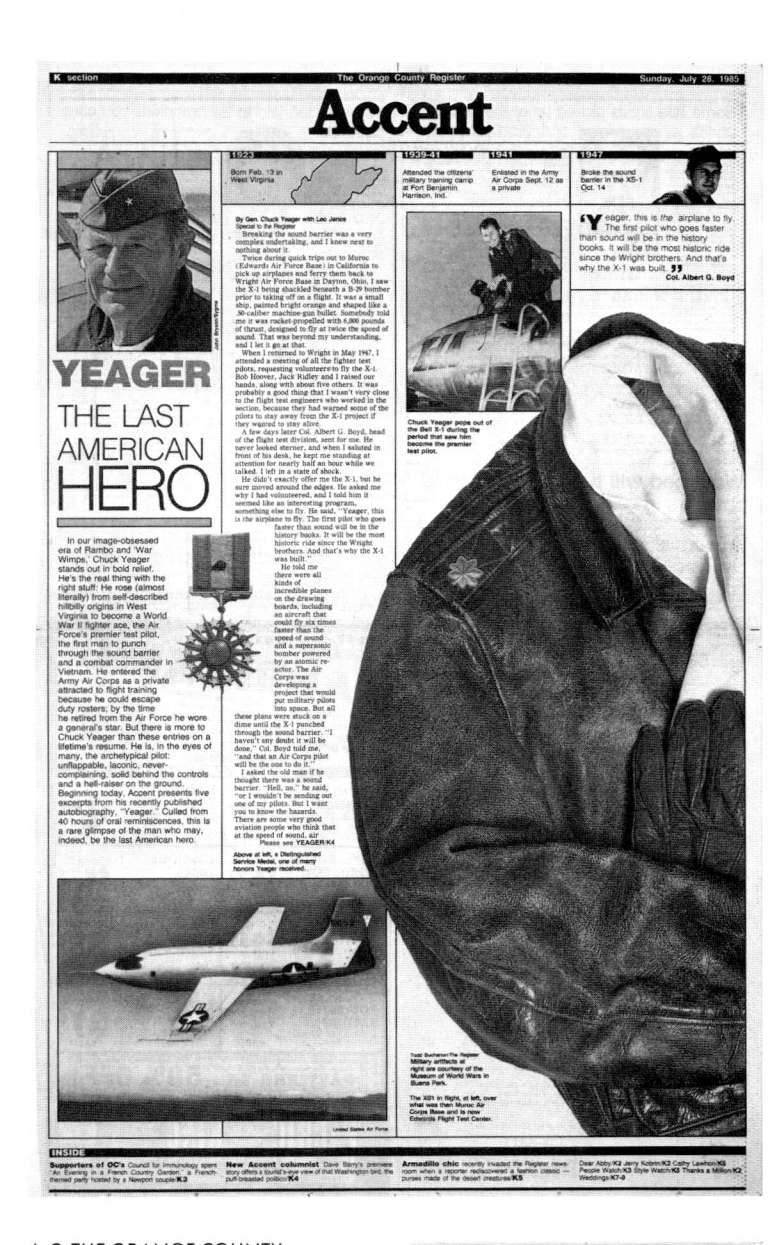

A-C THE ORANGE COUNTY REGISTER
Gwen Wong

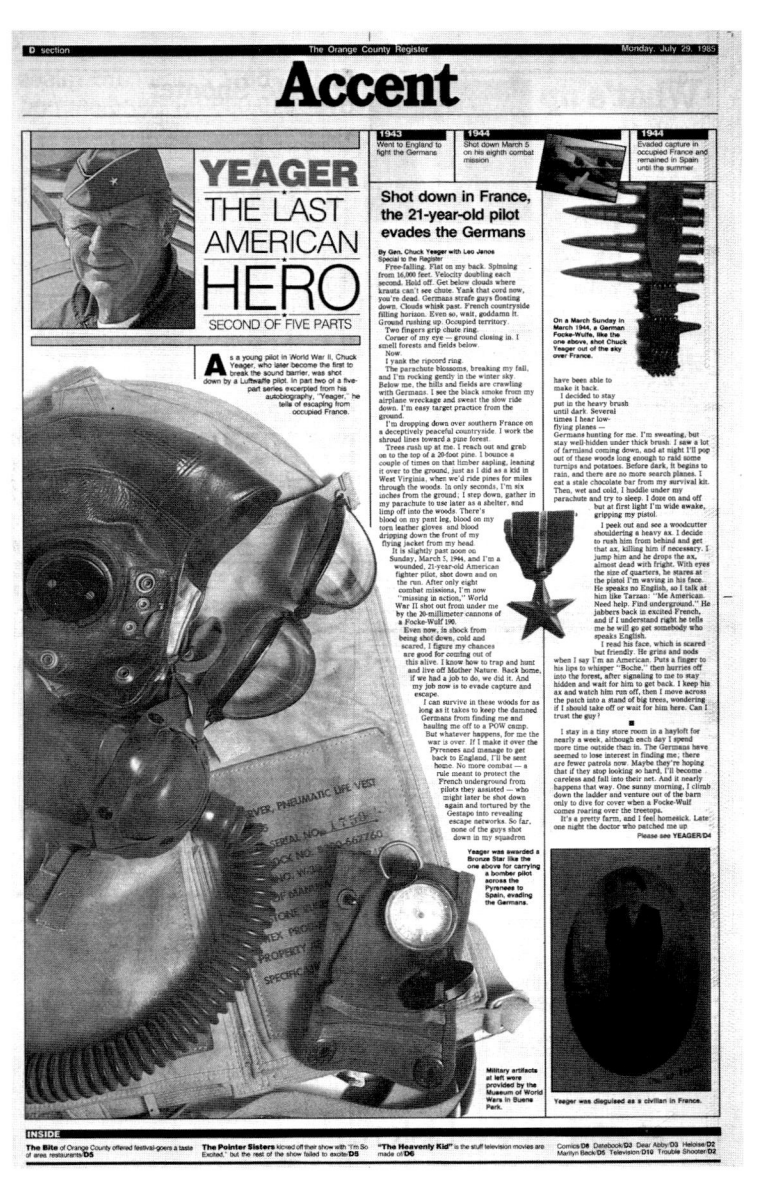

7
SINGLE SUBJECT

A,C THE CHRISTIAN SCIENCE MONITOR
Robin Jareaux

B,D THE CHRISTIAN SCIENCE MONITOR
Robin Jareaux

7
SINGLE SUBJECT

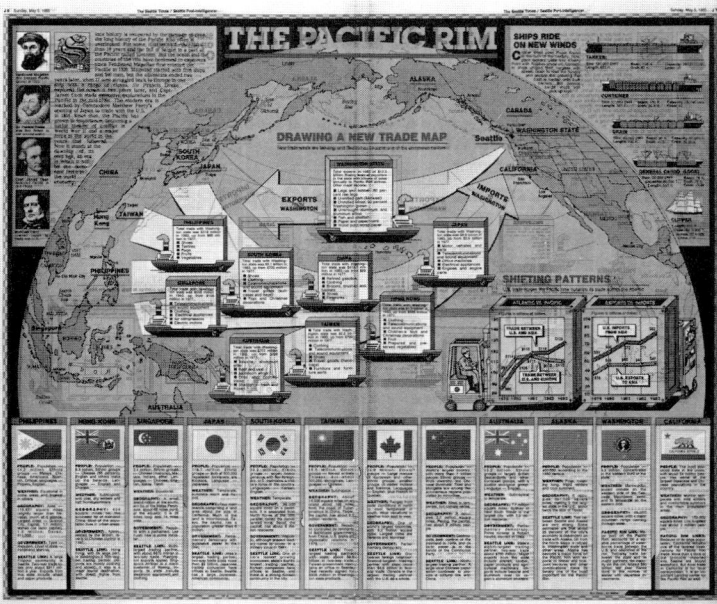

A–D THE SEATTLE TIMES
Robert Massa

7
SINGLE SUBJECT

A,B,D BERGENS TIDENDE
Staff

C,E,F THE PRINCE GEORGE'S
COUNTY JOURNAL
Linda Searing

94   The Best of Newspaper Design

8
NEWSPAPER SPECIAL SECTIONS

Entries consisted of complete news or feature sections published as part of the regular run of the press.

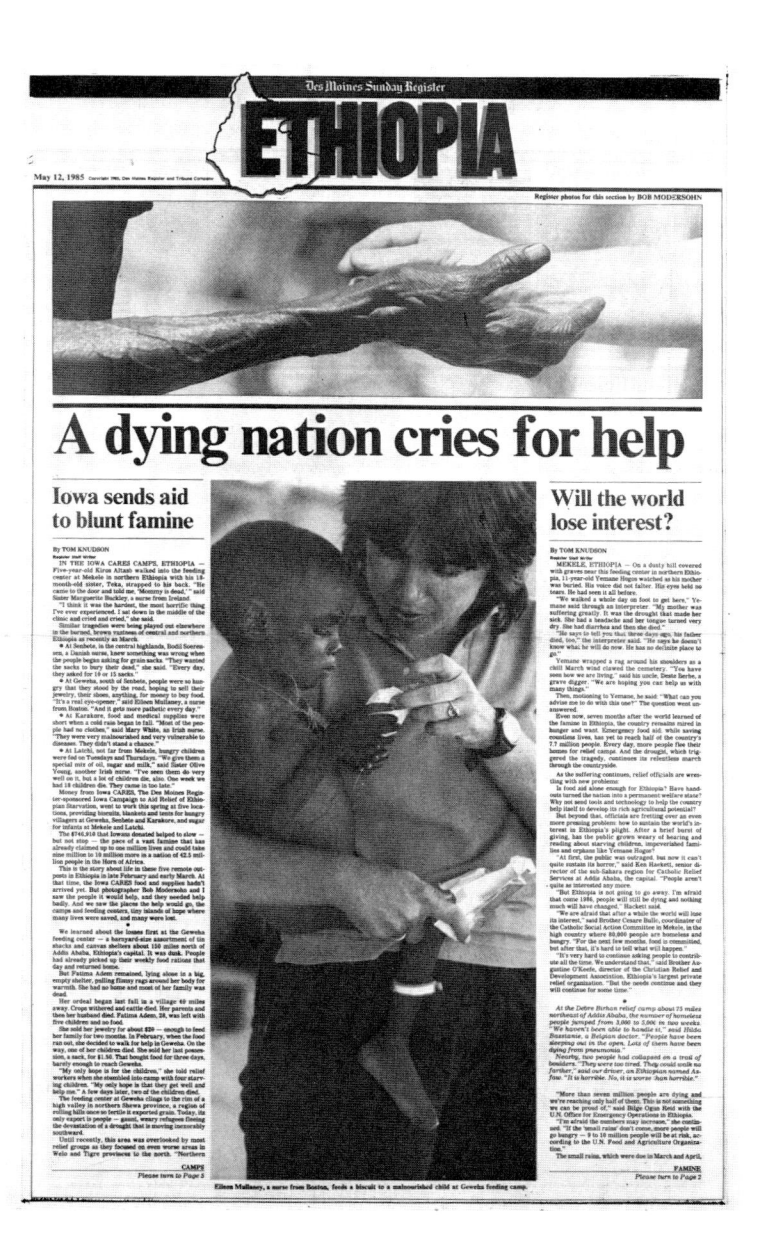

SILVER AWARD
A-D REGISTER AND TRIBUNE
Lyle Boone

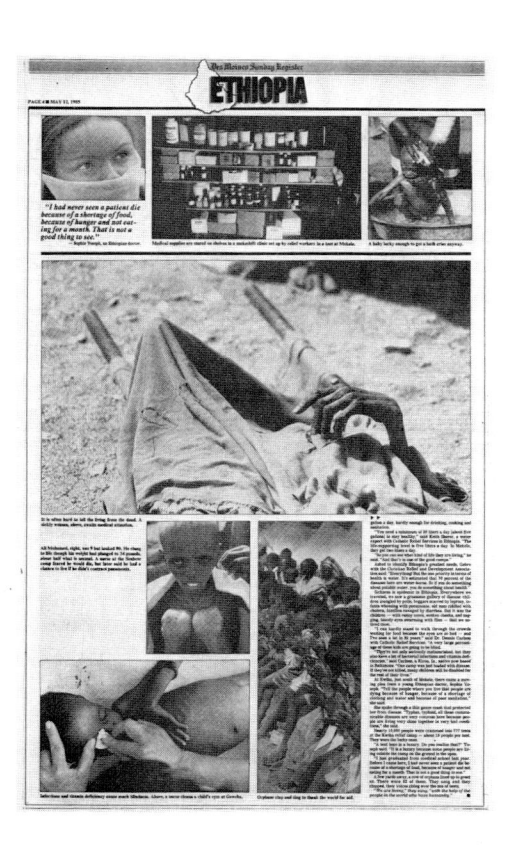

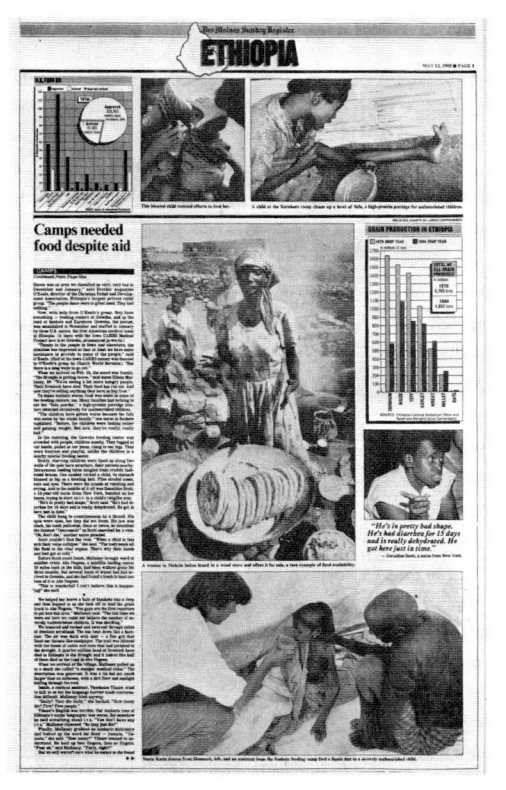

8

SPECIAL SECTIONS

A-D ST. PAUL PIONEER
PRESS/DISPATCH
Susie Eaton Hopper

96 ■ The Best of Newspaper Design

8
SPECIAL SECTIONS

SILVER AWARD

A-F THE WASHINGTON TIMES
Jane Paiecek

Seventh Edition 97

8
SPECIAL SECTIONS

A B C
D E

A-C THE CHICAGO TRIBUNE
Staff

D, E THE FLORIDA TIMES-UNION AND JACKSONVILLE JOURNAL
John Gold, John Hansen

98   The Best of Newspaper Design

8
SPECIAL SECTIONS

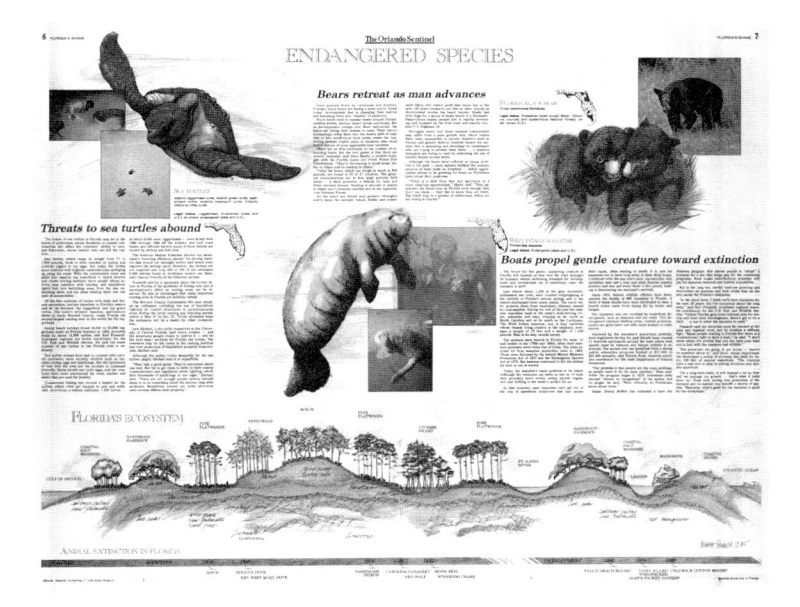

SILVER AWARD

A THE COURIER JOURNAL
Johnny Maupin, Jerry Ryan

B,C THE ORLANDO SENTINEL
Mark Williams

Saving the Land

A flood of relief and rains that dampened the parched soil have not brought an end to the crisis in Africa. Drought continues, and the sands of the Sahara march relentlessly toward a conquest of what little land is capable of sustaining human life.

By Mervin Aubespin / Photos by Durell Hall Jr.

A-D THE COURIER JOURNAL
Jerry Ryan

SPECIAL SECTIONS

A-D FAEDRELANDSVENNEN
Sven Hoiland

8
SPECIAL SECTIONS

A-F AFTENPOSTEN
Tom B. Fallsen, Roland Jorgensen,
Svein Hansen, Kjell Iversen,
Rolf Linneberg, Jens Erik Syversen

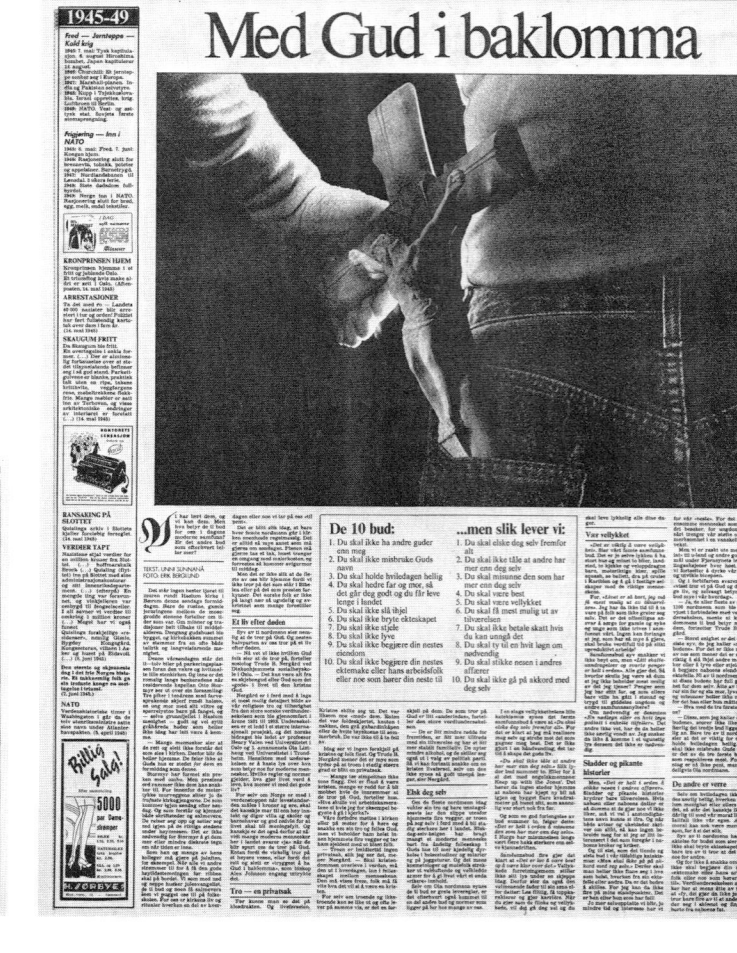

A THE NEW YORK TIMES
Ron Couture, Art Director

B,C THE NEW YORK TIMES
Mike Todd, Designer;
Ron Couture, Art Director

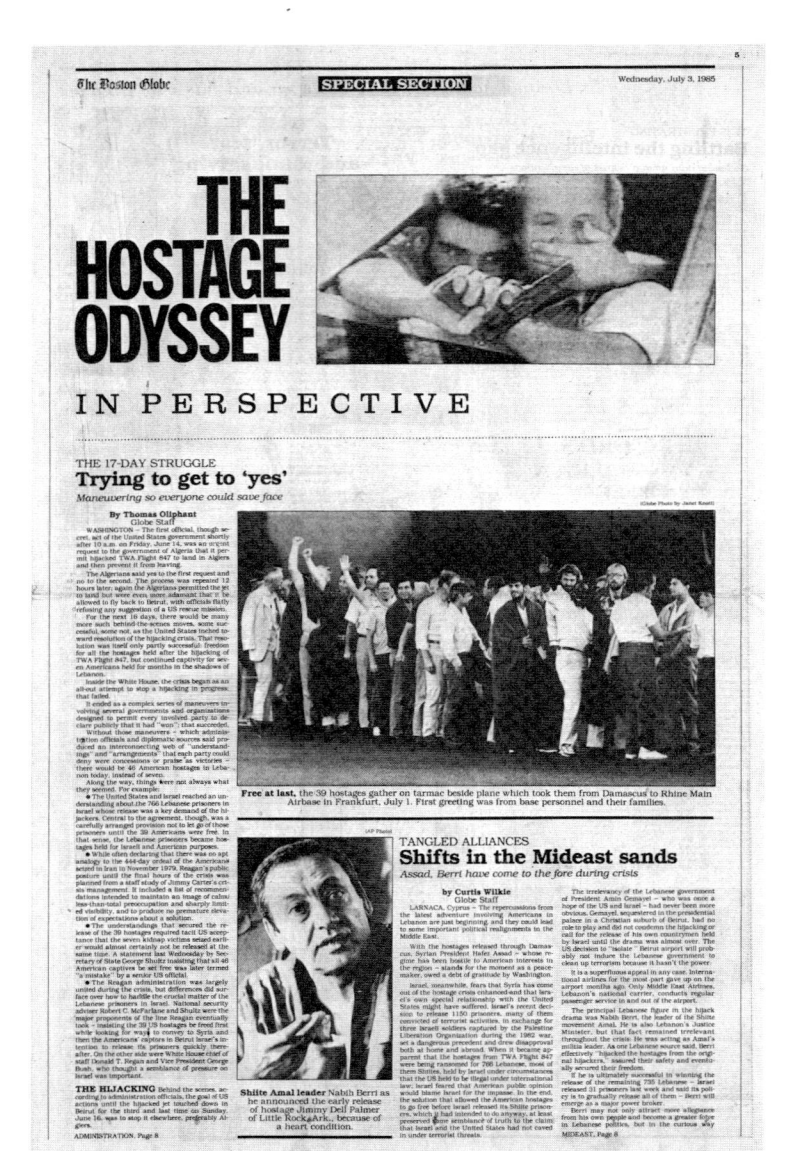

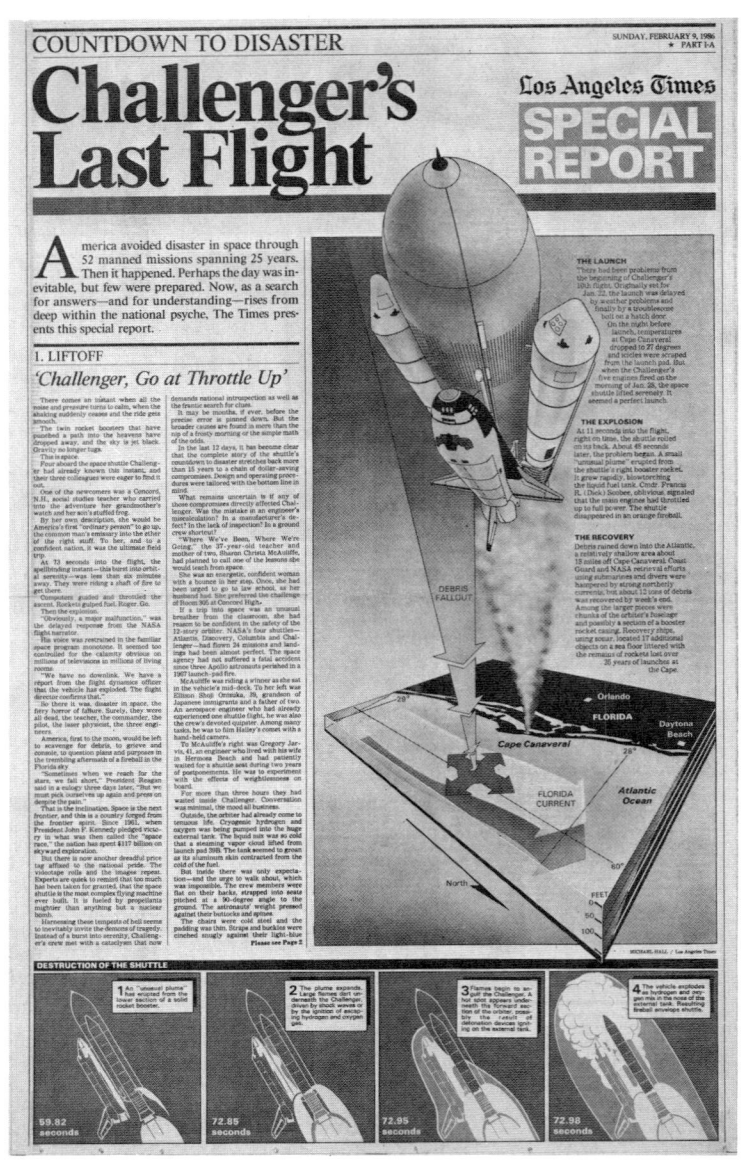

8
SPECIAL SECTIONS

A LOS ANGELES TIMES
Tom Trapnell, Terry Schwadron,
Michael Hall, David Puckett,
Patricia Mitchell

B-D THE BOSTON GLOBE
Ronn Campisi

104 The Best of Newspaper Design

8
SPECIAL SECTIONS

A-E THE DALLAS MORNING NEWS
Kathleen Vincent, Designer;
George Benge, Art Director

8
SPECIAL SECTIONS

A
B C

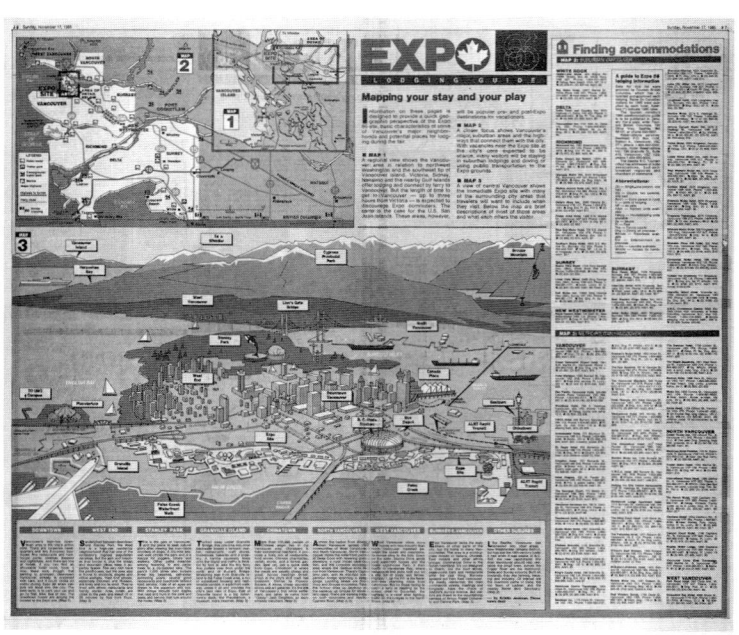

A THE SEATTLE TIMES
Robert Massa

B,C THE SEATTLE TIMES
Celeste Ericsson,
Steve McKinstry

106   The Best of Newspaper Design

8
SPECIAL SECTIONS

A B C D

A-C THE NEW YORK TIMES
Pamela Vassil, Art Director

D THE SAN DIEGO UNION
Chris Ross, Ray Downey-Laskowitz, Ken Marshall

Seventh Edition 107

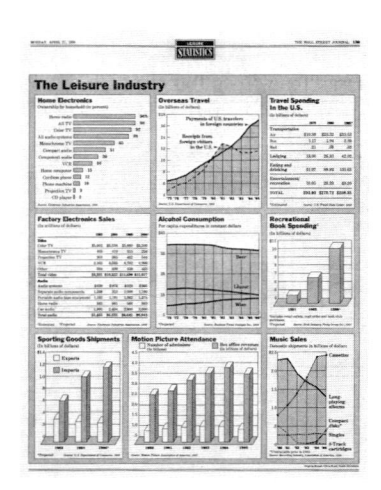

8
SPECIAL SECTIONS

SILVER AWARD
A,B THE WALL STREET JOURNAL
Greg Leeds

SILVER AWARD
C-E THE WALL STREET JOURNAL
Greg Leeds

SILVER AWARD
F-H THE WALL STREET JOURNAL
Greg Leeds

108   The Best of Newspaper Design

A-D THE WASHINGTON TIMES
Michael Good, Kevin T. Gilbert

E-G THE NEW YORK TIMES
Ron Couture, Richard Yeend,
Art Directors

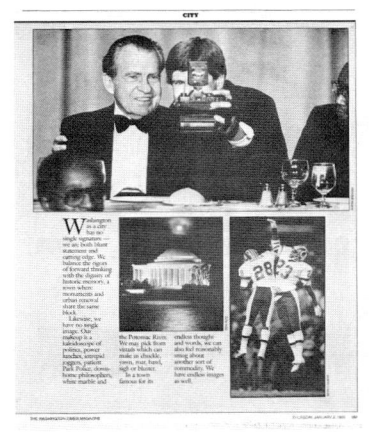

9
NEWSPAPER
MAGAZINE
REPRINTS

Entries consisted of special reprints of news or feature stories originally published as part of the run of the press.

A THE SEATTLE TIMES
Steve McKinstry

B THE CHICAGO TRIBUNE
Staff

C,D THE CHRISTIAN SCIENCE MONITOR WEEKLY WORLD EDITION
Robin Jareaux

110 The Best of Newspaper Design

9 SPECIAL REPRINTS

A-G THE BALTIMORE SUN
Donna Albano

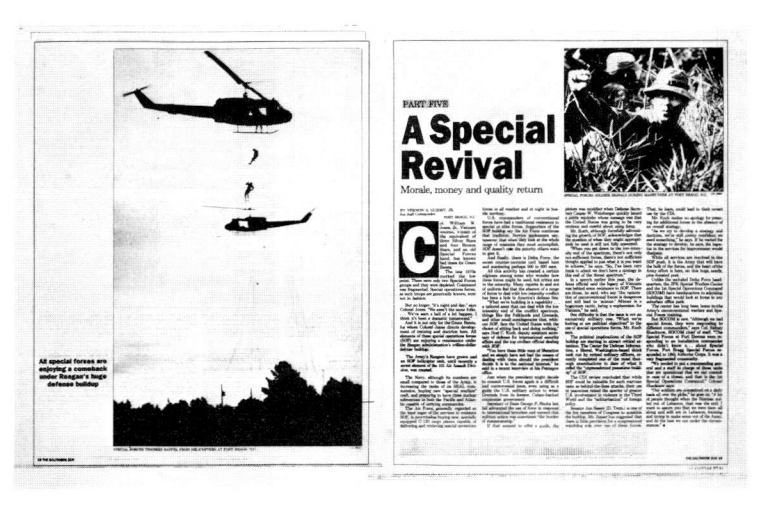

Seventh Edition 111

10

NEWSPAPER OVERALL DESIGN

Entries consisted of complete newspapers from three consecutive publication dates. Circulation • 150,000 and over • 75,000-150,000 • 75,000 and under and non-daily publications.

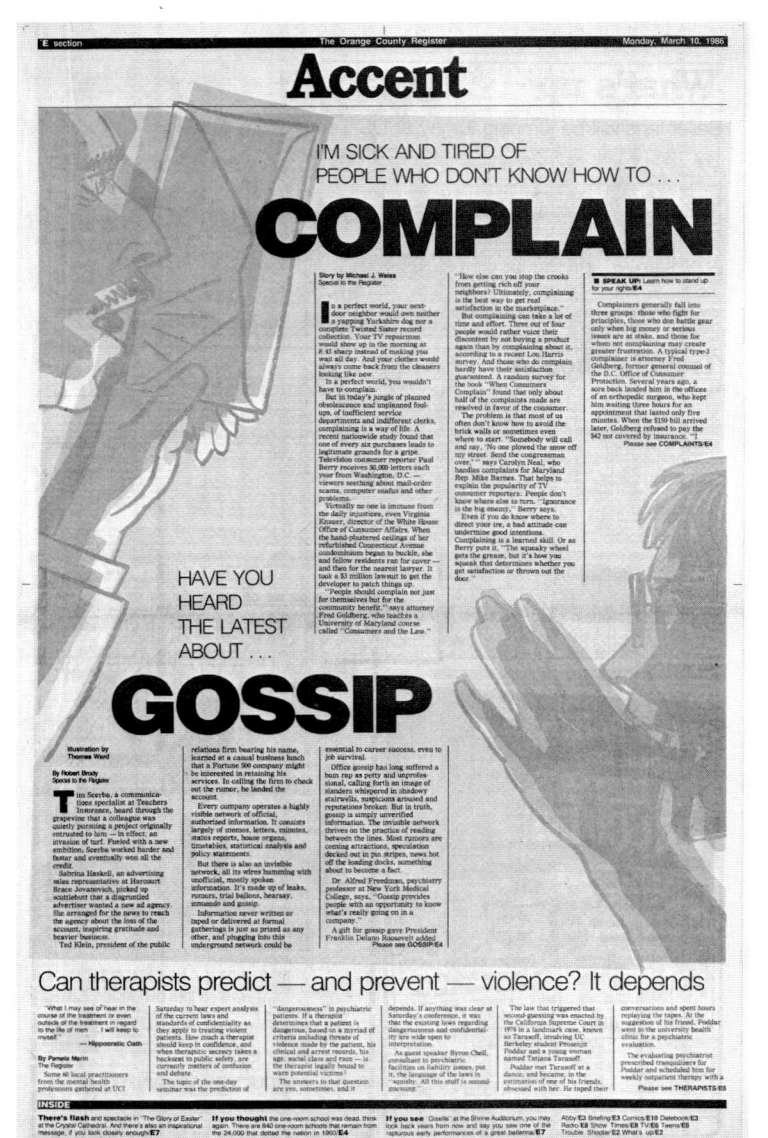

A-E THE ORANGE COUNTY REGISTER
N. C. Anderson, Staff

112   The Best of Newspaper Design

10
CIRCULATION
OVER 150,000

ⒶⒷ
ⒸⒹ

SILVER AWARD

A-D NOVEDADES
Roger Black, Mario Garcia,
Designers; Claudio Rodriguez,
Art Director

Seventh Edition 113

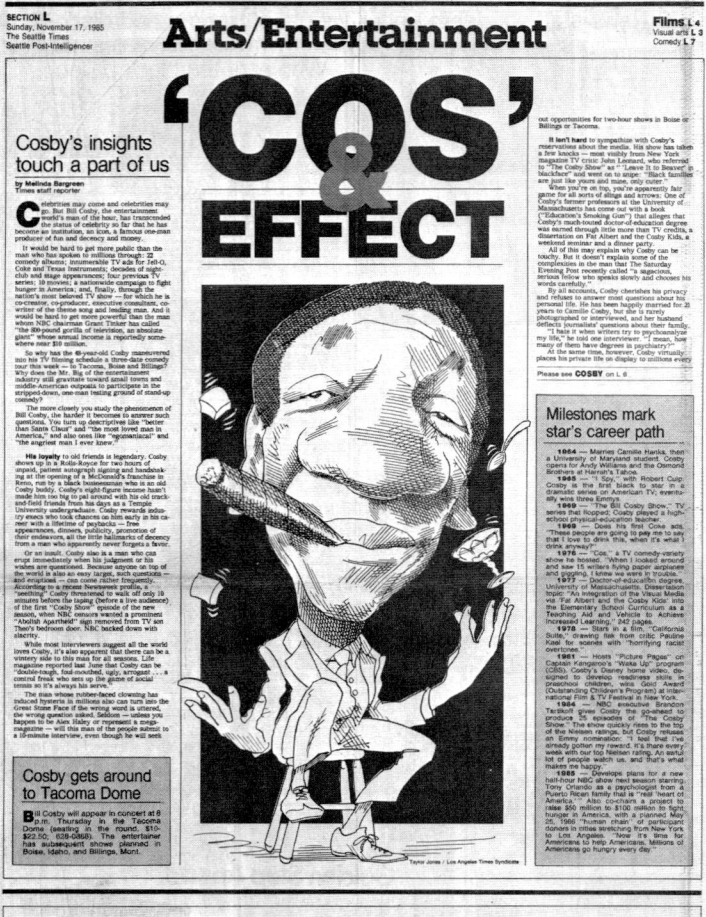

10

CIRCULATION OVER 150,000

A B C D

A-D THE SEATTLE TIMES
Rob Covey, Staff

114 The Best of Newspaper Design

A-D THE BALTIMORE SUN
Richard C. D'Agostino,
Design Director

10 CIRCULATION OVER 75,000

A B C D

SILVER AWARD
A-D THE WASHINGTON TIMES
Staff

11

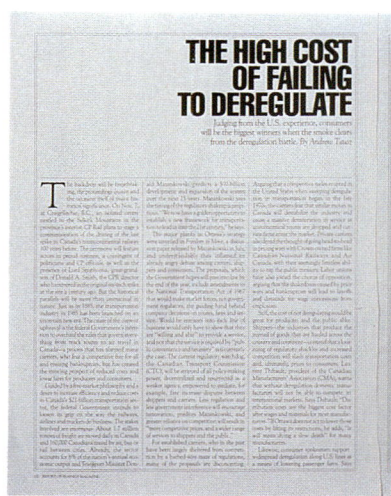

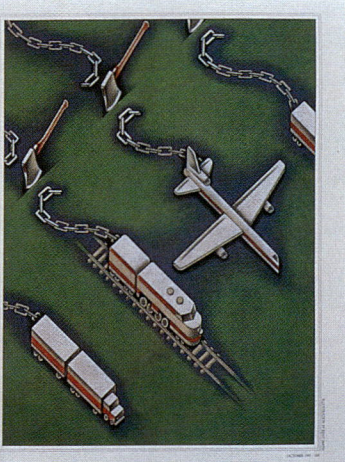

MAGAZINE OVERALL DESIGN

Entries consisted of three complete magazine issues from three different dates.

SILVER AWARD
A-E THE GLOBE AND MAIL
Peter Enneson, Jim Ireland,
Frank Teskey, Mark Danzig

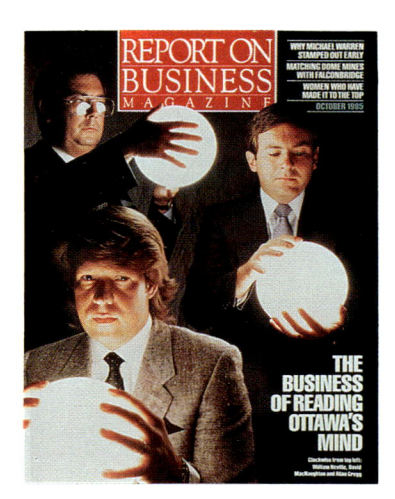

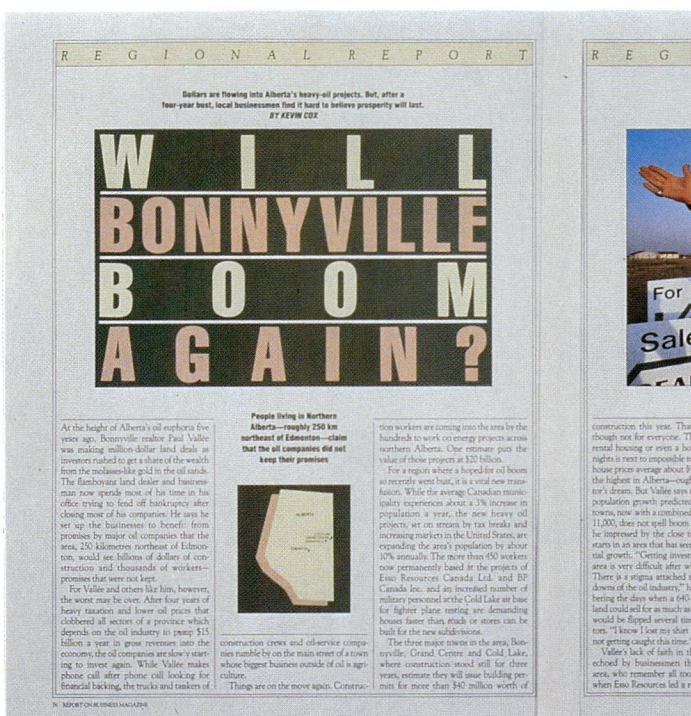

11
OVERALL DESIGN

A-E AFTENPOSTEN
Ashley Booth, Armin Beu, Bjørn Johannessen, Jan Mikalsen, Hilde B. Bang Ellingsen

11
OVERALL DESIGN

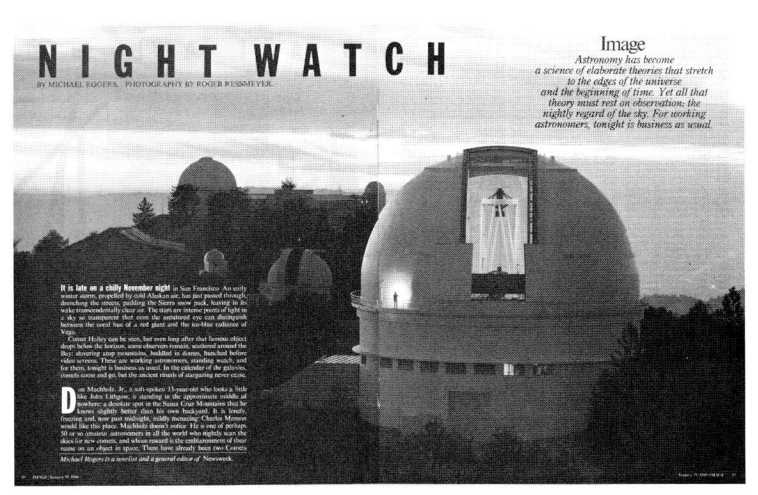

A,B EL NUEVO DIA
Carlos Castaneda, Jose L. Diaz de Villegas Jr.

C,D THE SAN FRANCISCO EXAMINER
Susan Brenneman, Editor;
Veronique Vienne, Art Director

E NOVEDADES
Roger Black, Claudio Rodriguez, Designers; Claudio Rodriguez, Art Director

F RESUME
Tommy Sundstrom,
Hans Wigstrand

Seventh Edition 119

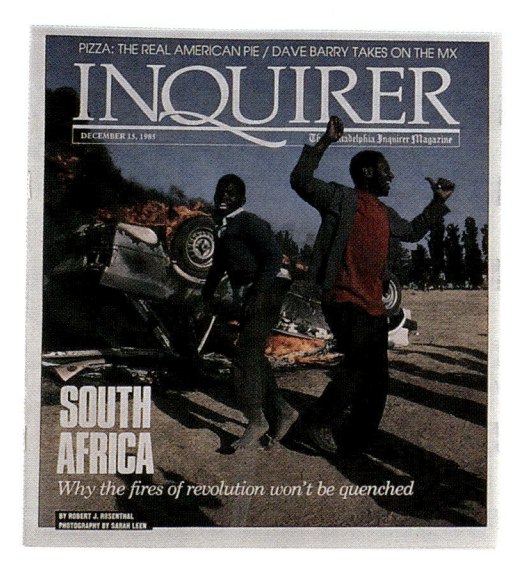

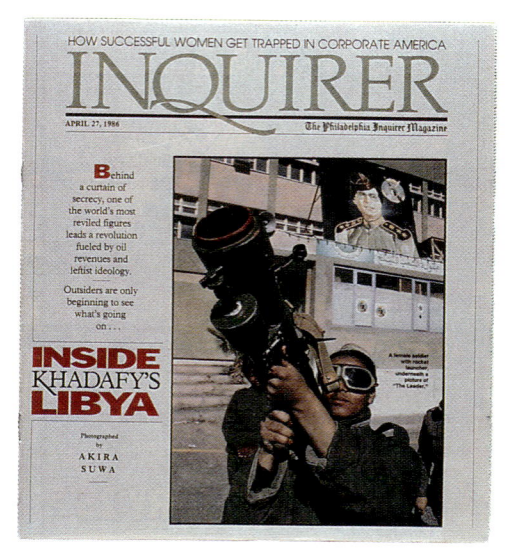

11
OVERALL DESIGN

A-C PHILADELPHIA INQUIRER
David Griffin, Bill Marr

120   The Best of Newspaper Design

11

OVERALL DESIGN

A B C D E

SILVER AWARD

A-E THE GLOBE AND MAIL
Barbara Solowan, Mark Danzig,
Frank Teskey, Jim Ireland

Seventh Edition   121

12 MAGAZINE SPECIAL SECTIONS

Entries consisted of complete special editions of regularly appearing news or feature magazines.

A-C FAEDRELANDSVENNEN
Svein S. Tybakken

12
SPECIAL SECTIONS

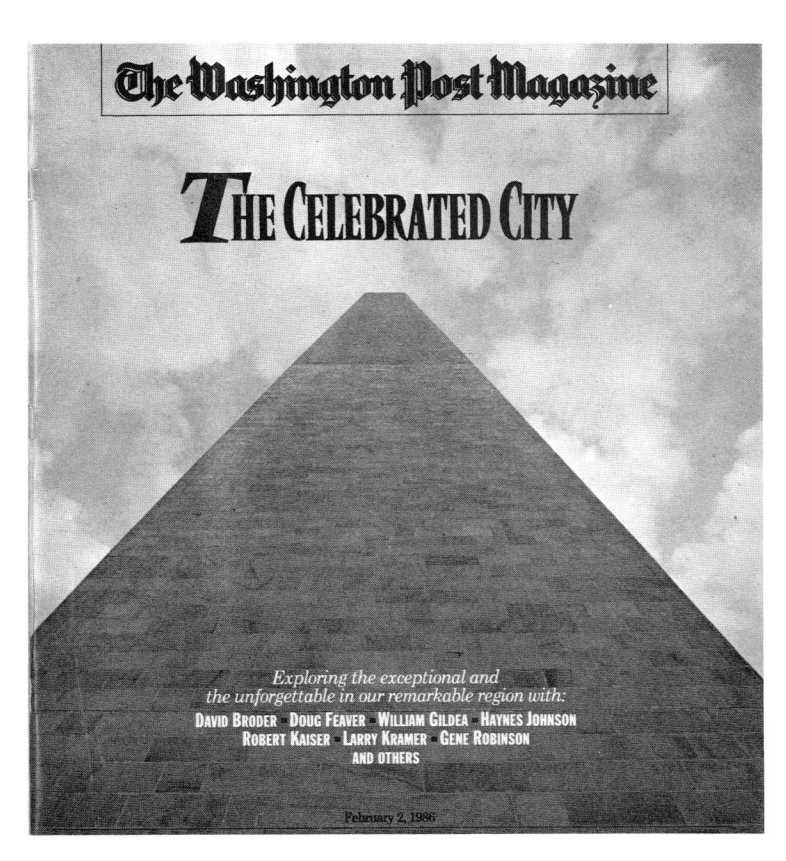

A B
C D
E F

A-F THE WASHINGTON POST
Jann Alexander

Seventh Edition 123

12
SPECIAL SECTIONS

SILVER AWARD

A-D THE NEW YORK TIMES
Ellen Burnie, Art Director

SILVER AWARD

E,F THE GLOBE AND MAIL
Anna James, Jim Ireland, Frank Teskey

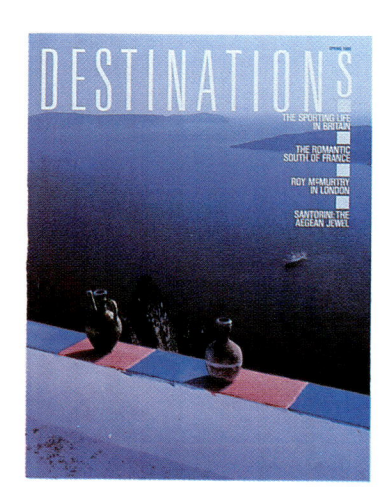

124 The Best of Newspaper Design

A-F THE BOSTON GLOBE
Ronn Campisi

12
SPECIAL SECTIONS

A-D THE BOSTON GLOBE
Ronn Campisi

13

MAGAZINE COVER DESIGN

Entries consisted of individual cover designs, judged separately for single and full color.

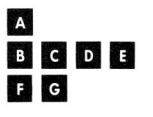

A THE PLAIN DEALER MAGAZINE
Gerard Sealy

B THE SAN FRANCISCO EXAMINER
Susan Brenneman, Editor; Veronique Vienne, Art Director

C THE BOSTON GLOBE
Lucy Bartholomay

D THE BOSTON GLOBE
Ronn Campisi

E THE GLOBE AND MAIL
Barbara Solowan, Mark Danzig, Joseph Chiu, Frank Teskey

F THE WASHINGTON POST
Kathy Legg, Art Director; John Pack, Illustrator

G ATLANTA WEEKLY MAGAZINE
Guy Billout, Illustrator; Peggy Robertson, Art Director

Seventh Edition

13
FULL COLOR

A THE BOSTON GLOBE
Lynn Staley

B SAN JOSE MERCURY NEWS
Bambi Nicklen

C THE CHICAGO TRIBUNE
Brad Holland, Illustrator; Dan Jursa, Art Director

D PHILADELPHIA INQUIRER
Bill Marr

E THE NEW YORK TIMES
Ken Kendrick

F THE NEW YORK TIMES
Ken Kendrick, Art Director; Sheldon Greenberg, Illustrator

G THE NEW YORK TIMES
Nancy Kent, Art Director

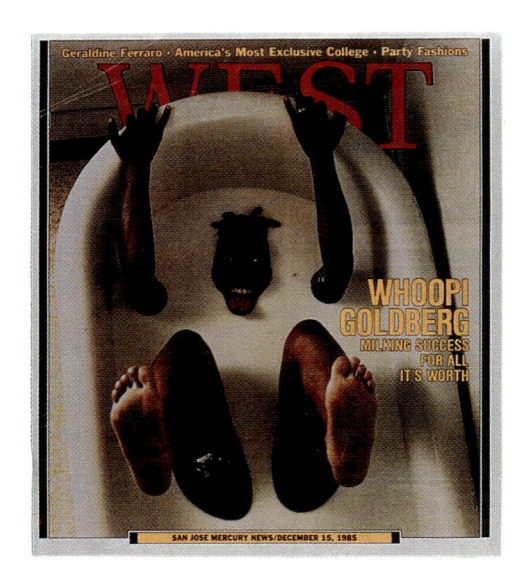

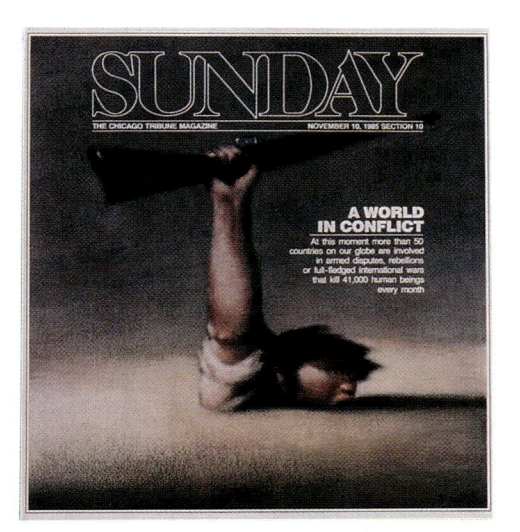

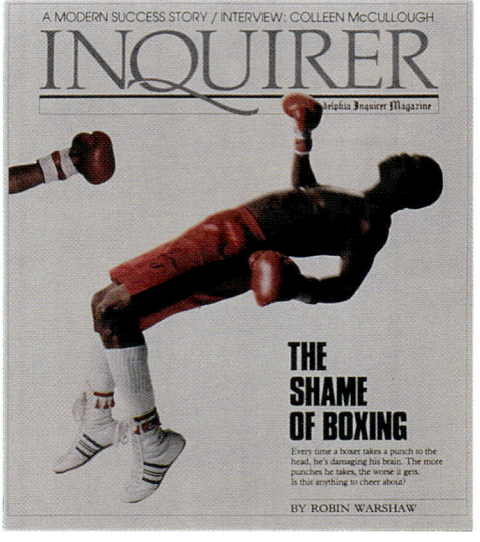

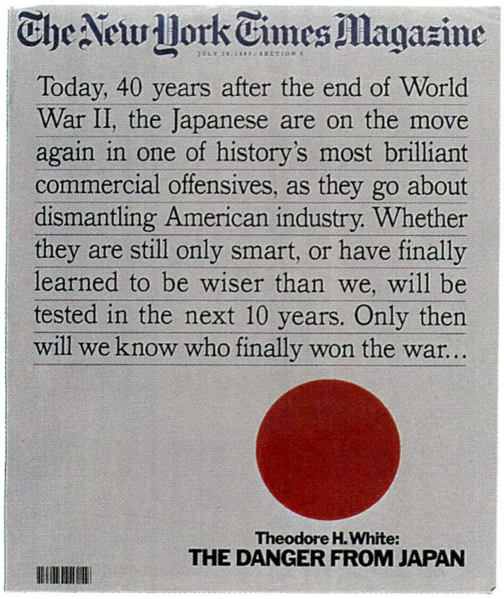

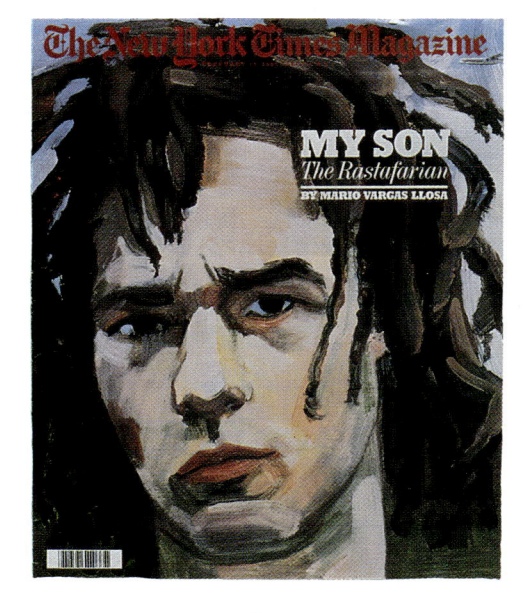

128 The Best of Newspaper Design

13
FULL COLOR

A B
C D E

A THE DETROIT NEWS
Michael Walsh, Denise Chapman

B THE BOSTON GLOBE
Lynn Staley

C THE NEW YORK TIMES
Nancy Kent, Art Director

D THE BOSTON GLOBE
Lynn Staley

E RESUME
Tommy Sundstrom

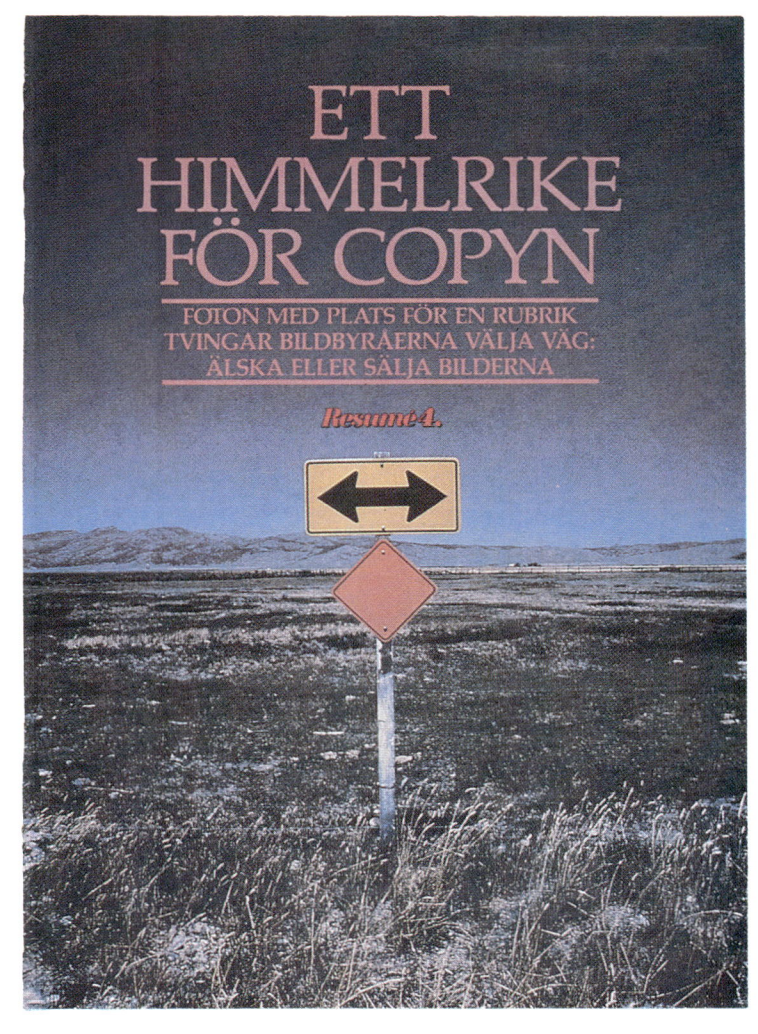

Seventh Edition   129

14
MAGAZINE
PAGE DESIGN

Entries consisted of two or more pages, and single page designs.

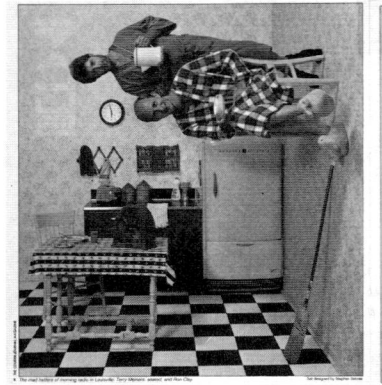

A THE COURIER JOURNAL
Gary S. Chapman, Stephen D. Sebree

B NEWS/SUN-SENTINEL
Kent H. Barton, Art Director; John Parky, Editor

C THE BOSTON GLOBE
Lynn Staley

D THE BOSTON GLOBE
Lynn Staley

130   The Best of Newspaper Design

14
TWO OR MORE PAGES

A
B C
D

A THE BOSTON GLOBE
Ronn Campisi

B THE KANSAS CITY STAR
Ted Pitts, Artist; Bill Gaspard, Art Director

C EL NUEVO DIA
Carlos Castaneda

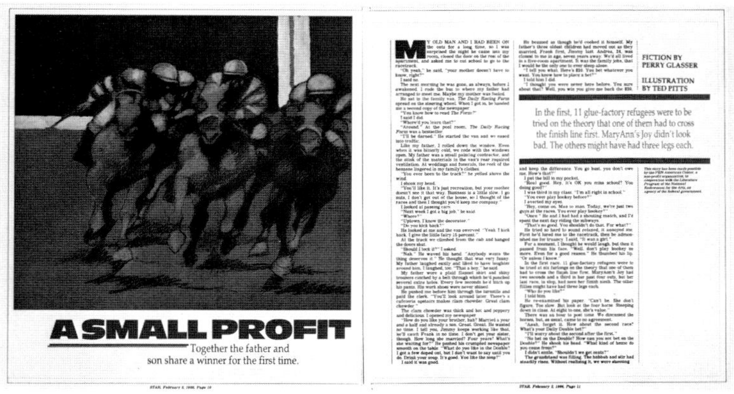

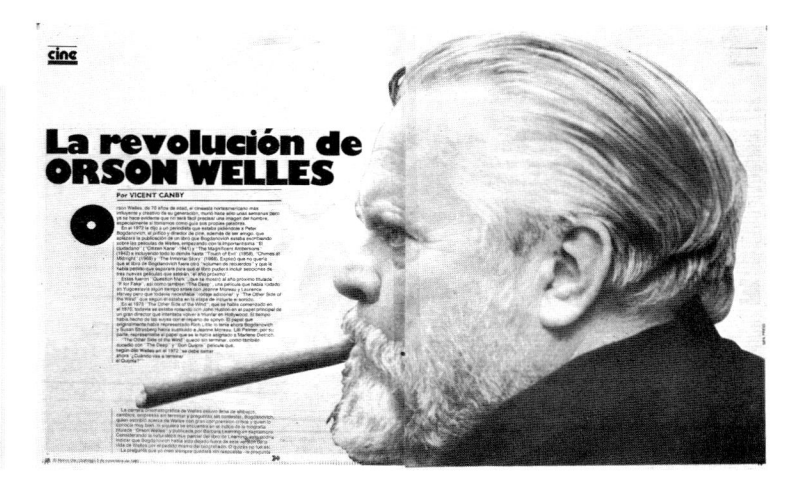

D THE COLUMBUS DISPATCH
Scott Minister; Stephen Castleberry

Seventh Edition 131

14
TWO OR MORE PAGES

A NEWSDAY
Miriam Smith, Dale Gottlieb

B THE SAN FRANCISCO EXAMINER
Susan Brenneman, Editor;
Veronique Vienne, Art Director

C,D DAILY NEWS MAGAZINE
Janet Froelich

132   The Best of Newspaper Design

14
TWO OR MORE PAGES

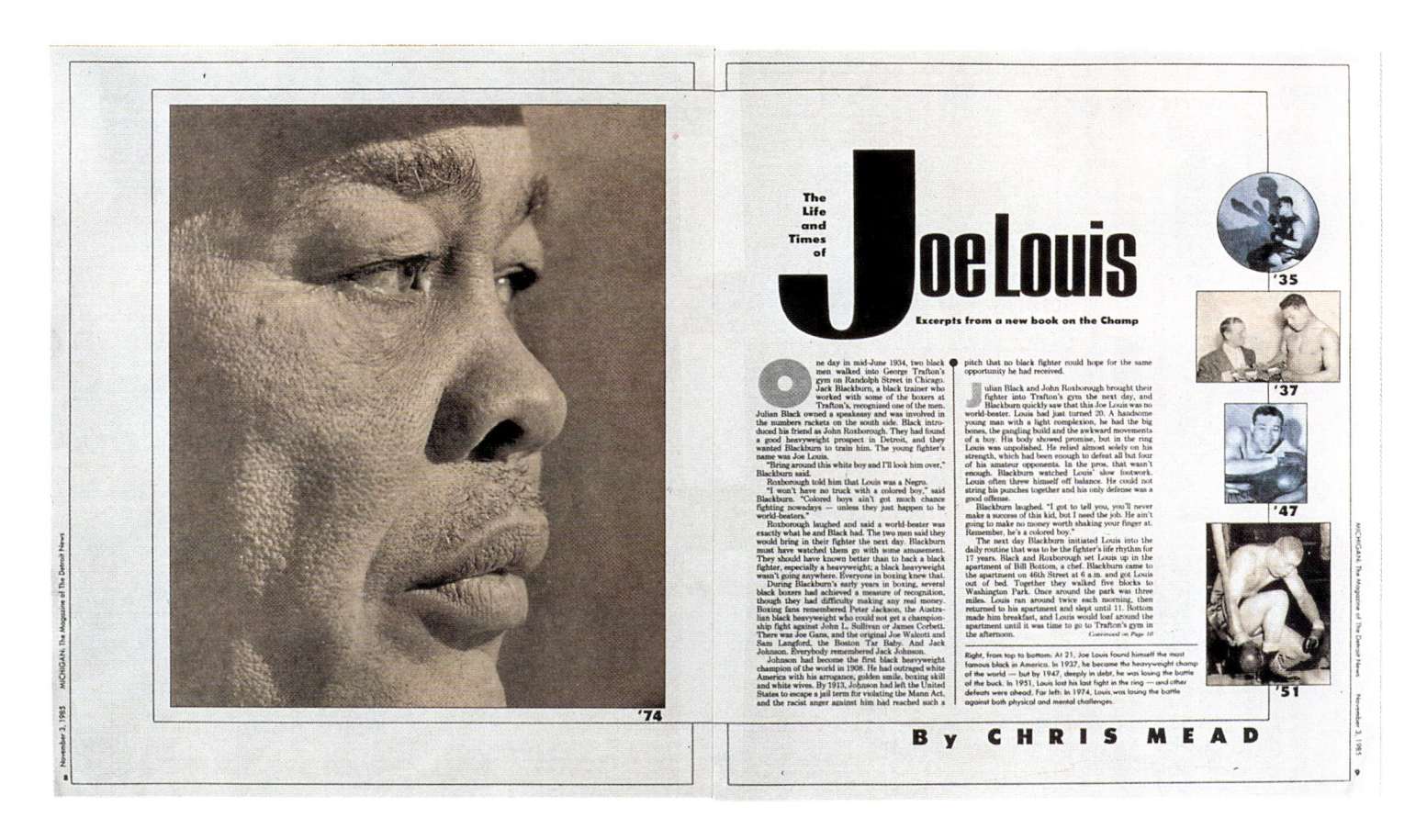

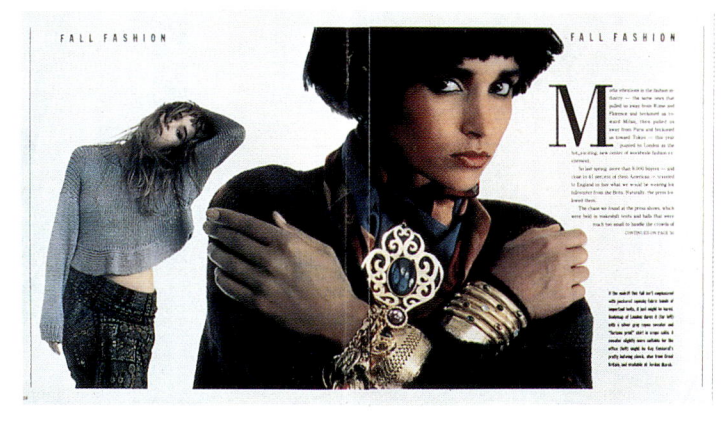

A THE DETROIT NEWS
Michael Walsh, Art Director

B THE SAN FRANCISCO EXAMINER
Susan Brenneman, Editor;
Veronique Vienne, Art Director

C THE BOSTON GLOBE
James Pavlovich

D THE BOSTON GLOBE
Lynn Staley

Seventh Edition 133

14
TWO OR MORE PAGES

A-D SAN JOSE MERCURY NEWS
Bambi Nicklen

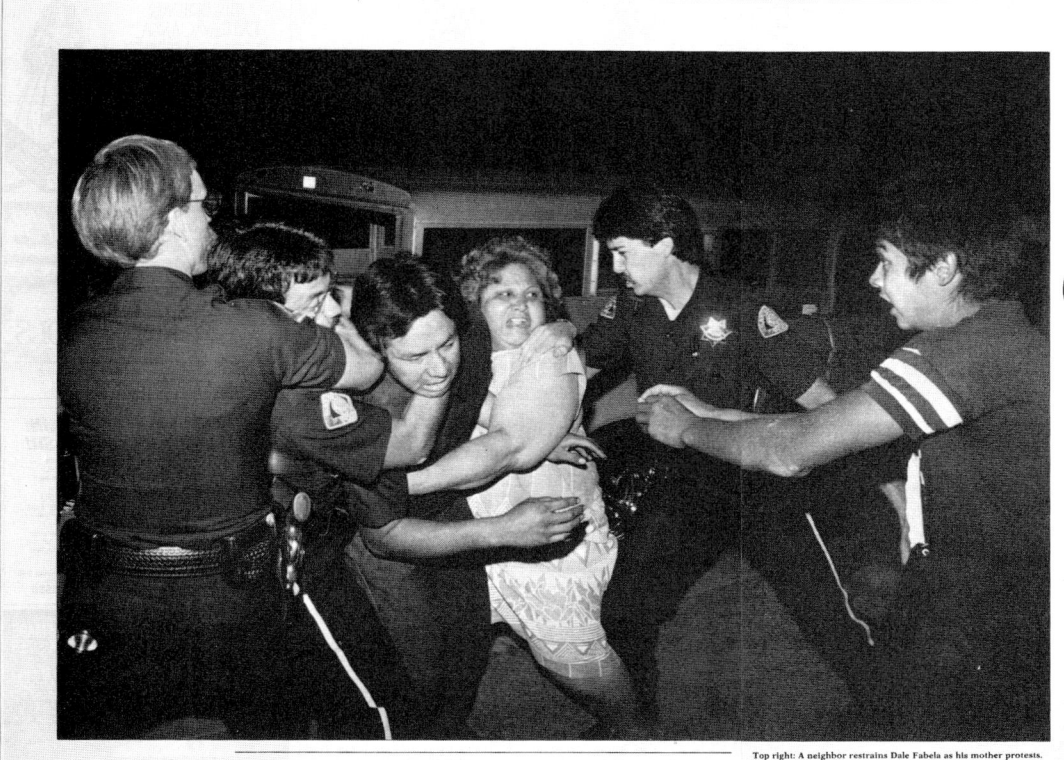

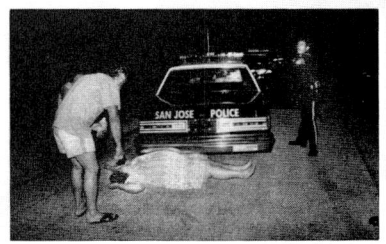

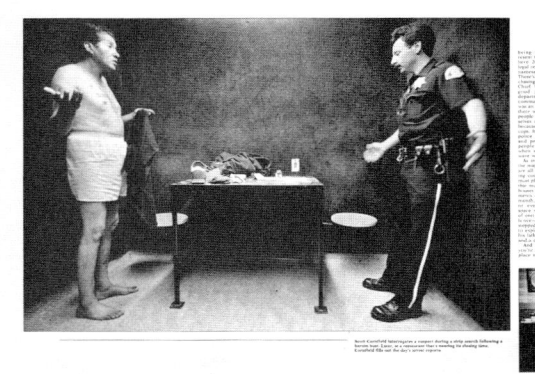

14

TWO OR MORE PAGES

A-D SAN JOSE MERCURY NEWS
Bambi Nicklen

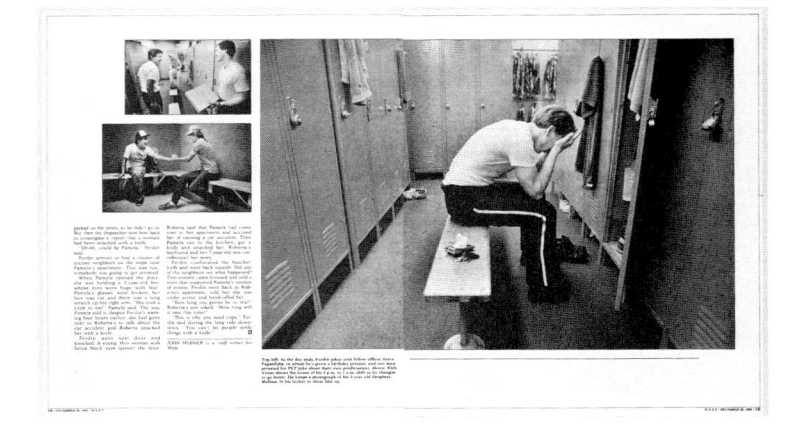

A
B
C
D

Seventh Edition 135

14
TWO OR MORE PAGES

A-D THE NEW YORK TIMES
Ellen Burnie, Art Director

A
B
C
D

136 The Best of Newspaper Design

14
TWO OR MORE PAGES

A,B PHILADELPHIA INQUIRER
David Griffin

C,D THE DENVER POST
Jack Atkinson

Seventh Edition 137

14
SINGLE PAGE

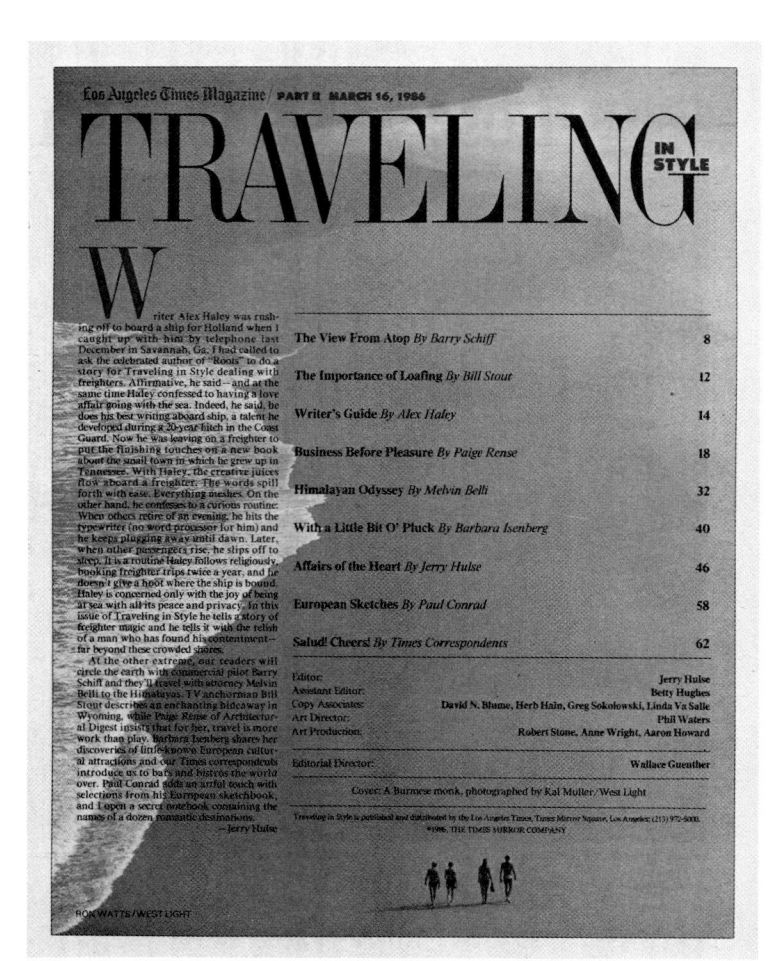

A THE NEW YORK TIMES
Ken Kendrick, Art Director;
Richard Samperi, Designer

B LOS ANGELES TIMES
Phil Waters, Art Director

C DALLAS TIMES HERALD
Dallas City Magazine

15

ART AND ILLUSTRATION

Illustrations were judged as they appeared on the full printed page and were separated into single- and full-color entries. Portfolios consisted of no more than six pages.

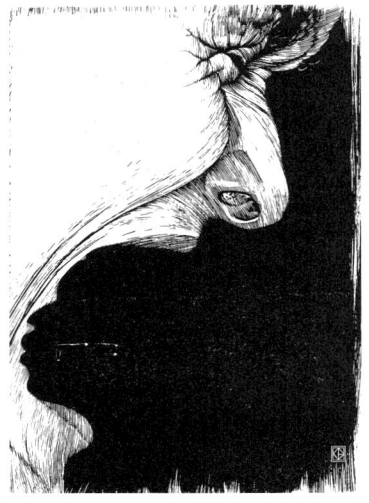

A B C D E

A THE NEW YORK TIMES
Jerelle Kraus, Art Director, Rafal Olbinski, Illustrator

B THE MIAMI HERALD
Kent Barton

C NEWSDAY
Bob Newman

D THE NEW YORK TIMES
Jerelle Kraus, Art Director; Brad Holland, Illustrator

SILVER AWARD
E THE DENVER POST
Bonnie Timmons

Seventh Edition 139

15
FULL COLOR

A	
B	C	D

SILVER AWARD

A THE CHICAGO TRIBUNE
Brad Holland, Illustrator; Dan Jursa, Art Director

B THE NEW YORK TIMES
Ken Kendrick, Art Director; Richard Samperi, Designer; Anita Kunz, Illustrator

C THE COURIER JOURNAL
Herman Wiederwohl

D THE KANSAS CITY STAR
Susan Wise, Illustrator; Bill Gaspard, Art Director

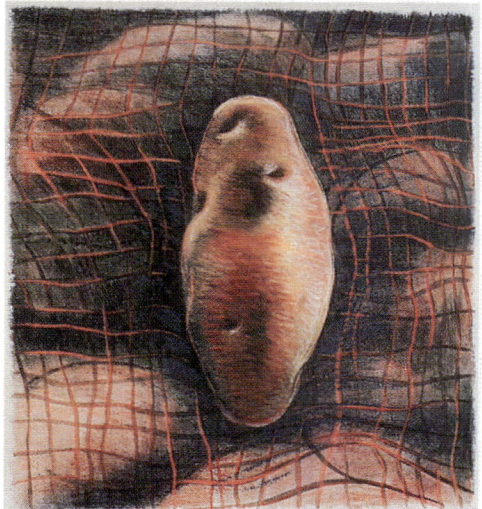

140   The Best of Newspaper Design

15
FULL COLOR

A THE KANSAS CITY STAR
Dick Daniels, Artist; Bill Gaspard, Art Director

B THE MIAMI HERALD
Frank Rakoncay

C THE NEW YORK TIMES
Ken Kendrick, Art Director; Diana La Guardia, Designer; Jeffrey Smith, Illustrator

D DALLAS TIMES HERALD
David Harris, Art Director; Terry Widener, Illustrator

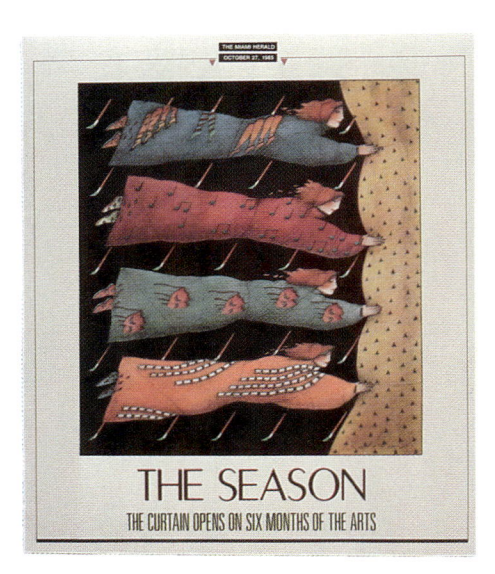

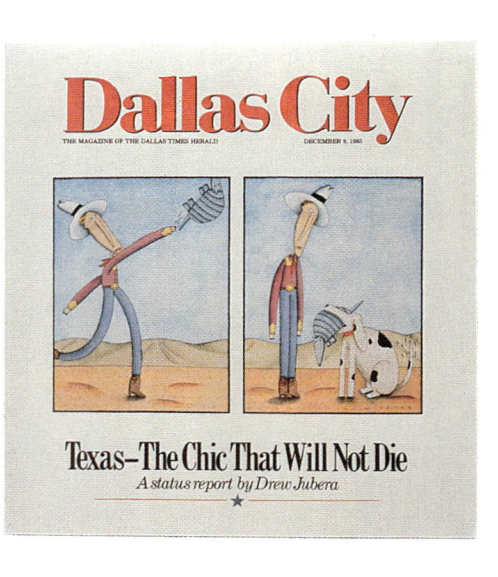

Seventh Edition 141

15
FULL COLOR

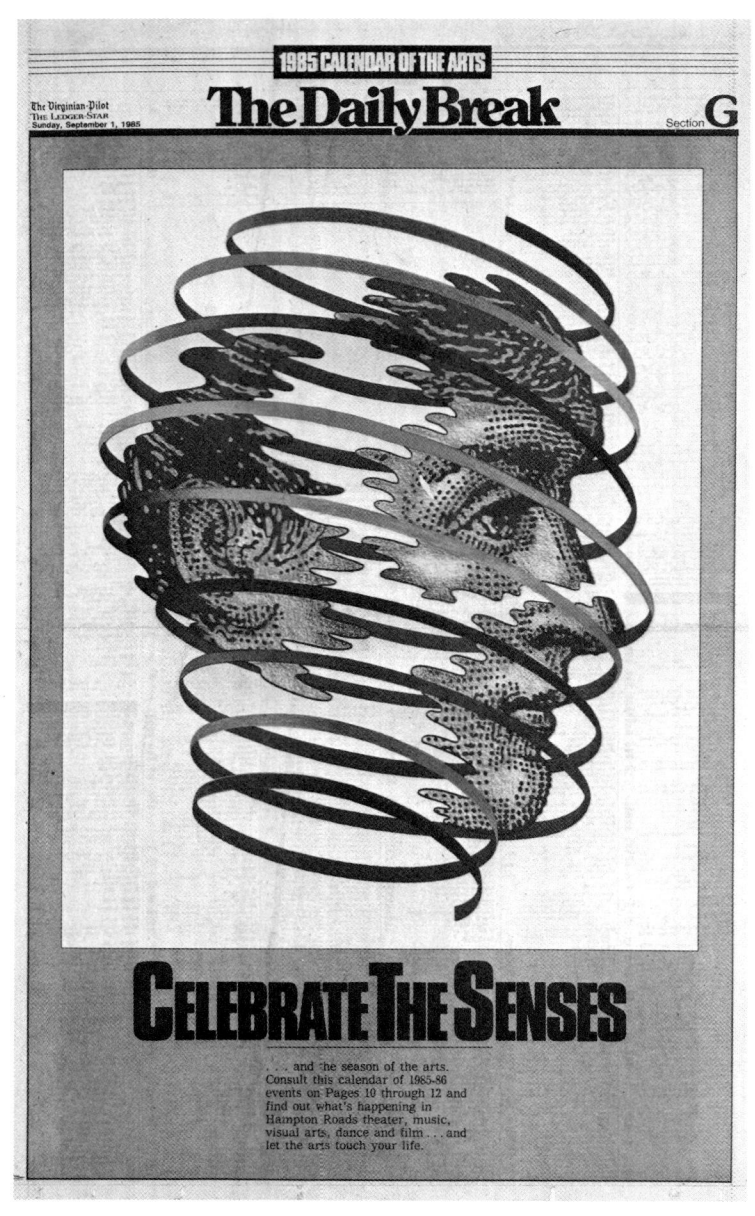

A ATLANTA WEEKLY MAGAZINE
Guy Billout, Illustrator; Peggy Robertson, Art Director

B THE WASHINGTON POST
Beth Rubin, Illustrator; Peggy Robertson, Art Director

C THE DENVER POST
Bonnie Timmons

D THE VIRGINIAN-PILOT/LEDGER-STAR
Sam Hundley

E EL NUEVO DIA
Jose L. Diaz de Villegas, Jr.

F DALLAS TIMES HERALD
Deborah Withey-Culp

142   The Best of Newspaper Design

A THE NEW YORK TIMES
Jerelle Kraus, Art Director; David Suter, Illustrator

B THE NEW YORK TIMES
Jerelle Kraus, Art Director; Horacio Fidel Cardo, Illustrator

C THE CHARLOTTE OBSERVER
Al Phillips

D THE NEW YORK TIMES
Steve Heller, Art Director; David Johnson, Illustrator

15
SINGLE COLOR

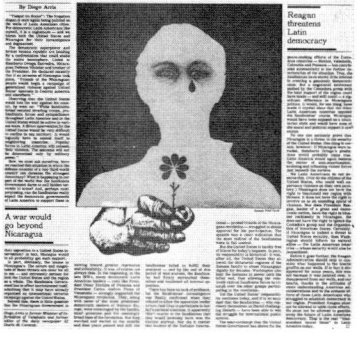

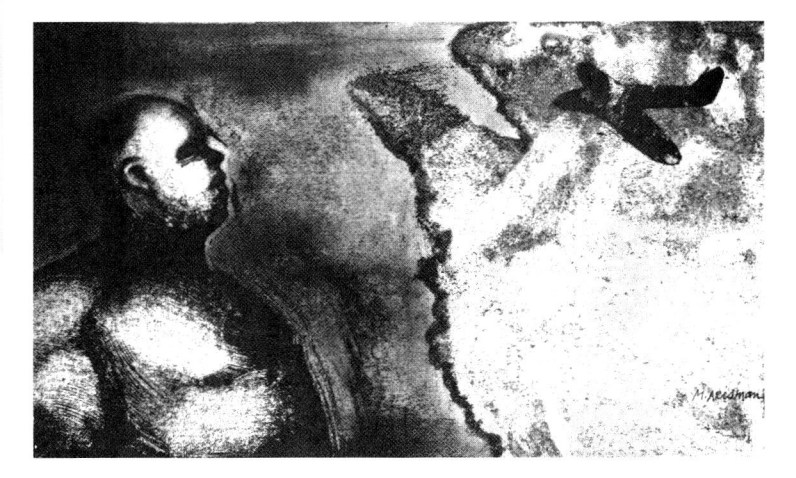

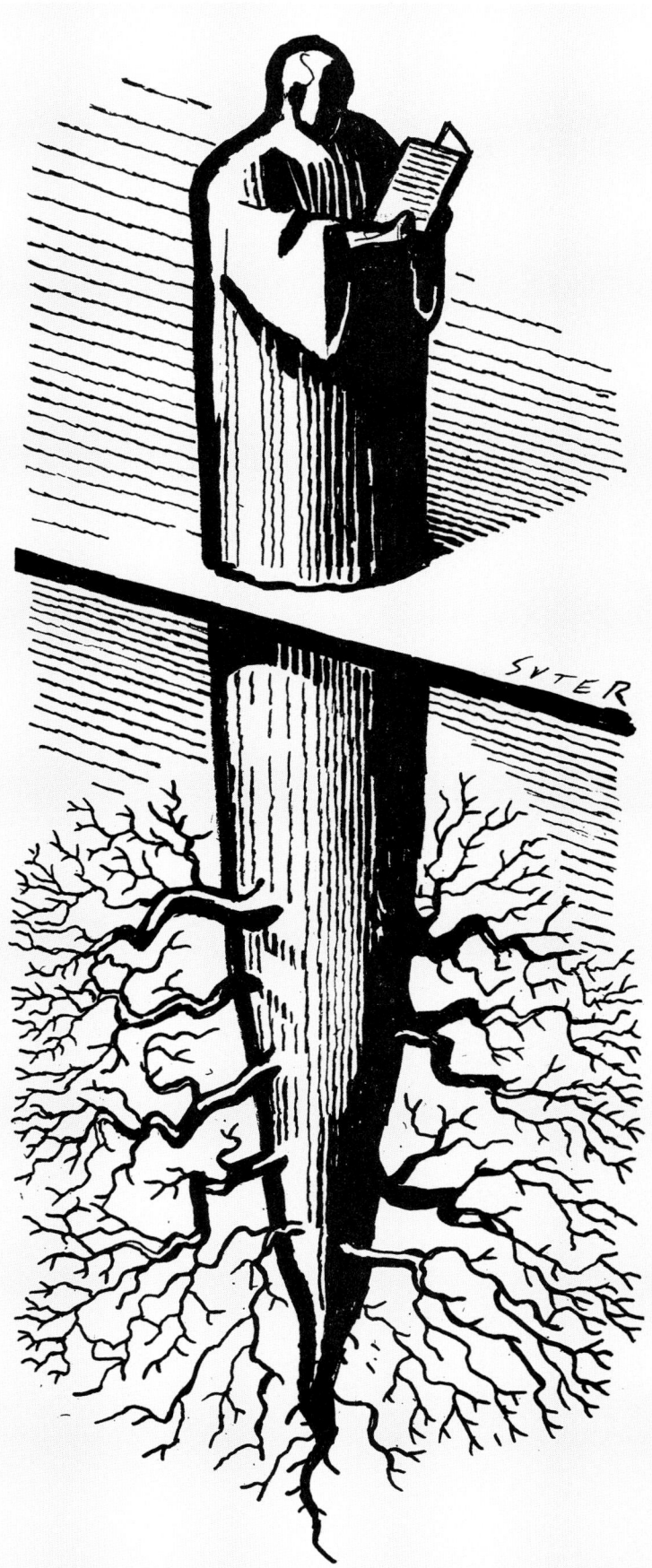

E THE BALTIMORE SUN
Donna Albano

F NEWSDAY
Bob Newman

G THE HARTFORD COURANT
Bob Gallagher

H THE NEW YORK TIMES
Jerelle Kraus, Art Director; Marshall Arisman, Illustrator

Seventh Edition 143

15
FULL COLOR

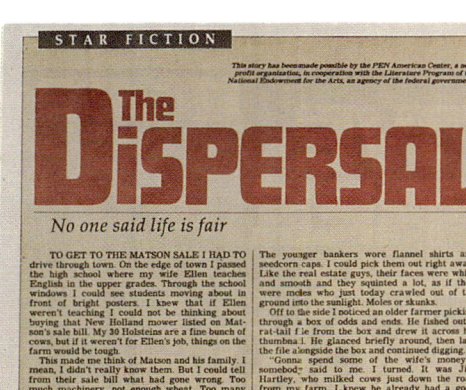

SILVER AWARD

A THE KANSAS CITY STAR
Tom Dolphens, Illustrator; Bill Gaspard, Art Director

B EL NUEVO DIA
Jose L. Diaz de Villegas, Jr.

C THE COURIER JOURNAL
Herman Wiederwohl

D THE SAN FRANCISCO EXAMINER
Susan Brenneman, Editor; Veronique Vienne, Art Director; Guy Billout, Illustrator

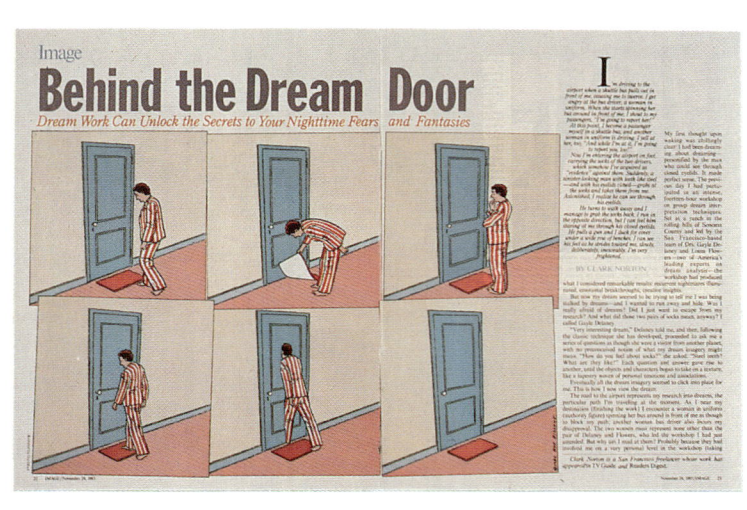

144 The Best of Newspaper Design

15
FULL COLOR

A DALLAS TIMES HERALD
Terry Widener, Illustrator

B THE CHICAGO TRIBUNE
David Beck, Illustrator;
Dan Jursa, Art Director

C THE KANSAS CITY STAR
Tom Dolphens, Illustrator; Bill
Gaspard, Art Director

D THE NEW YORK TIMES
Ken Kendrick, Art Director;
Audrone Razgaitis, Designer; Eric
Velasquez, Illustrator

E ATLANTA WEEKLY
MAGAZINE
Matt Mahurin, Illustrator;
Peggy Robertson, Art Director

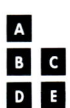

Seventh Edition   145

15
SINGLE COLOR

TRUE VIRTUE

The author says he's had his fill of the 'virtucrat', that prig with cold contempt for all who disagree with him.

By Joseph Epstein

THE LANGUAGE, IF MY RECENT EXperience be any guide, badly needs a new word. The word needed is one to describe those people who are extremely confident about their own virtue and whose spectacular confidence nicely feeds their general feeling of superiority. They are superior to me, or so they have made plain, and they are probably superior to you, if only you will give them the opportunity to demonstrate it.

The people I have in mind have a superiority complex; they are completely convinced of their own moral superiority. I think of them as "virtucrats," for they are empowered by the unfaltering sense of their own virtue.

Roughly a year and a half ago, in the midst of the Democratic primaries, I went to lunch with an old acquaintance, a Chicago journalist. It was at an Italian restaurant and both the food and the talk seemed fine. All was humming along jollily when the journalist began extolling Gary Hart, who at that point in the primaries had begun showing remarkably well. Normally, I prefer to let sleeping dogmas lie, my own and the next person's, but I have this thing about Gary Hart. In four words — I dislike him intensely. I dislike his self-righteousness, his promises to make government "compassionate" again, his general virtuousness, so often self-proclaimed and so endlessly implied.

As my luncheon companion went on and on about what a helluva guy Gary Hart was, I felt this sentence gurgling in my throat — a sentence I have used, in the mostly liberal circles in which I travel, to enliven dull parties and, sometimes, to end lively ones — and then, whoosh, it was out. "I voted for Reagan in 1980," I said, "and shall probably do so again." There, you might say, went the lunch. To the veal limone on the plate before me was now added an ample side order of political bile.

After I had allowed that I had voted for Ronald Reagan and would probably do so again, my lunch companion said he thought Reagan dangerously stupid. I requested examples of his stupidity, but none was forthcoming. He added that the men around Reagan were a terrible and dangerous lot, yet here, too, impressive examples were wanting. He brought up Central America. I said I thought it worth defending, even with its wretched regimes, especially since the Communists were willing to go to such lengths to put and sometimes to keep leftist governments in power there. He said that we drive these people into the arms of the Communists. I said it seemed to me that it doesn't usually turn out to be a very long drive.

When the salad arrived, I went on the offensive. I claimed that, despite the frequent Laurel and Hardy-like antics of the C.I.A., despite the patent interests of American business abroad, I thought the humanitarianism of the United States in its dealings with other nations, through the supplying of food and money and technical assistance, was impressively generous and in fact unsurpassed by any other modern nation I knew. He brought up multinational corporations. I responded that multinationals didn't quite seem to represent the worst the world (Continued on Page 86)

Joseph Epstein is editor of The American Scholar and the author, most recently, of "The Middle of My Tether" and "Plausible Prejudices."

ILLUSTRATION BY PETER DE SEVE

A THE NEW YORK TIMES
Peter De Seve, Illustrator; Ken Kendrick, Art Director; Kevin McPhee, Designer

B THE DENVER POST
Bonnie Timmons

C THE DENVER POST
Bonnie Timmons

D DAYTON DAILY NEWS
Ted Pitts

E THE DENVER POST
Bonnie Timmons

F THE NEW YORK TIMES
Jerelle Kraus, Art Director; Horacio Fidel Cardo, Illustrator

146   The Best of Newspaper Design

15
SINGLE COLOR

A PHILADELPHIA INQUIRER
Sam Hundley

B THE NEW YORK TIMES
John Cayea, Art Director; Istvan Ventilla, Illustrator

SILVER AWARD
C THE WALL STREET JOURNAL
Kevin Sprouls

D THE BALTIMORE SUN
Donna Albano

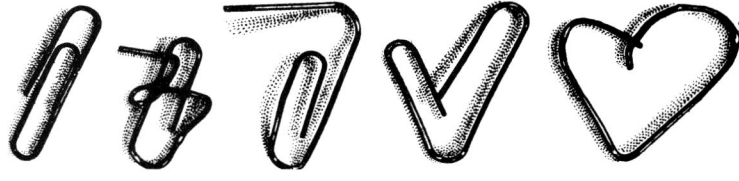

Seventh Edition 147

15
FULL COLOR

A DALLAS TIMES HERALD
David Harris, Art Director;
Elwood H. Smith, Illustrator

B THE SAN FRANCISCO EXAMINER
Susan Brenneman, Editor;
Veronique Vienne, Art Director;
Andrzej Dudzinski, Illustrator

C THE NEW YORK TIMES
Ken Kendrick, Art Director; Tim Lewis, Illustrator

D THE NEW YORK TIMES
Ken Kendrick, Art Director;
Robert Goldstrom Illustrator

E THE DENVER POST
Bonnie Timmons

F THE ROCKET
Jim Christie, Illustrator;
Rick Jost, Art Director

G DAYTON DAILY NEWS
Ted Pitts

H PHILADELPHIA INQUIRER
Sam Hundley

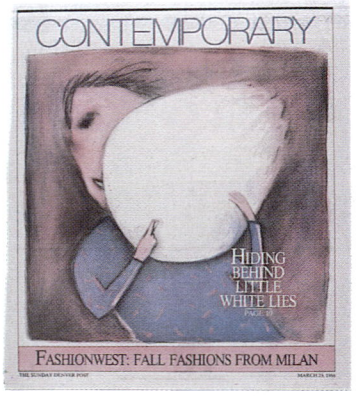

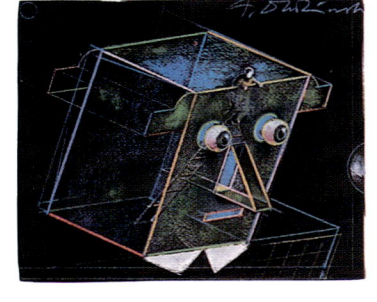

148 The Best of Newspaper Design

A THE KANSAS CITY STAR
Kerry Meyer, Illustrator; Bill Gaspard, Art Director

B THE NEW YORK TIMES
Ken Kendrick, Art Director; Richard Samperi, Designer; Peter De Seve, Illustrator

C THE WASHINGTON TIMES
Peter Steiner

D ATLANTA WEEKLY MAGAZINE
Matt Mahurin, Illustrator; Peggy Robertson, Art Director

E THE NEW YORK TIMES
Ken Kendrick, Art Director; Audrone Razgaitis, Designer; Paul Yalowitz, Illustrator

SILVER AWARD
F THE NEW YORK TIMES
Ken Kendrick, Art Director; Audrone Razgaitis, Designer; Robert Goldstrom, Illustrator

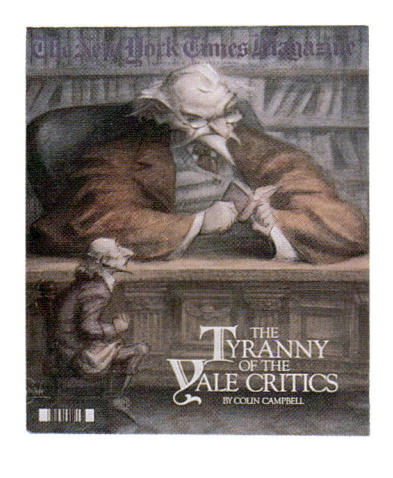

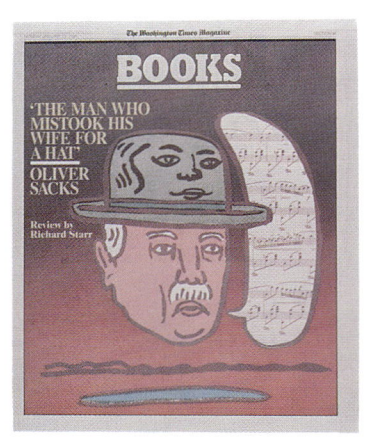

15
PORTFOLIO OF WORK

A-D THE WALL STREET
JOURNAL
Kevin Sprouls

A
B
C D

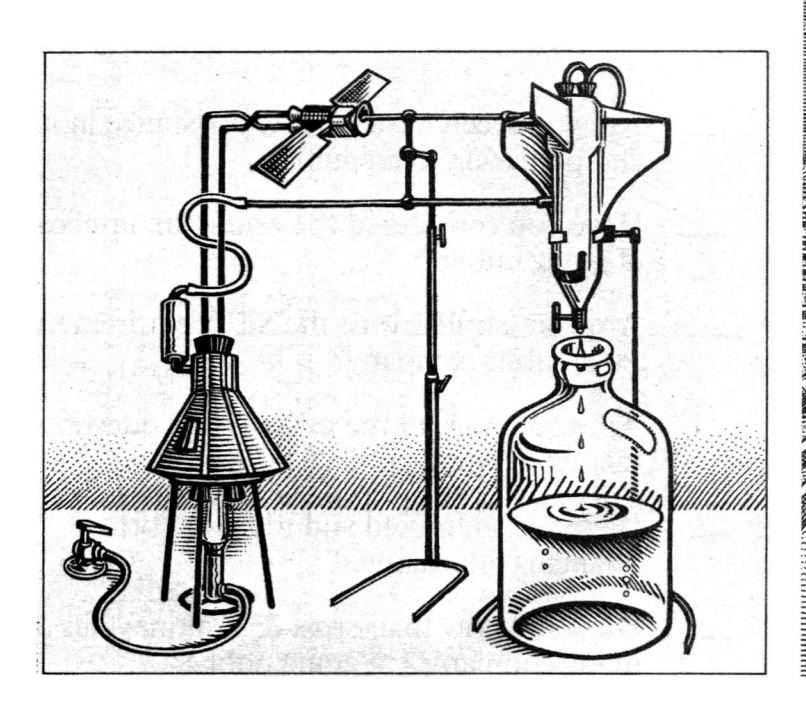

150 The Best of Newspaper Design

15

PORTFOLIO OF WORK

A-D THE SAN FRANCISCO CHRONICLE
William Cone

Seventh Edition 151

15
PORTFOLIO OF WORK

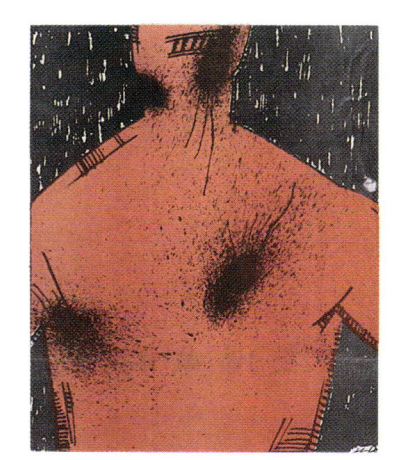

SILVER AWARD
A-D EL NUEVO DIA
Jose L. Diaz de Villegas, Jr.

15
PORTFOLIO OF WORK

A	B	
C	D	
E	F	G
H		

A–D THE KANSAS CITY STAR
Tom Dolphens

E–H THE HARTFORD COURANT
Merle Nacht

15
PORTFOLIO OF WORK

A-D THE ORANGE COUNTY REGISTER
Craig Pursley

154   The Best of Newspaper Design

15
PORTFOLIO OF WORK

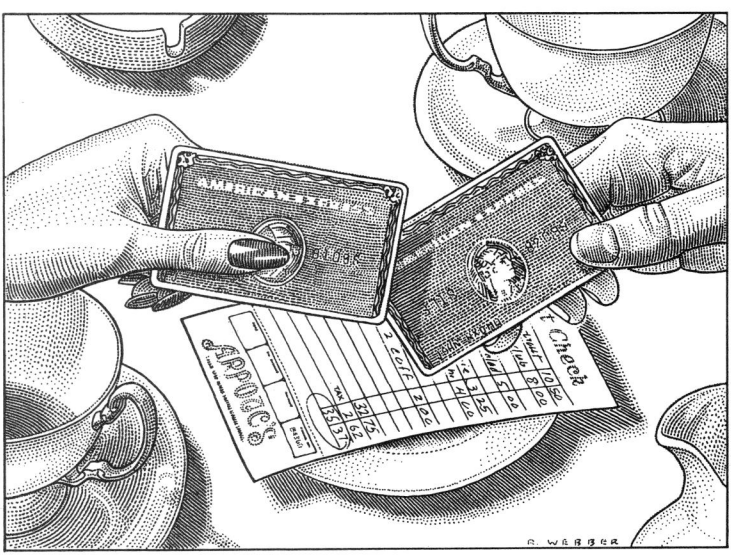

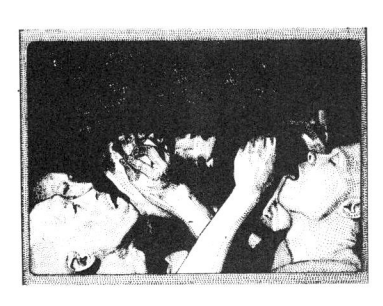

A	B
C	D
E	F
G	H

A-D THE WALL STREET JOURNAL
Rosemary Webber

E-H THE WALL STREET JOURNAL
Laura Lou Levy

Seventh Edition 155

16

PHOTOGRAPHY AND PHOTOJOURNALISM

Entries consisted of full pages as published in four categories • Spot News Photography • Photo Story • Feature Photography • Portfolio of Work.

156 The Best of Newspaper Design

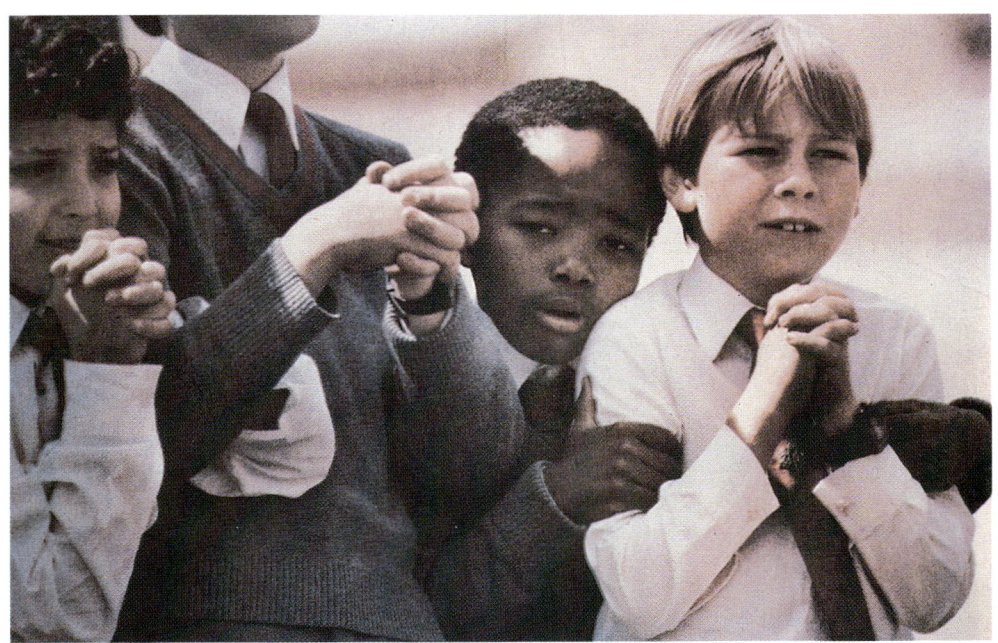

GOLD AWARD

A-D THE DALLAS MORNING NEWS
David Leeson

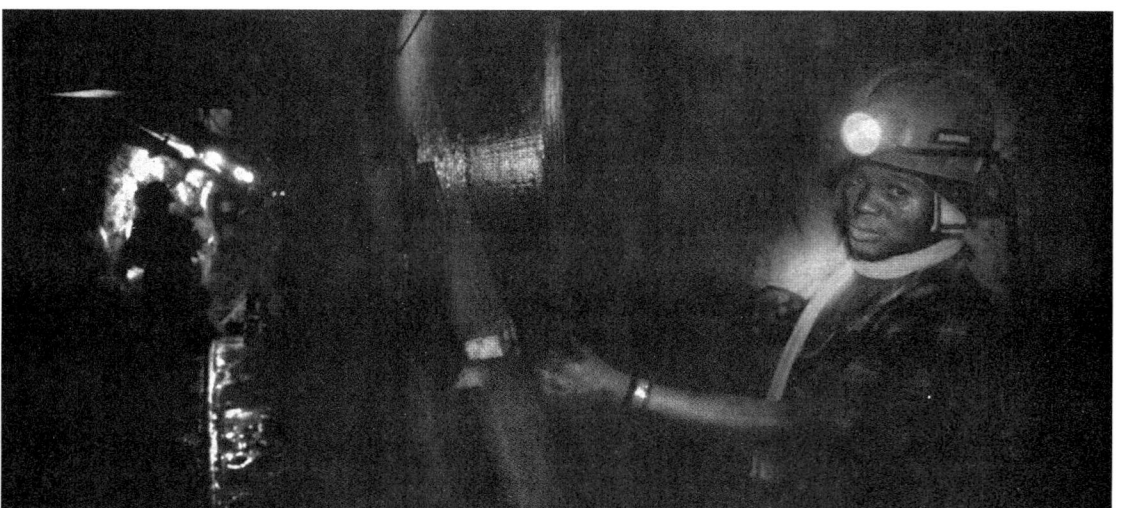

16
PHOTO STORY

GOLD AWARD

A,B THE DALLAS MORNING NEWS
David Leeson

16
PHOTO STORY

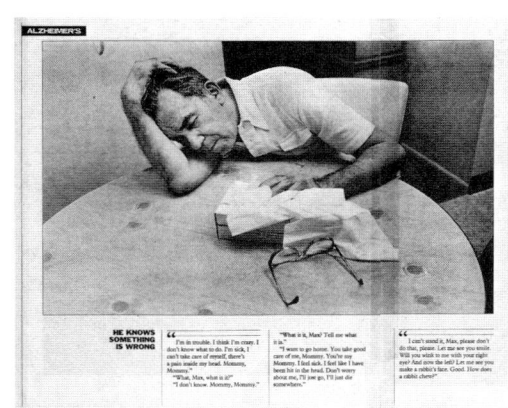

SILVER AWARD
A-D PHILADELPHIA INQUIRER
Sarah Leen

16
PHOTO STORY

A B
C D

An American Farm Family

A-D ST. PAUL PIONEER PRESS-DISPATCH
Joe Rossi

160 The Best of Newspaper Design

16
PHOTO STORY

A-E THE PHOENIX GAZETTE
Mike Rynearson

Seventh Edition 161

16
PHOTO STORY

A-D THE SEATTLE TIMES
Harley Soltes

162   The Best of Newspaper Design

16
PHOTO STORY

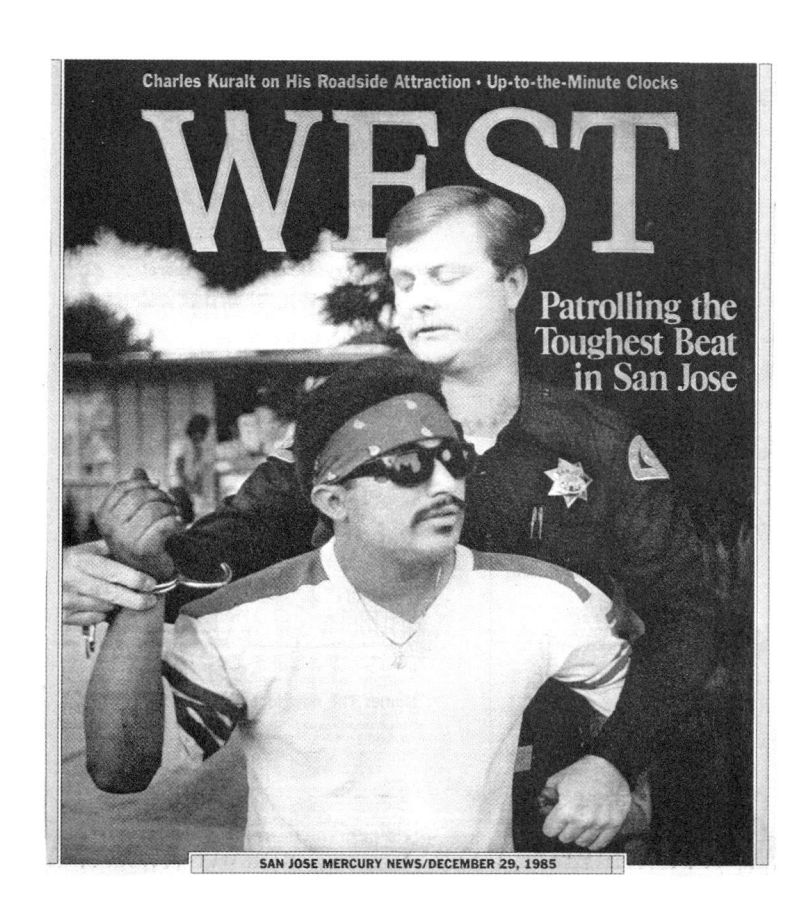

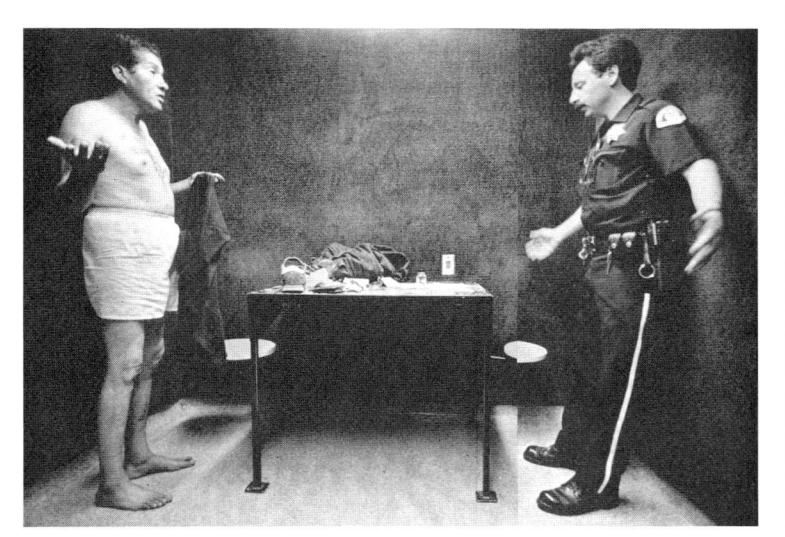

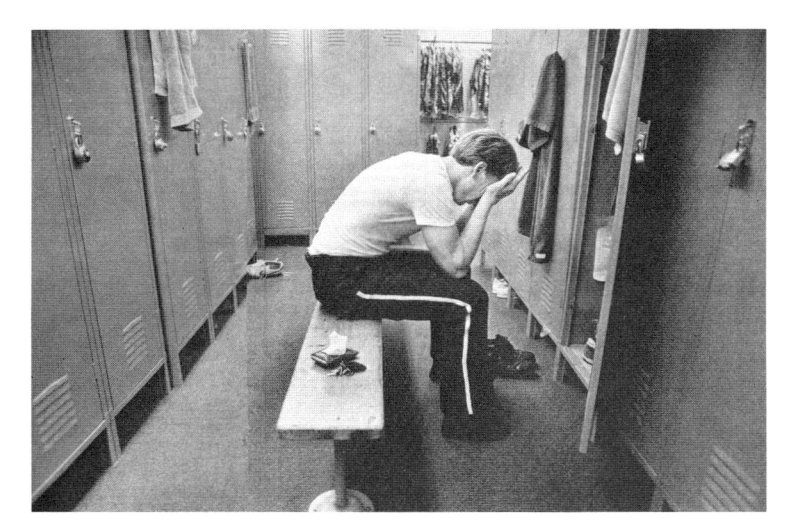

A-E SAN JOSE MERCURY NEWS
Jim Gensheimer

Seventh Edition 163

16
PHOTO STORY

A-D THE SACRAMENTO BEE
Michael Williamson, Photographer; George Wedding, Designer

16
PHOTO STORY

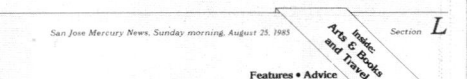

A B
C D

A-D SAN JOSE MERCURY NEWS
Cheryl Nuss

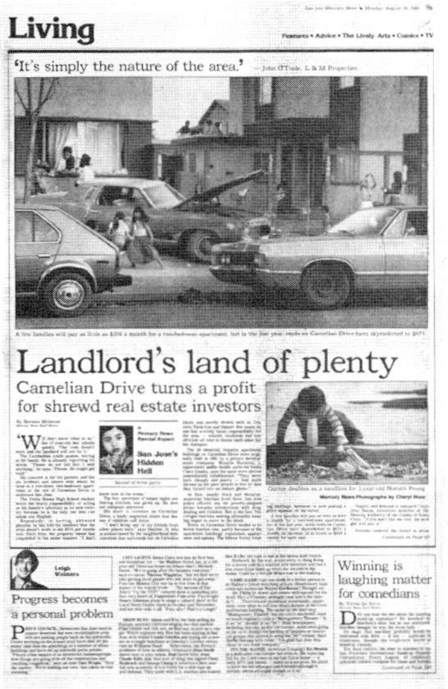

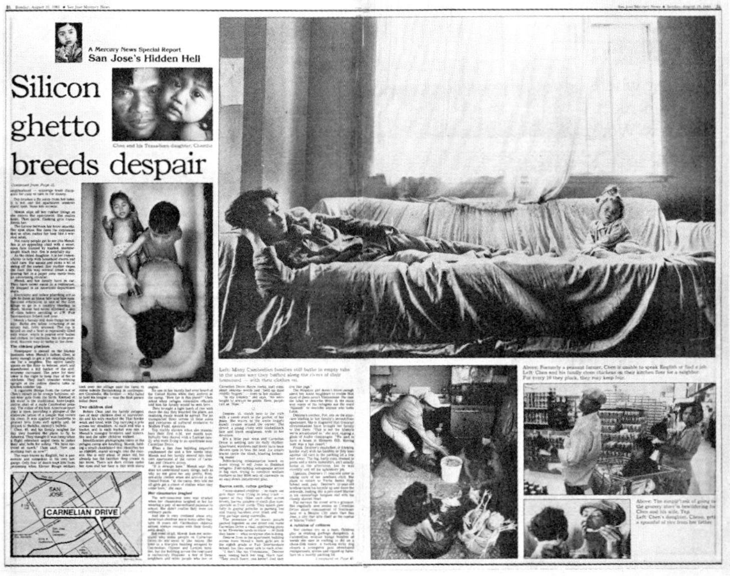

Seventh Edition 165

16
PHOTO STORY

A B
C D

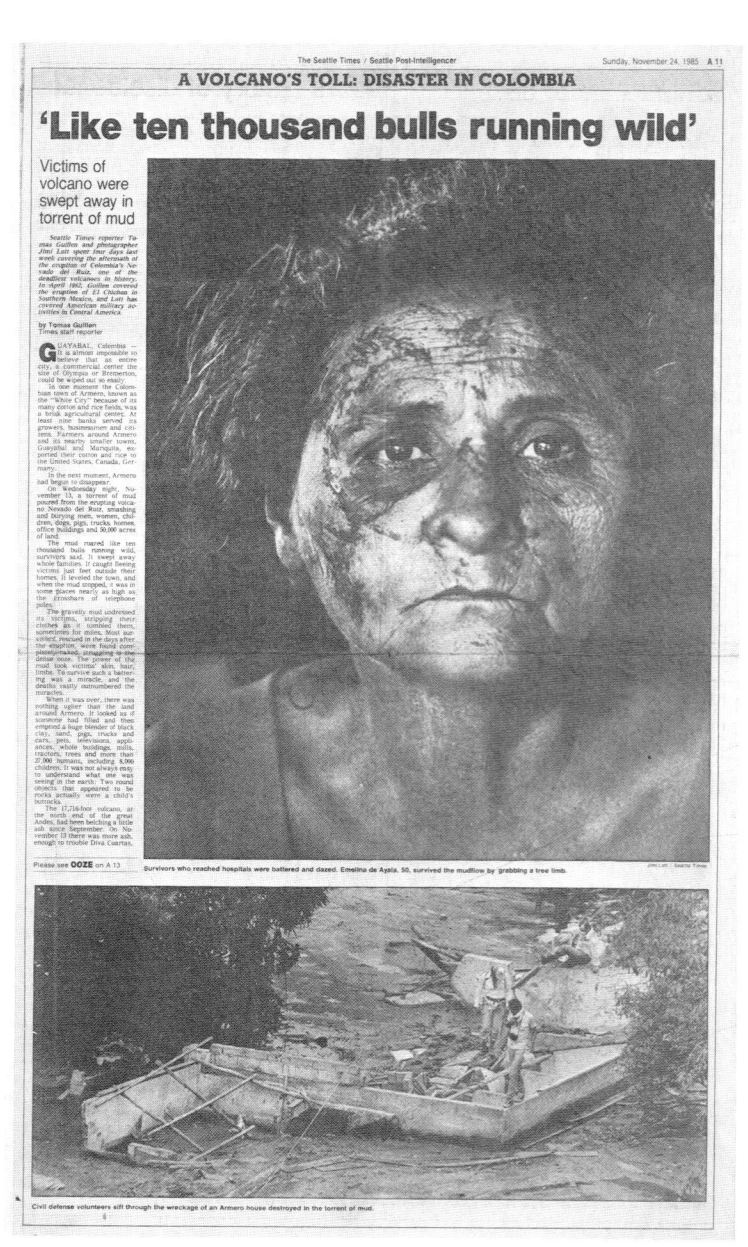

A-D THE SEATTLE TIMES
Jimi Lott

166   The Best of Newspaper Design

PHOTO STORY

Helen retrieves the luncheon salads left to cool in a screened porch off the kitchen.

A,B THE KANSAS CITY STAR
Patrick Sullivan, Photographer; Bill Gaspard, Art Director

give to children as they came up to him."

There were friends, an occasional party, and good relations with most of the neighbors. But for a variety of reasons, the Seelyes became isolated. Some in town resented the grandeur of their home. The merits of patent medicines increasingly were in doubt. And Mrs. Seelye and her daughters weren't predisposed to active socializing.

"I guess we were more or less retiring, I think, rather hesitant. Don't you think so?" Helen asked her sister.

"Yes, I believe so," Marion said.

"Mother . . . she liked to stay at home," Helen said. "The three of us went around together a lot. We seemed to enjoy people who were mother's age more than those who were our age."

Marion was valedictorian of the class of 1914. She remembers a young future-president named Dwight David Eisenhower doing preparatory work for West Point.

Helen was salutatorian of the Class of '17. It took her six years to graduate; twice she'd had surgery to remove malignant abdominal tumors, and she'd missed a lot of school convalescing.

She remembers a senior class gathering in which the class members put on a circus.

"Milton Eisenhower was a clown," Helen said. "And I think Earl was the ringmaster. But I didn't really mingle with [her classmates] very much. I kind of drew into a shell. I couldn't talk to people in those days."

Marion went to the University of Kansas and studied at the School of Fine Arts. She later studied music in St. Louis and at the Kansas City Conservatory of Music. But at the close of classes each term, she returned home. And ultimately, she stayed.

She performed for friends around the county, was the first secretary of the county historical society and was an officer in the local chapter of the Daughters of the American Revolution.

When her mother became an invalid from the strokes she'd suffered, Marion cared for her. Mrs. Seelye died in 1951 at the age of 77. Dr. Seelye had died three years earlier of heart disease and a brain tumor. He too had been 77.

Helen attended KU as well, studying pharmacy. But after less than a year there, she, like many people across the country in 1917 and 1918, contracted the Spanish flu. She returned home to recuperate and stayed to work in her father's laboratory in downtown Abilene.

continued on page 14

No swimming pool? Well, legend wouldn't be legend if it were all true.

February 16, 1986, Page 11

A
B

THE HOUSE

She stands in Abilene, the grand dame of Victorian excess. And now, for the first time in 80 years, we are all invited inside.

BY MIKE DeARMOND

THE LINE BEGAN TO FORM about noon just outside the front door, and in the next 60 minutes backed across the a tennis-court-sized porch, down the stone steps, turned left and undulated half a block along North Buckeye. Enveloped in the chill of a Sunday in December, the people spoke in whispers that represented decades of wondering.

Where is the swimming pool?
Did you know about the secret passages? The bowling alley in the basement?
This is the house that patent medicine built. Cost $50,000 back in 1905. Must be worth a couple of million now.
The daughters never married. Haven't been out of the place in years. You ever met them? You ever been inside the place?
'Course not. Don't know anybody who has.

These were the curious, who plunked down $10 each to take an organized peek inside the A.B. Seelye Mansion. Over two weekends, some 1,800 persons paid for the privilege. Two thousand fortunate enough not to have to pay—tour guides from the Dickinson County Historical Society, friends, a journalist or two—joined them.

If the Grand Dame of Abilene, Kansas, was willing to raise her skirts and cast off the veil of the years, there sure wasn't anything wrong with gawking a bit.

In groups of eight to 10, church manners on display, they inspected each of the mansion's 25 rooms. Accompanied by classical selections performed by a string quartet (in the music room, of course), they trod the hardwood floors covered by Oriental rugs and craned their necks to see the brass and crystal chandeliers hanging from the 10½-foot ceilings. Have-you-ever glances played across the concave, convex and leaded-glass windows and the wood-burning stove in the kitchen—still used for some of the cooking. Oh-look-at-this gasps resounded over

Photography by Patrick Sullivan

Helen (left) and Marion Seelye invited the public recently to come see their grand old house. (Top left) The light fixtures in the ballroom still have their original Edison bulbs.

16
SPOT NEWS

SILVER AWARD
A THE VIRGINIAN-PILOT/
LEDGER-STAR
Michael McDonald

SILVER AWARD
B THE WASHINGTON TIMES
Stephen Crowley

SILVER AWARD
C THE VIRGINIAN-PILOT/
LEDGER-STAR
Lois Bernstein

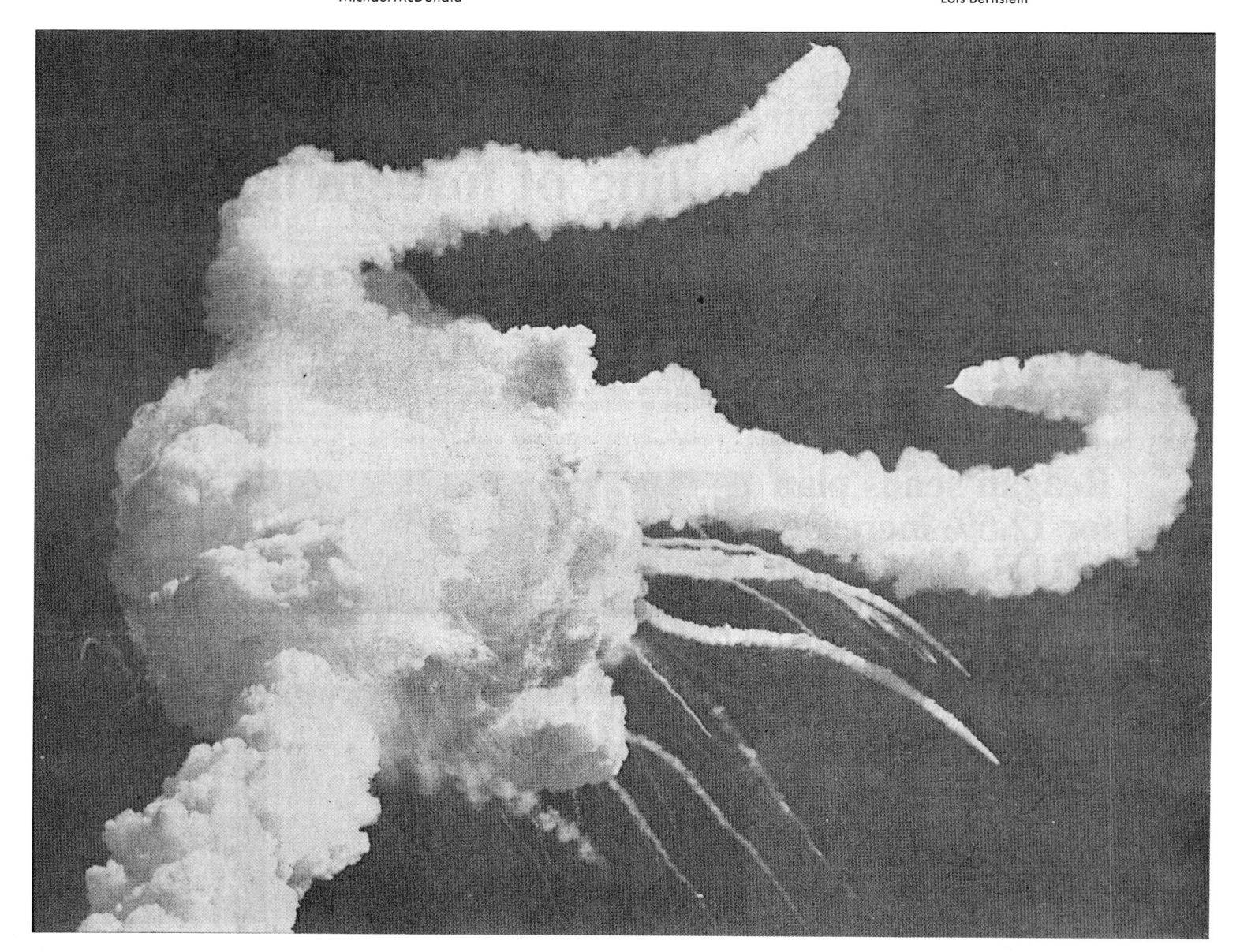

168   The Best of Newspaper Design

16
SPOT NEWS

A THE ORANGE COUNTY REGISTER
Jim Mendenhall

B THE SEATTLE TIMES
Jimi Lott

C THE DALLAS MORNING NEWS
Ken Geiger

D EL NORTE
Staff

E THE PRESS DEMOCRAT
Mary Carroll

16
FEATURE PHOTOGRAPHY

A THE NEW YORK TIMES
Michael O'Neill, Photographer;
Richard Samperi, Designer; Ken
Kendrick, Art Director

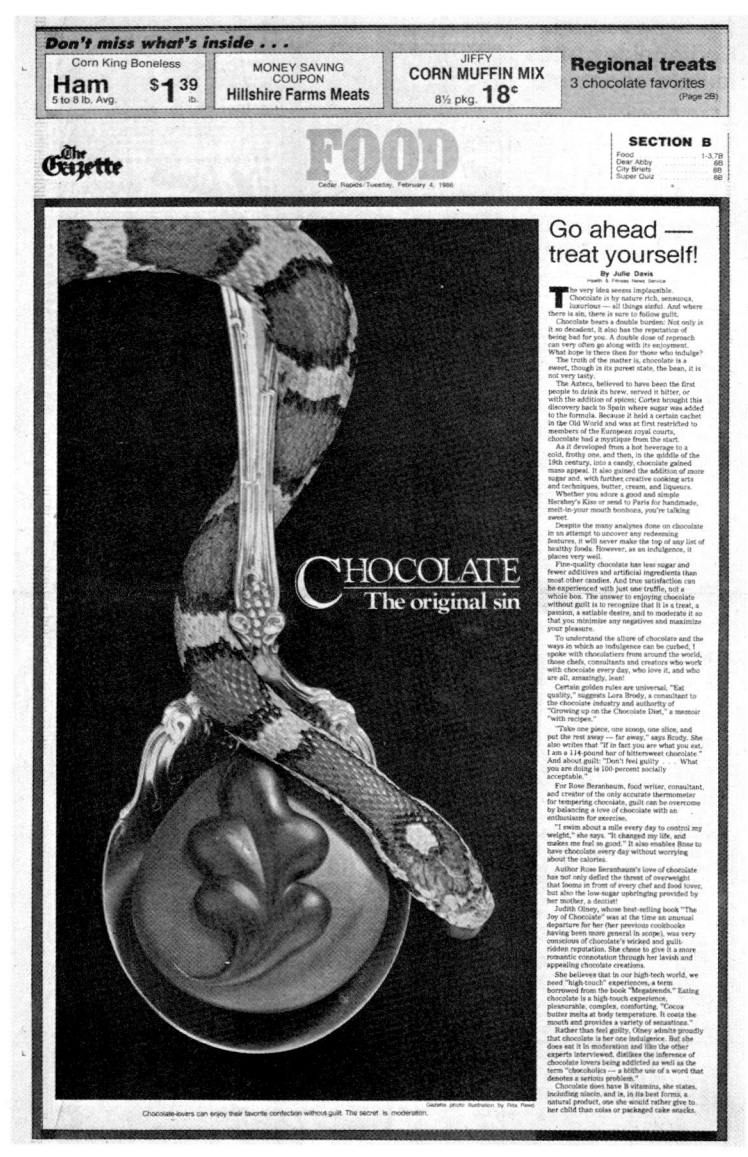

B THE ORANGE COUNTY
REGISTER
Jim Mendenhall

C THE CINCINNATI POST
Patrick Reddy

D THE GAZETTE
Rita Reed

E THE GLOBE AND MAIL
Frank Teskey, Cylla Von Tiedmann

F THE SUN-TATTLER
Judy Lutz

170 The Best of Newspaper Design

16 FEATURE PHOTOGRAPHY

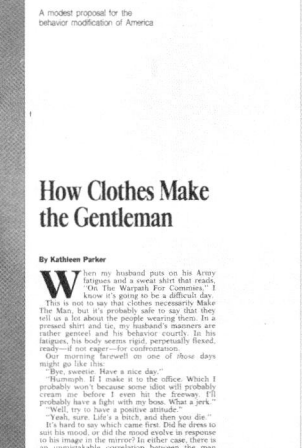

SILVER AWARD

A AFTENPOSTEN
Stein P. Aasheim

B THE NEW YORK TIMES
Lizzie Himmel, Photographer;
Audrone Razgaitis, Designer;
Ken Kendrick, Art Director

C SAN JOSE MERCURY NEWS
Michael J. Bryant

D DAILY NEWS MAGAZINE
Janet Froelich

E UPSTATE MAGAZINE
Michael Schwarz, Photographer;
Kate Weisskopf, Art Director

Seventh Edition 171

16
PORTFOLIO OF WORK

A B C
D E

A-E THE SEATTLE TIMES
Jimi Lott

172   The Best of Newspaper Design

16
PORTFOLIO OF WORK

A B C
D E F

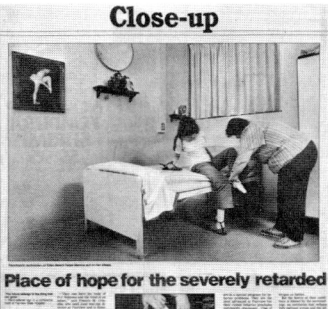

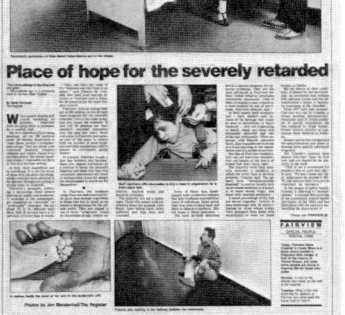

A-F THE ORANGE COUNTY REGISTER
Jim Mendenhall

Seventh Edition 173

16
POLTFOLIO OF WORK

A-D THE VIRGINIAN-PILOT/
LEDGER-STAR
Bill Kelley III

16
PORTFOLIO OF WORK

A-D SAN JOSE MERCURY NEWS
Tom Van Dyke

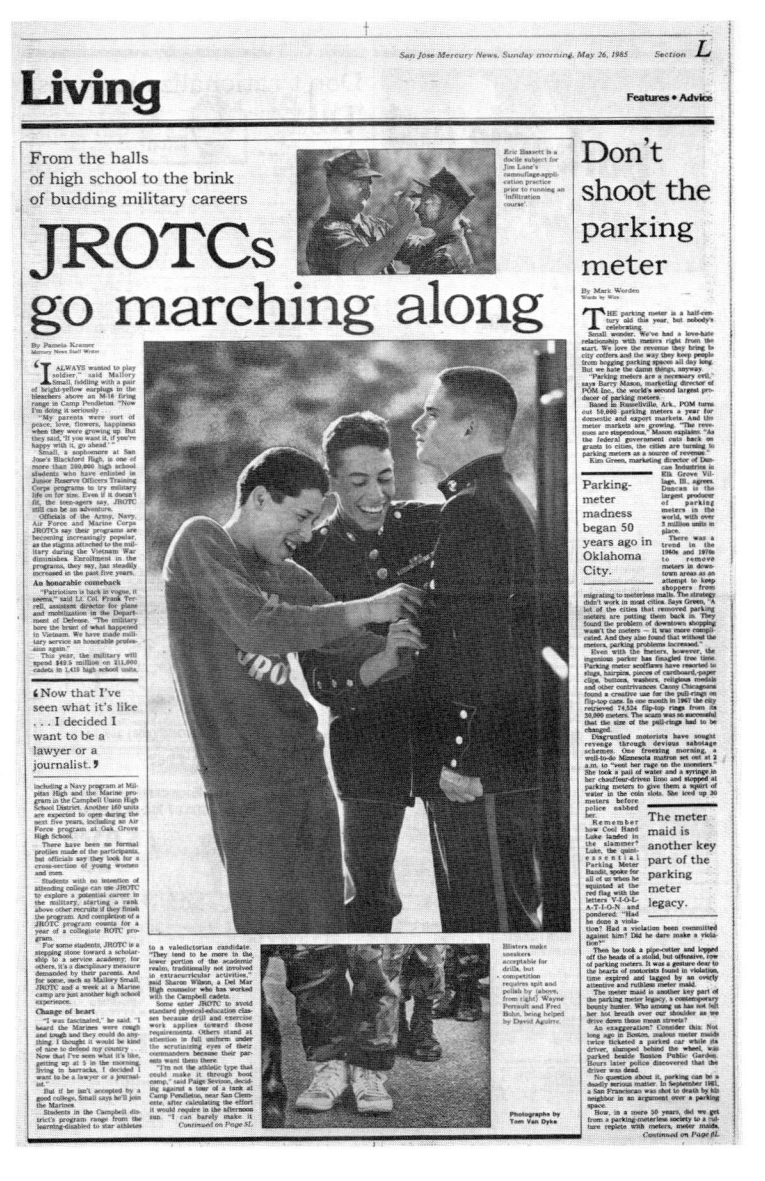

Seventh Edition 175

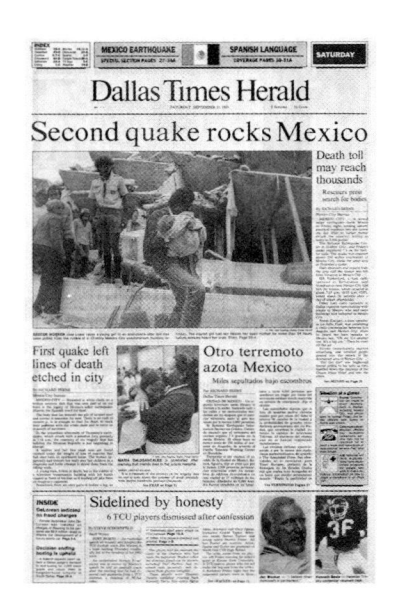

16
PORTFOLIO OF WORK

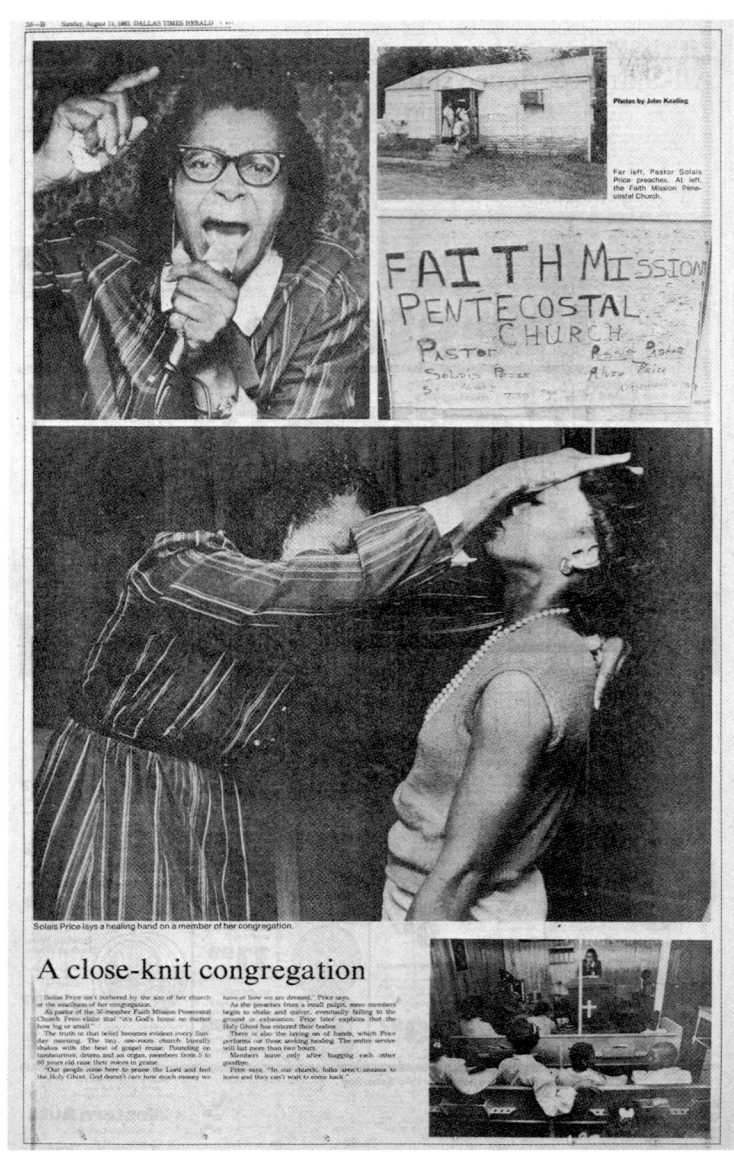

A-E DALLAS TIMES HERALD
John Keating

176   The Best of Newspaper Design

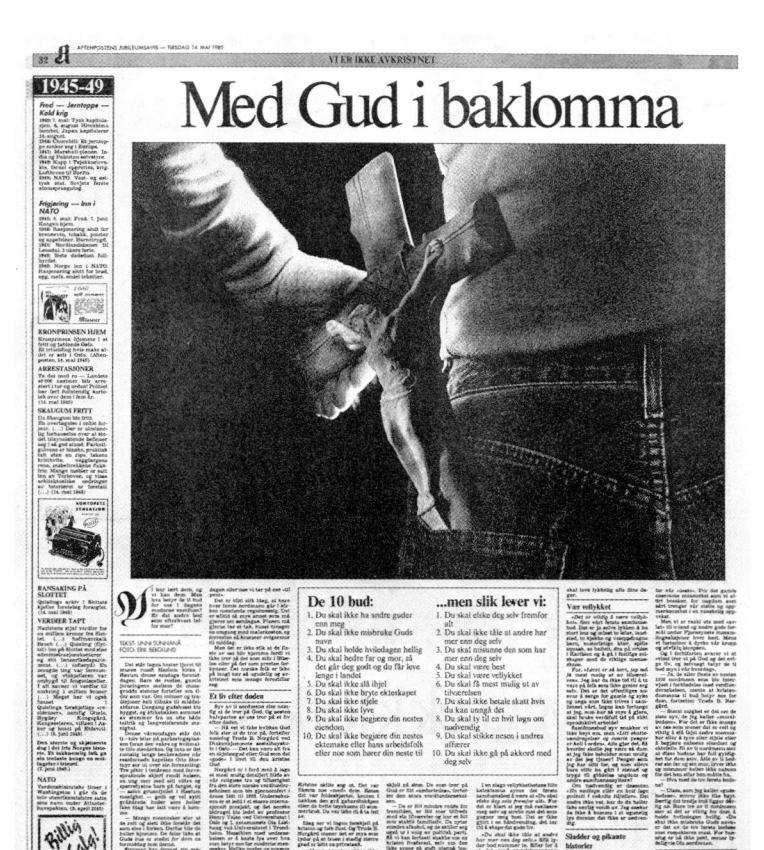

16
PORTFOLIO OF WORK

A-E AFTENPOSTEN
Erik Berglund

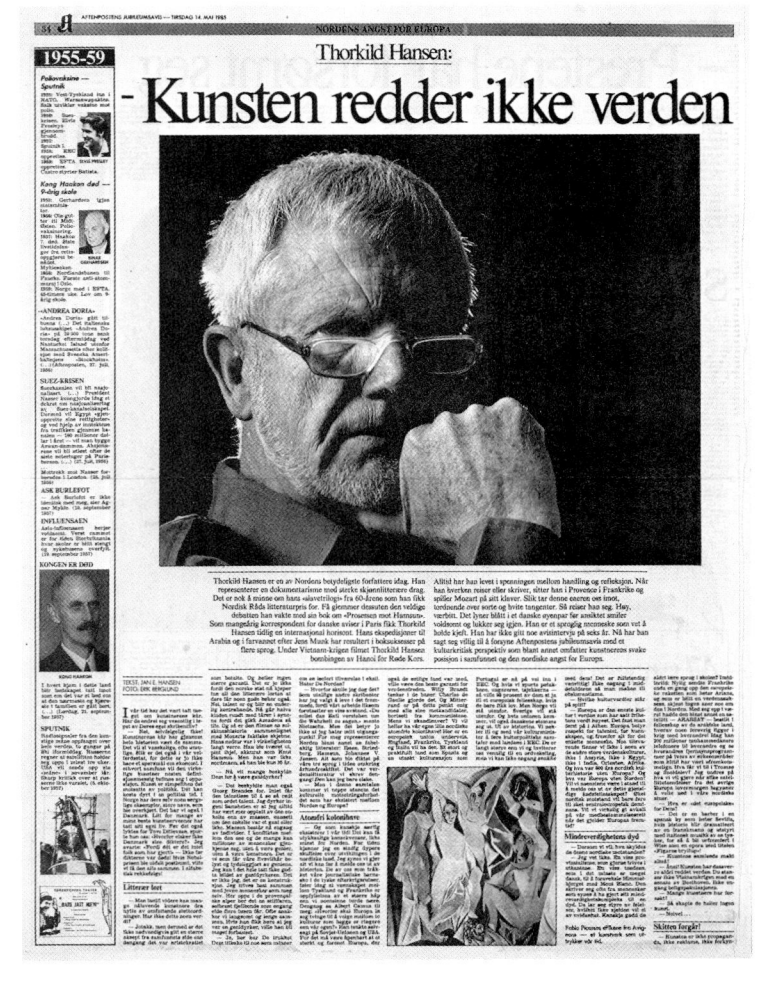

Seventh Edition 177

16
PORTFOLIO OF WORK

A B
C D

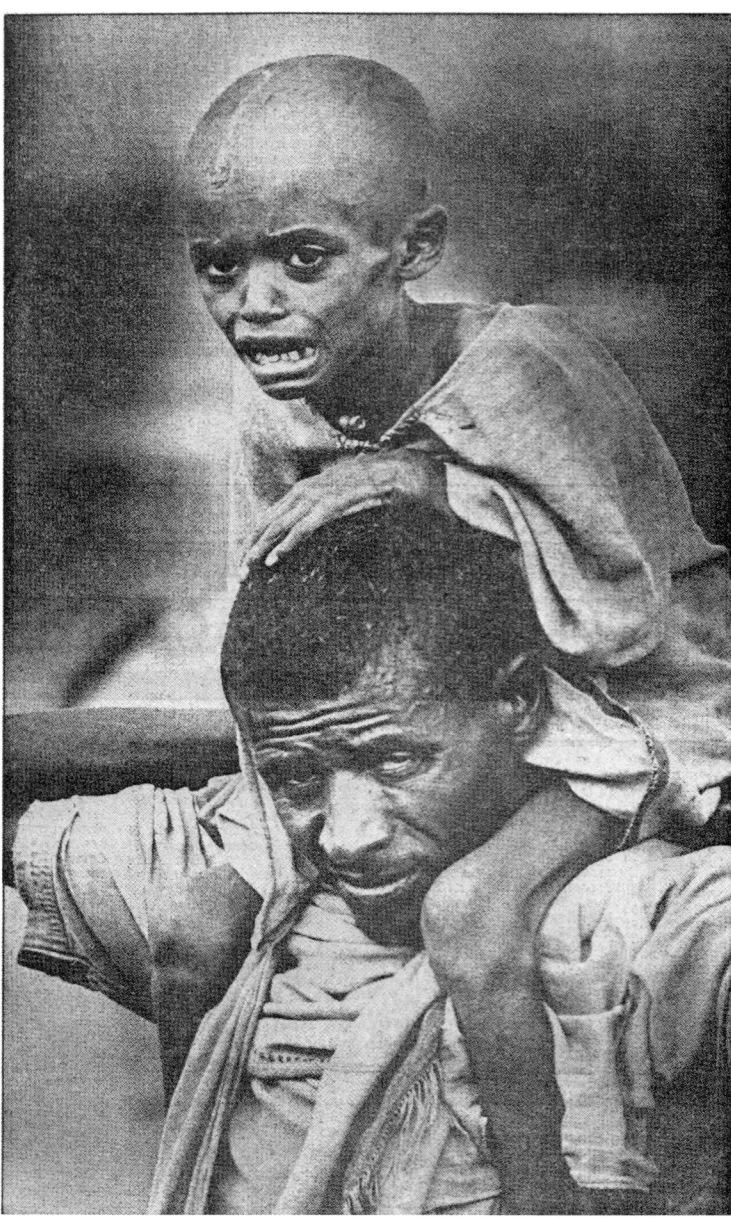

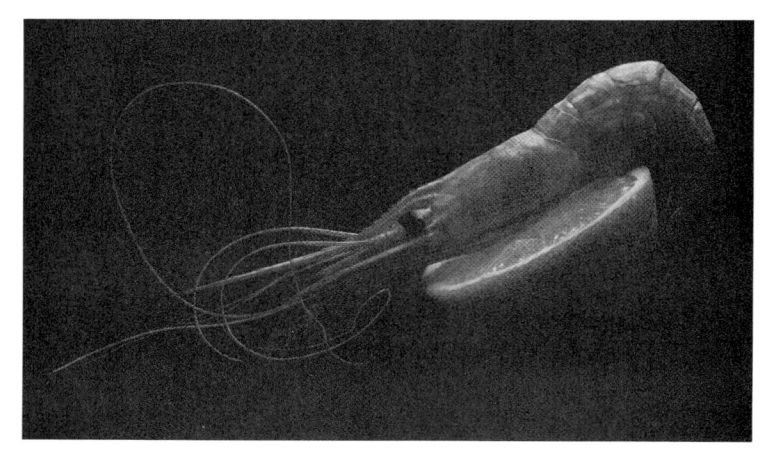

A-D THE SEATTLE TIMES
Alan Berner

178   The Best of Newspaper Design

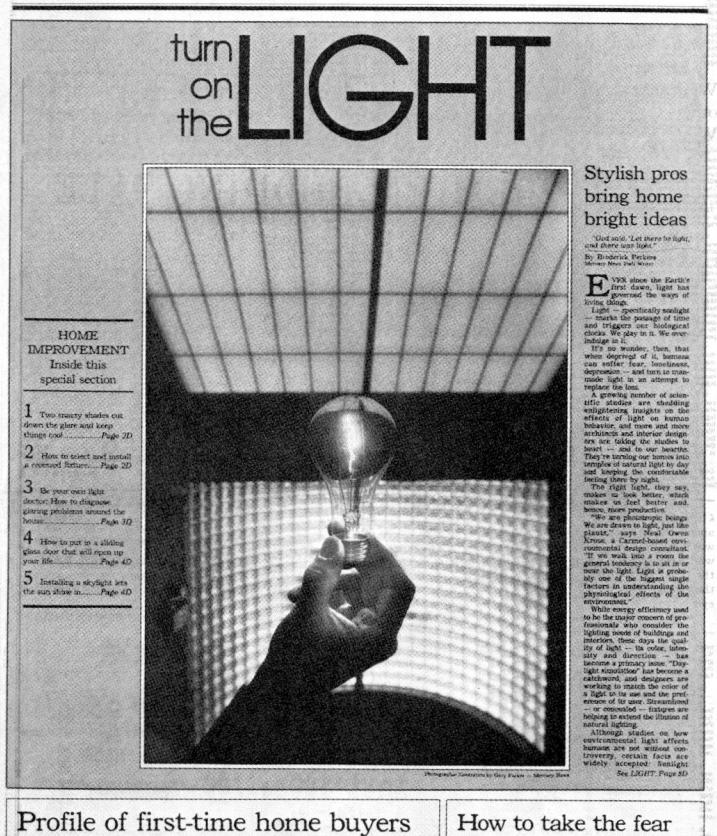

16
PORTFOLIO OF WORK

A B
C D

A-D SAN JOSE MERCURY NEWS
Gary Parker

Seventh Edition 179

16
PORTFOLIO OF WORK

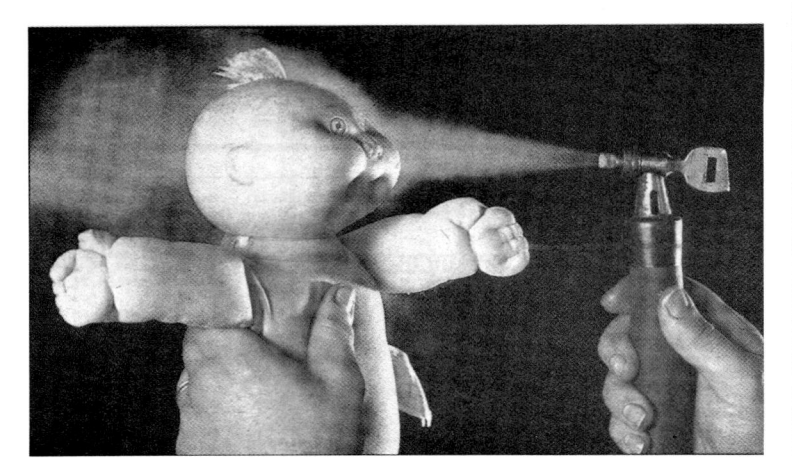

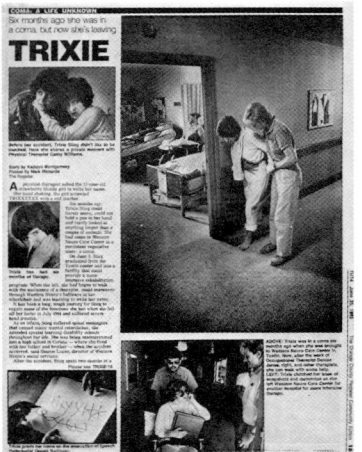

A-F THE ORANGE COUNTY REGISTER
Mark Richards

16
PORTFOLIO OF WORK

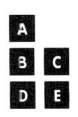

A-E AFTENPOSTEN
Rolf M. Aagaard

Seventh Edition 181

17
INFORMATIONAL GRAPHICS

Graphs, charts, maps, and diagrams were judged as part of the full page in three categories • Single Color • Full Color • Portfolio of Work.

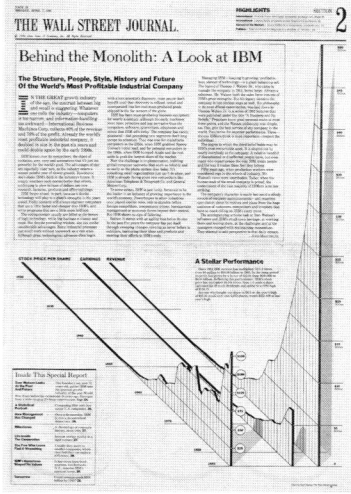

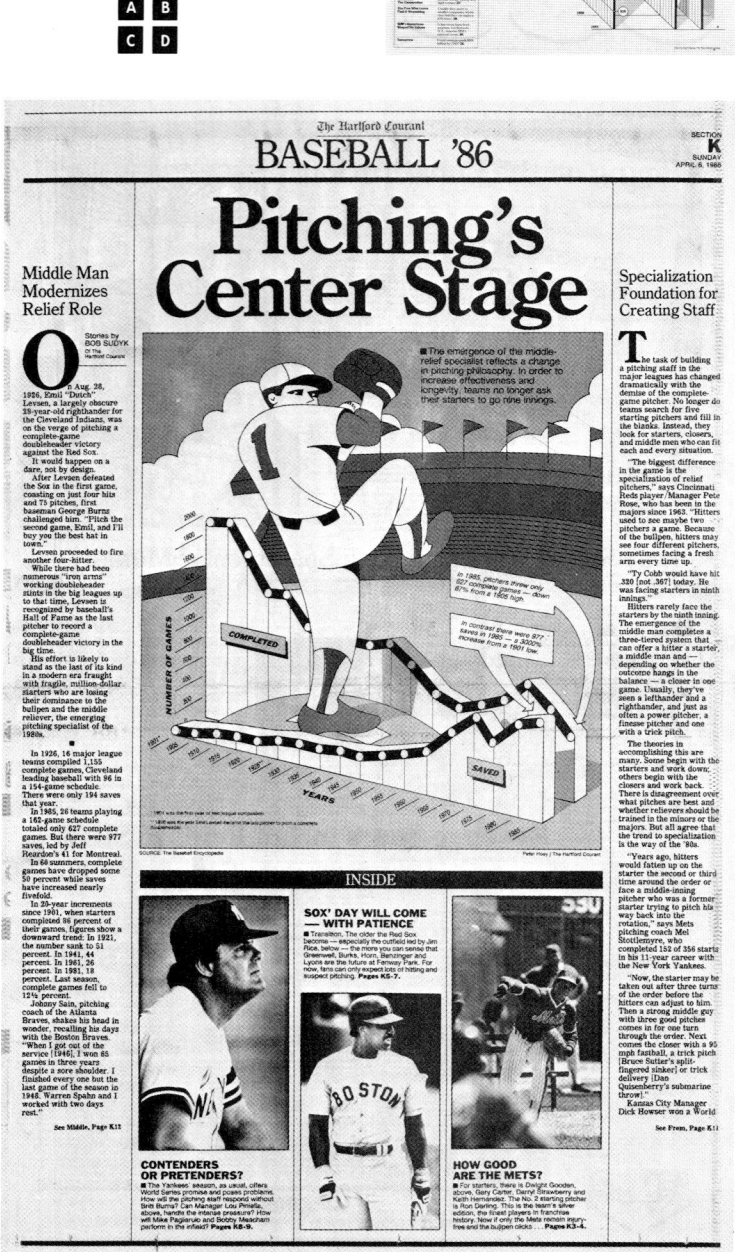

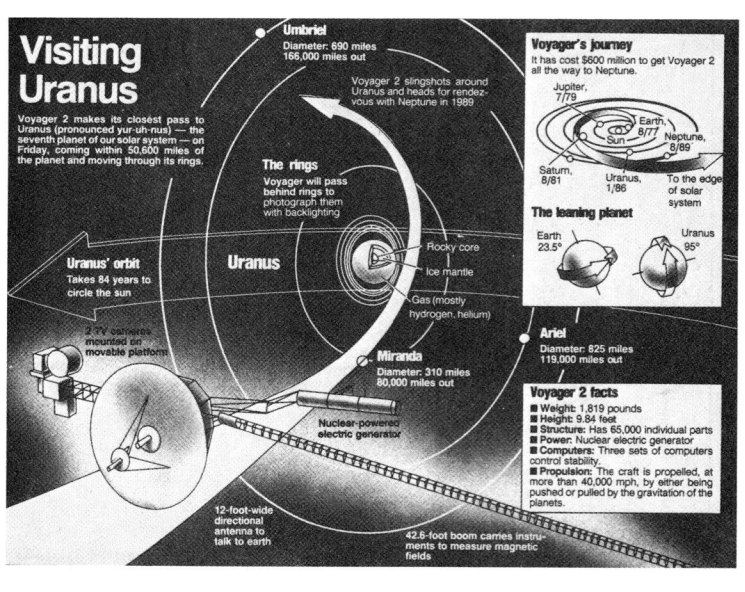

A THE WALL STREET JOURNAL
Karl Hartig

B PROVIDENCE JOURNAL
George M. Sylvia

C THE HARTFORD COURANT
Peter Hoey

D USA TODAY
Dale Glasgow

182   The Best of Newspaper Design

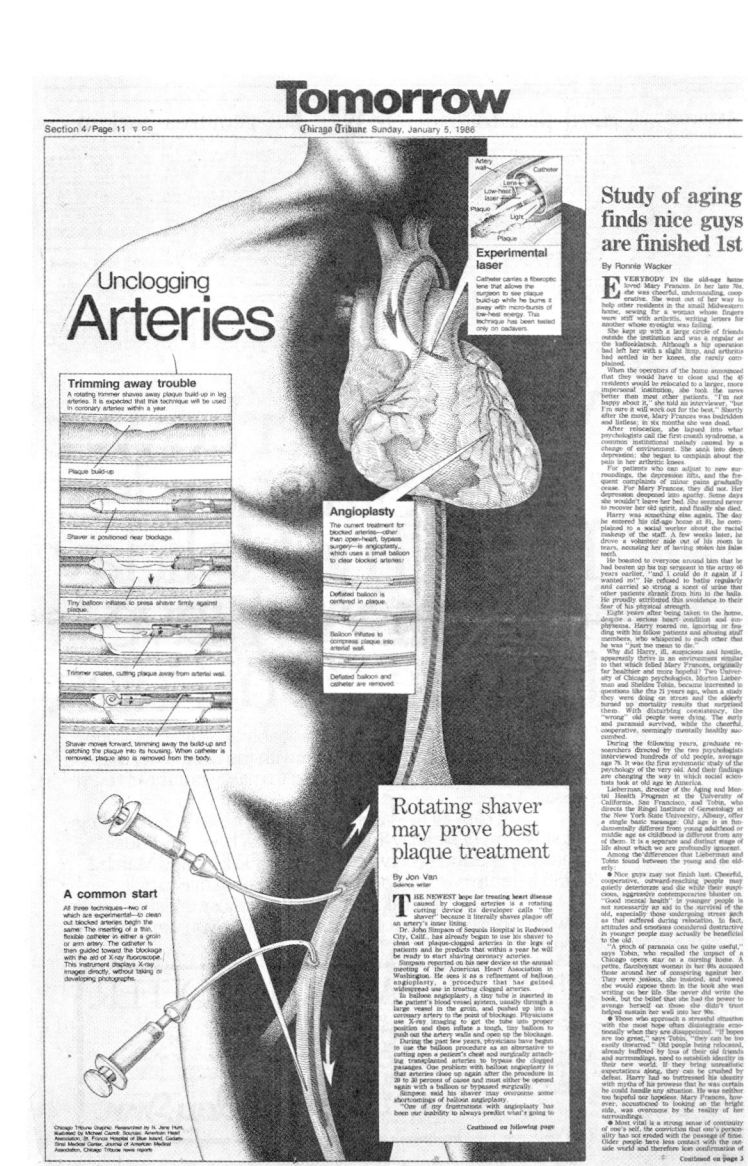

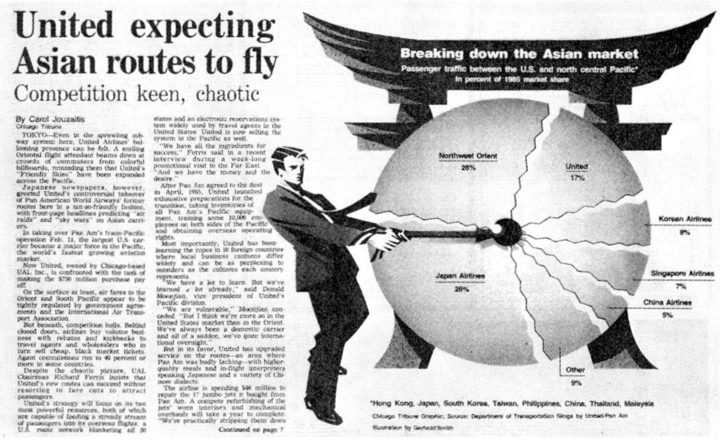

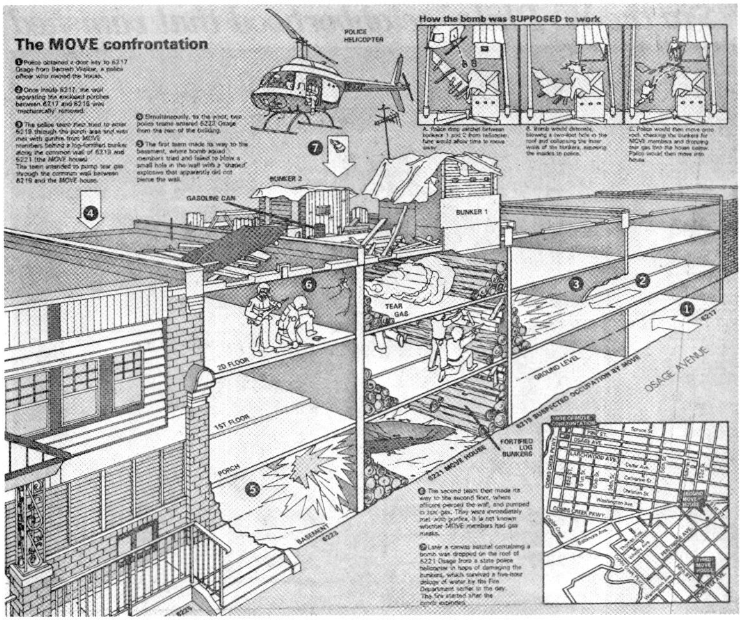

SINGLE COLOR

A B
C D

A THE CHICAGO TRIBUNE
Mike Carroll, Illustrator;
Earl Toledo, Jane Hunt, Art Directors

B THE CHICAGO TRIBUNE
Gerhold/Smith, Illustration;
Kevin Fewell, Art Director

C PHILADELPHIA INQUIRER
Helen Driggs

D THE NEW YORK TIMES
Randy Jones, Illustrator;
Greg Ryan, Art Director

Seventh Edition 183

17
SINGLE COLOR

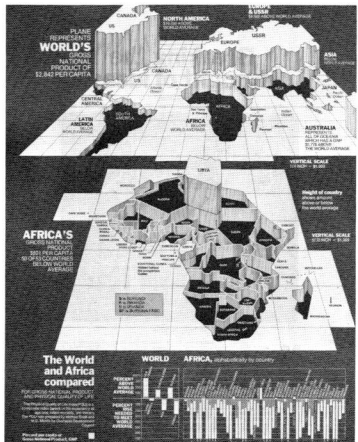

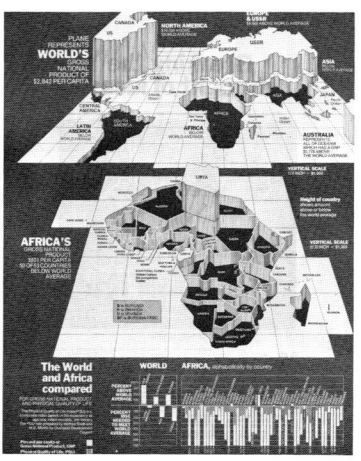

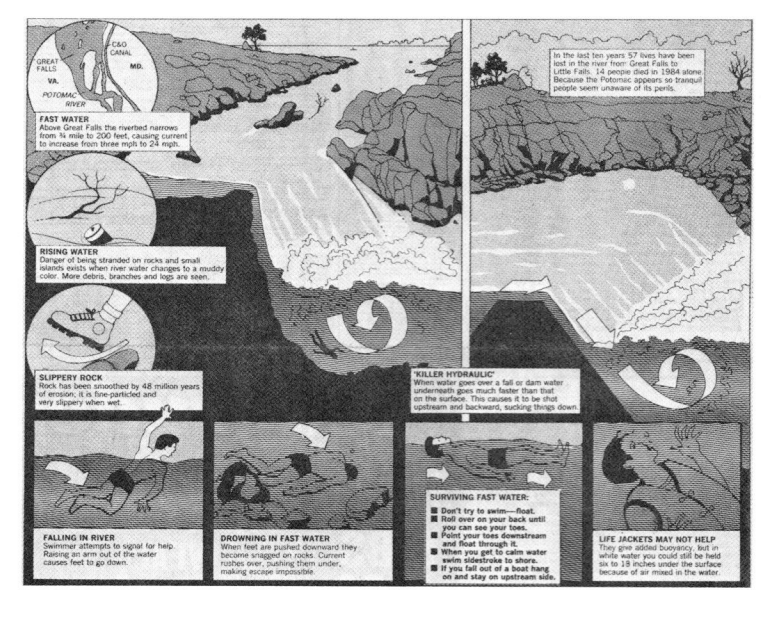

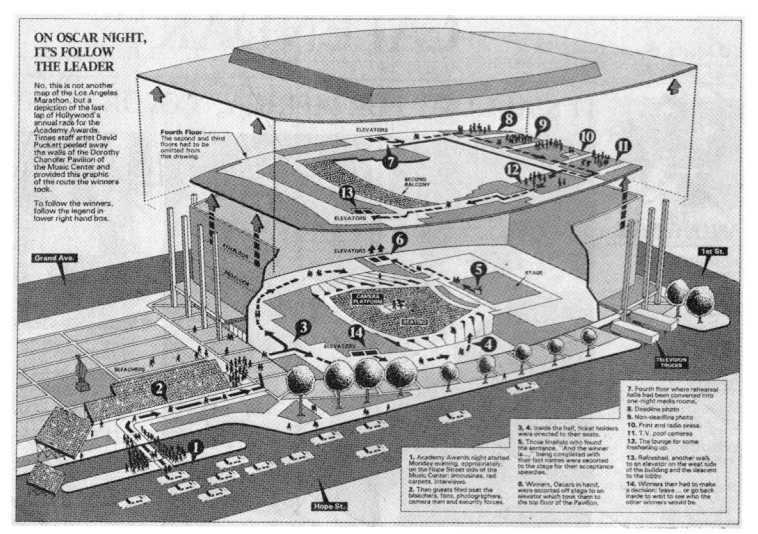

A   THE CHRISTIAN SCIENCE MONITOR
William Palmstrom, Jeff Carmel

B   THE WASHINGTON POST
Johnstone Quinan

C   DEMOCRAT AND CHRONICLE
Allen Dise

D   LOS ANGELES TIMES
David Puckett

184   The Best of Newspaper Design

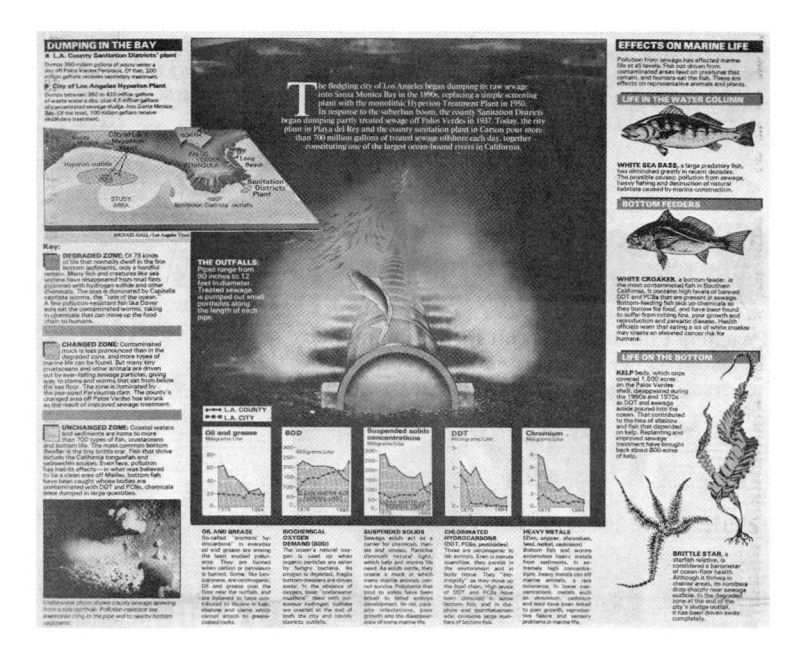

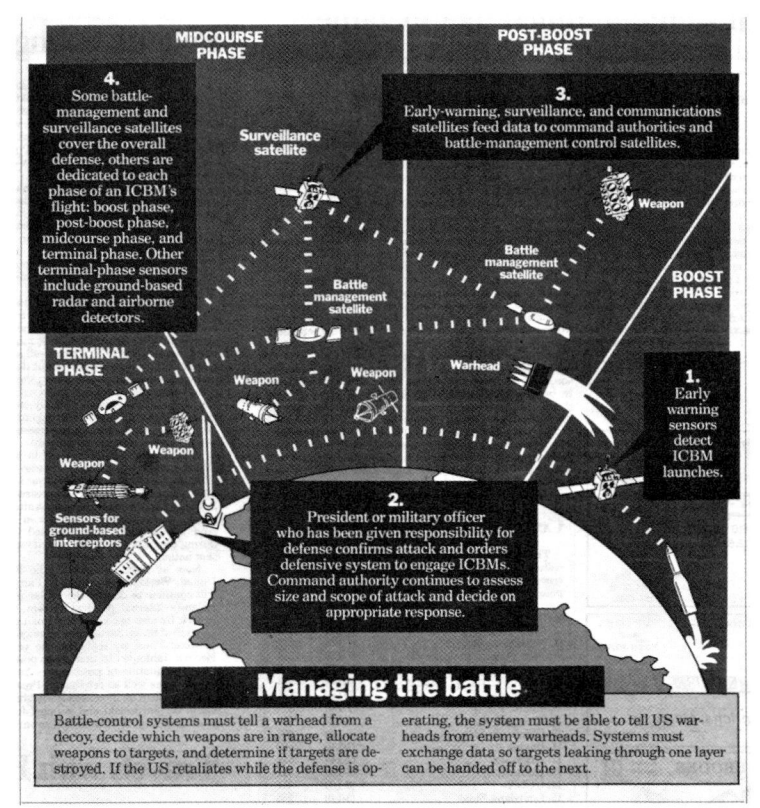

17
SINGLE COLOR

A LOS ANGELES TIMES
Michael Hall, Terry Schwadron

B,E THE CHRISTIAN SCIENCE MONITOR
Robin Jareaux

C THE MIAMI HERALD
Matt Walsh, Bob Barkin, Ana Lense, Randy Stano, Staff

D NEWSDAY
Brigitte Zimmer

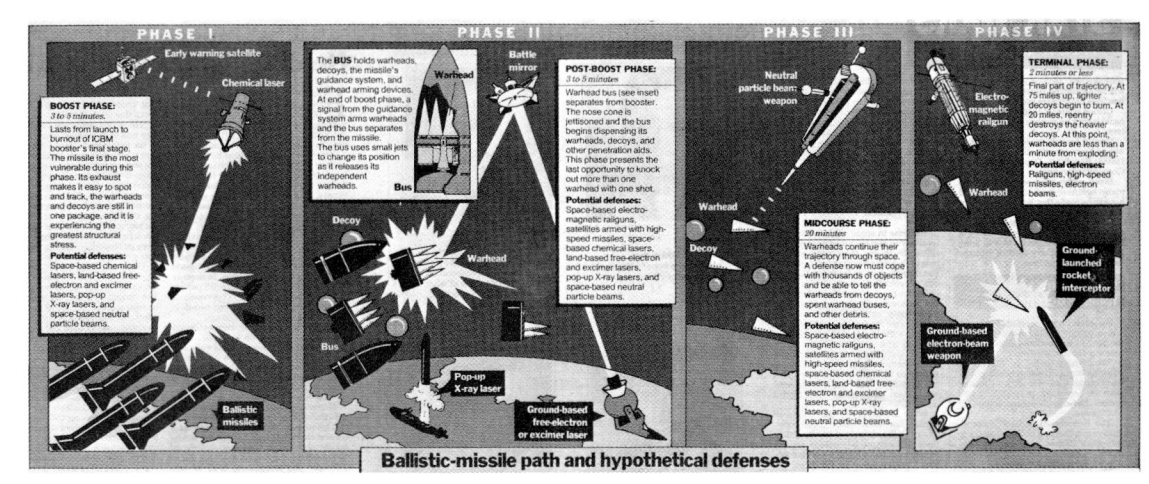

Seventh Edition 185

17
FULL COLOR

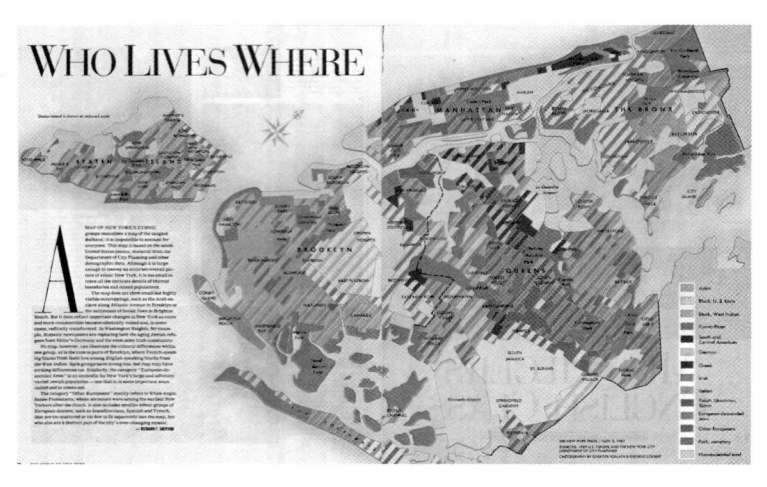

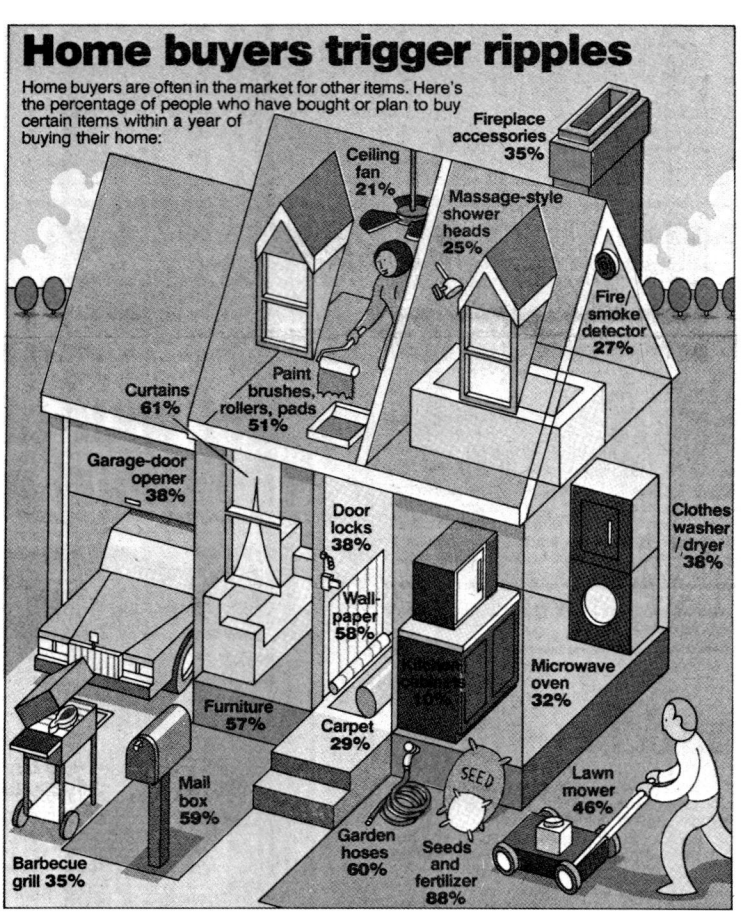

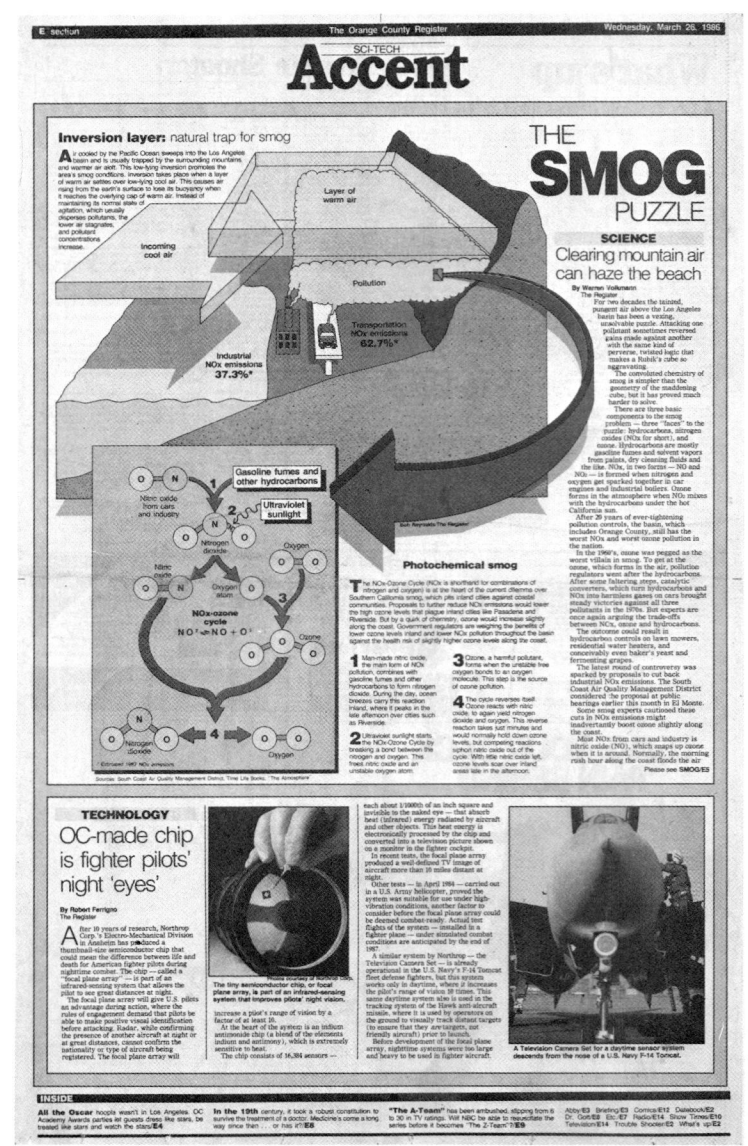

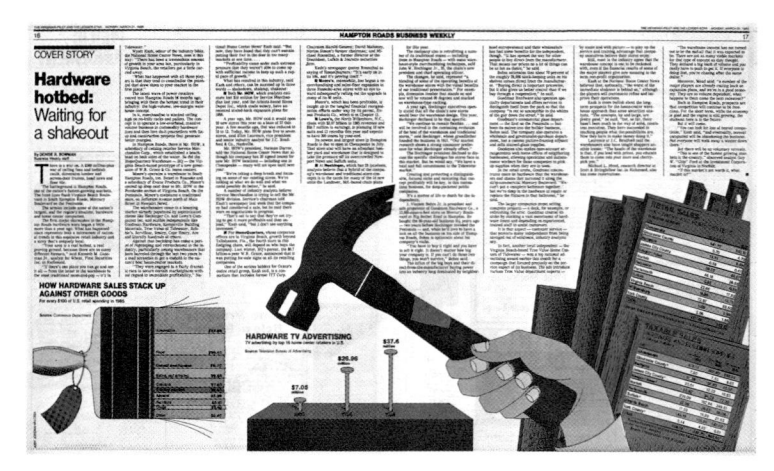

A THE NEW YORK TIMES
Tom Bodkin, Art Director;
Guenter Vollath, George Colbert,
Artists

B THE ORANGE COUNTY
REGISTER
Bob Reynolds

C USA TODAY
Dale Glasgow

D THE VIRGINIAN-PILOT/
LEDGER-STAR
Judy Jordan-Valoria

186   The Best of Newspaper Design

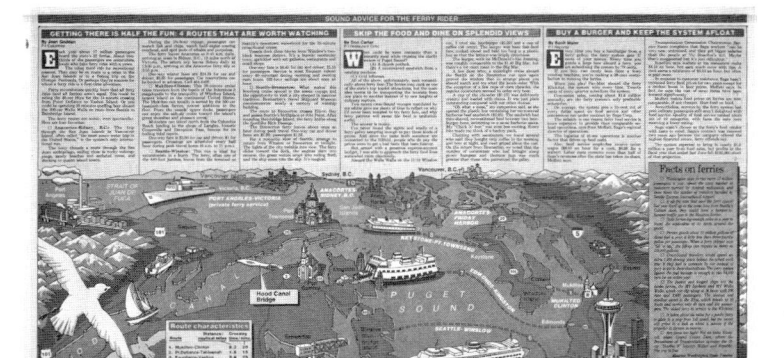

A THE DALLAS MORNING NEWS
Karen Blessen

B USA TODAY
Bob Laird

C REGISTER AND TRIBUNE
Dave Silk

D SEATTLE POST-INTELLIGENCER
Ben Garrison

E USA TODAY
Dale Glasgow

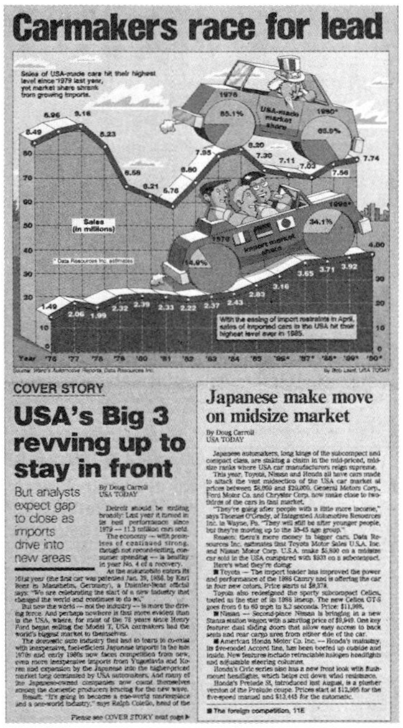

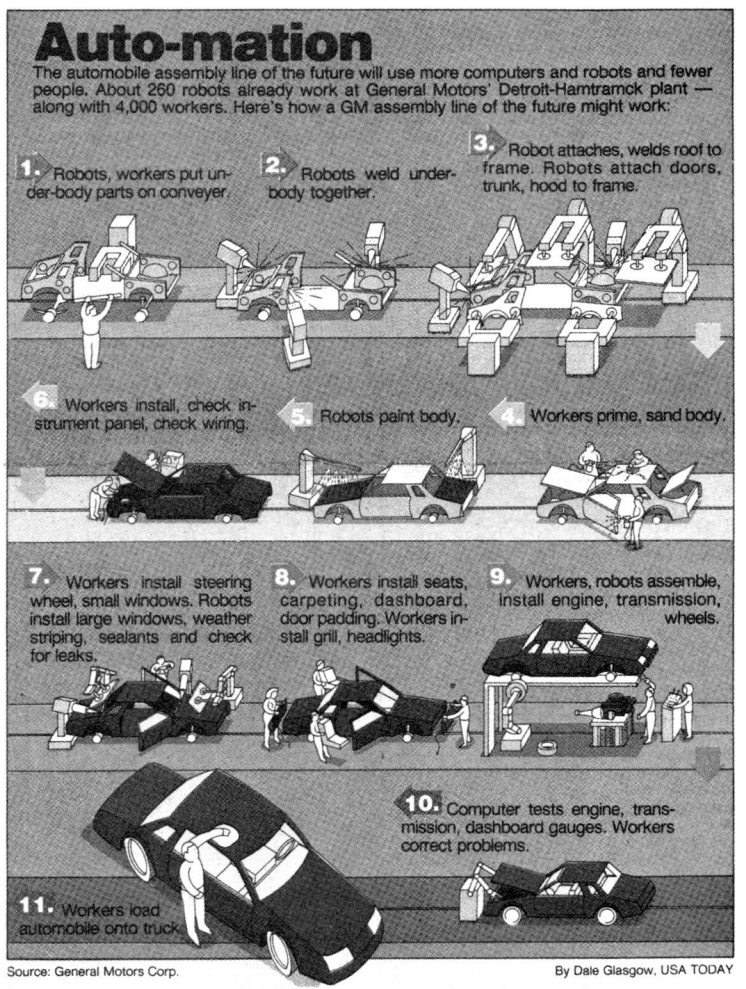

Seventh Edition 187

17
FULL COLOR

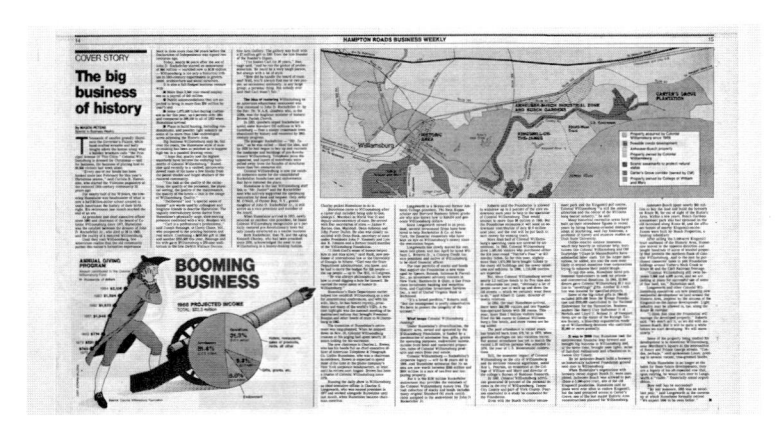

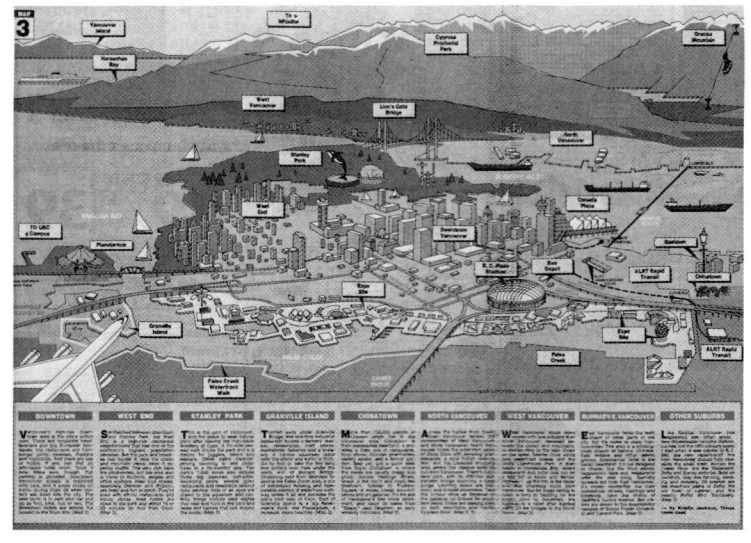

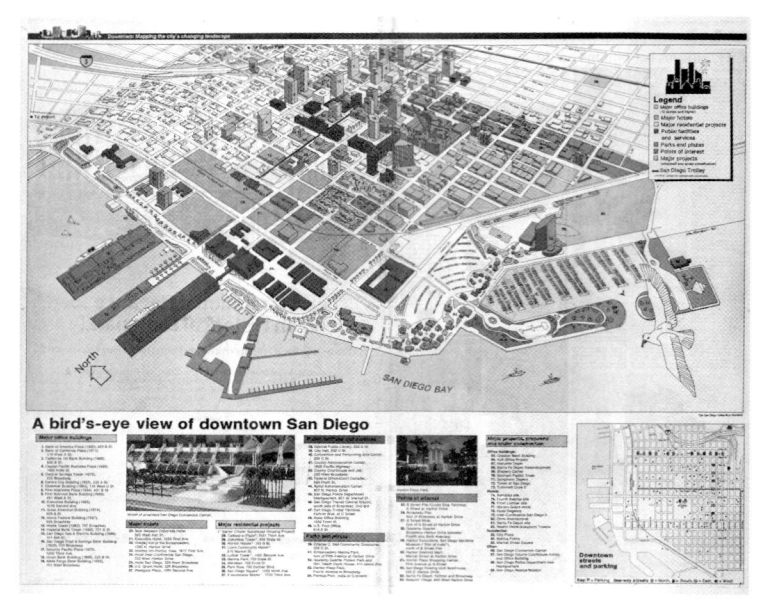

A THE VIRGINIAN-PILOT/
LEDGER-STAR
Judy Jordan-Valoria

B THE SEATTLE TIMES
James McFarlane

C THE COURIER JOURNAL
Stephen D. Sebree

D THE SAN DIEGO UNION
Ken Marshall

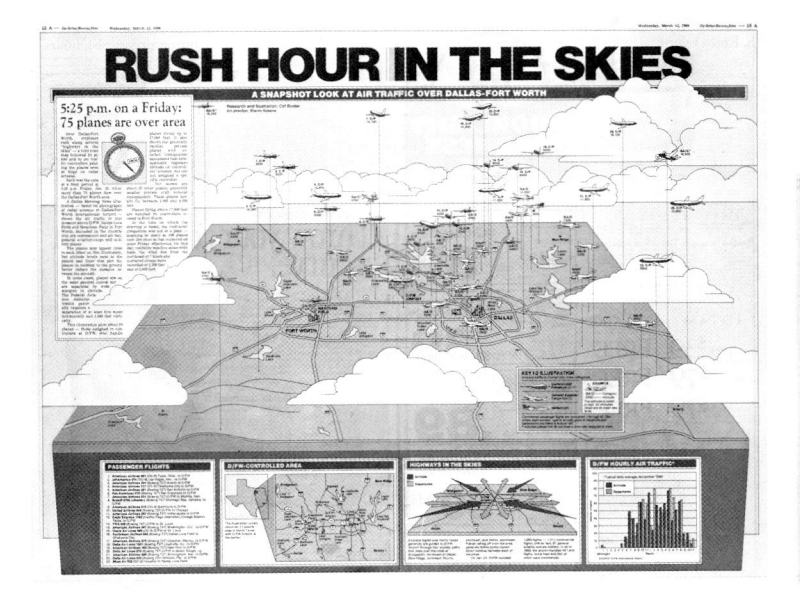

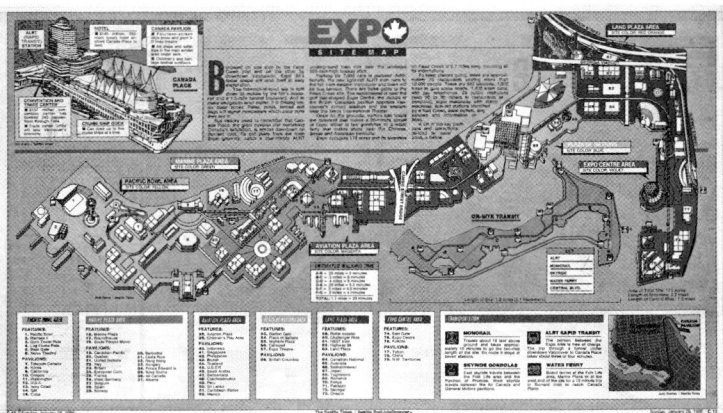

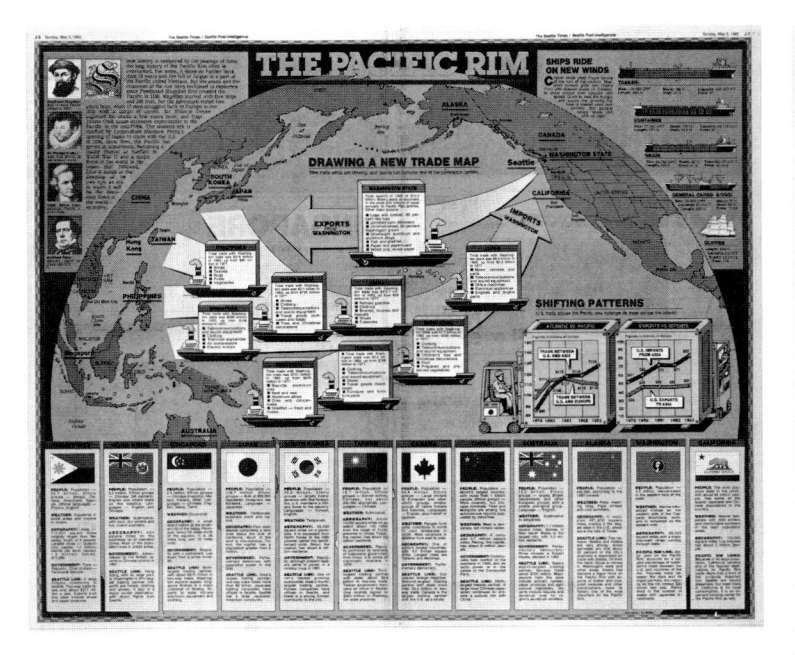

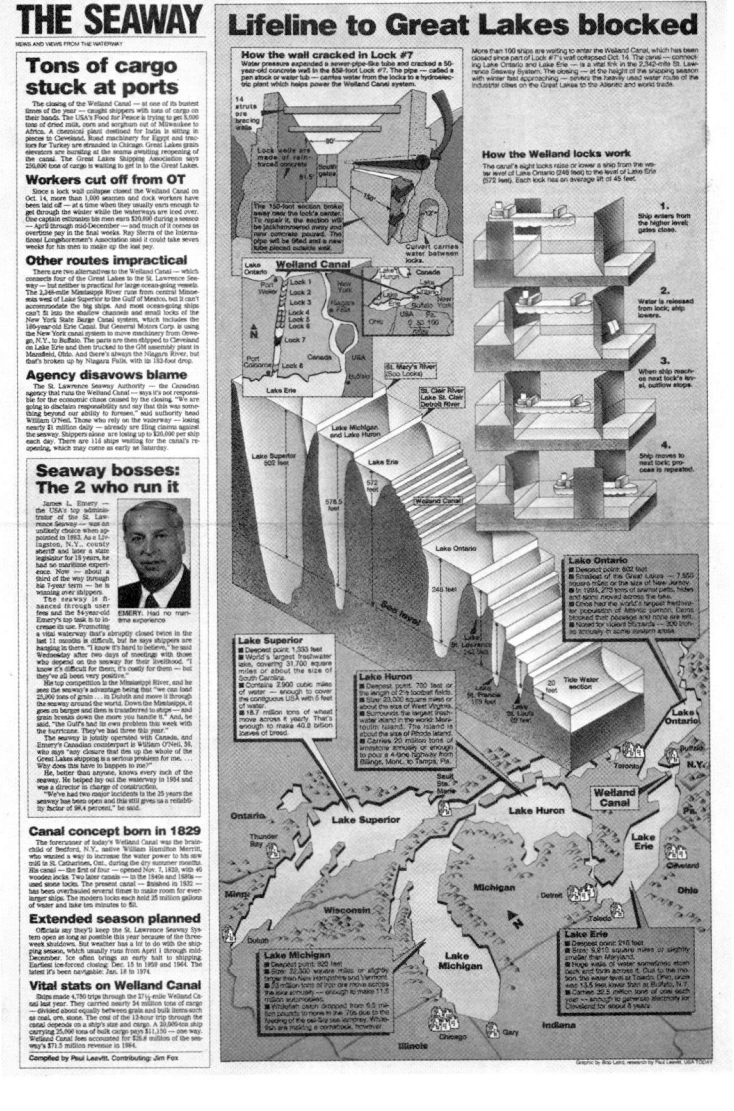

A THE DALLAS MORNING NEWS
Clif Bosler, Sharon Roberts

B,C THE SEATTLE TIMES
Rob Kemp

D USA TODAY
Bob Laird

17

PORTFOLIO OF WORK

A B C
D E F

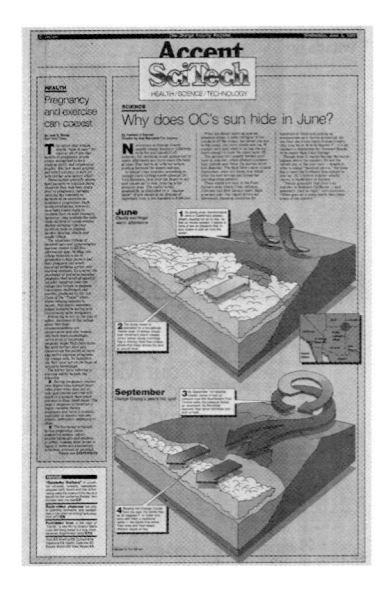

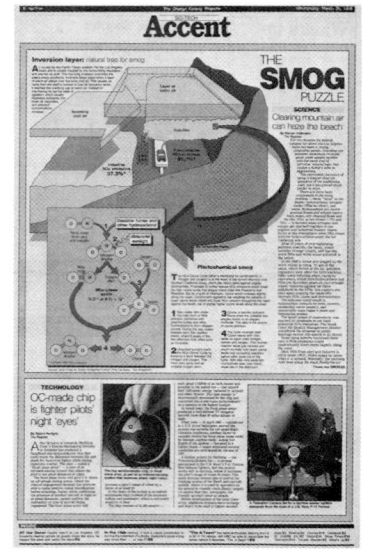

A-F THE ORANGE COUNTY REGISTER
Bob Reynolds

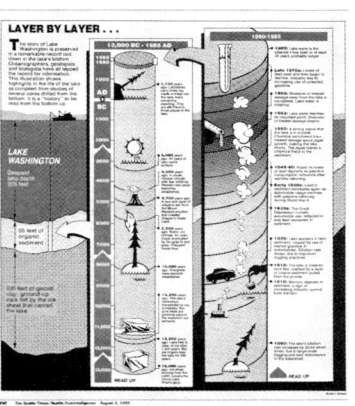

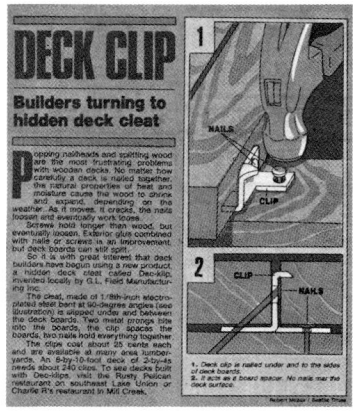

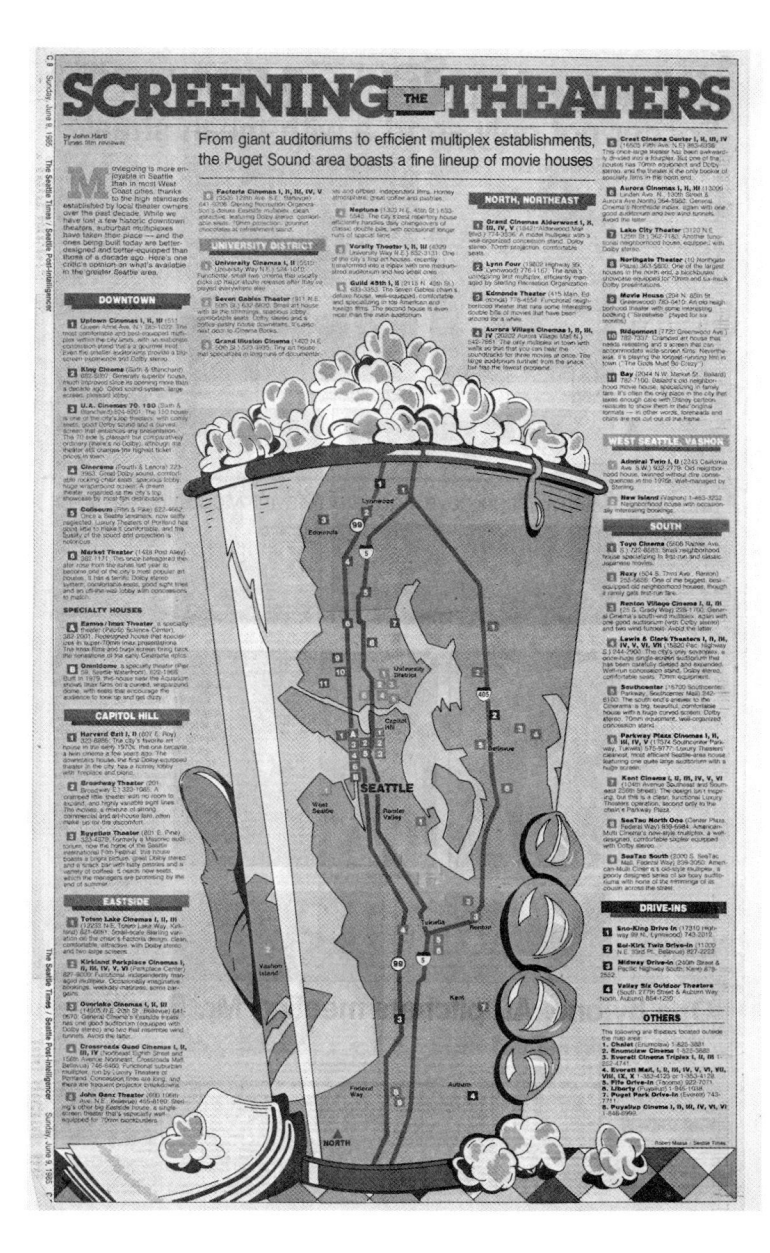

A-F THE SEATTLE TIMES
Robert Massa

17
PORTFOLIO OF WORK

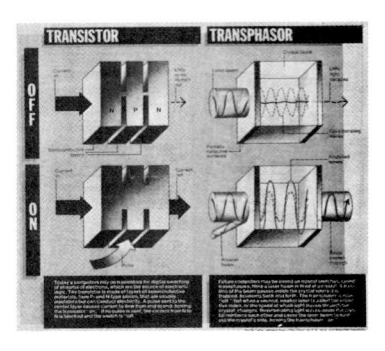

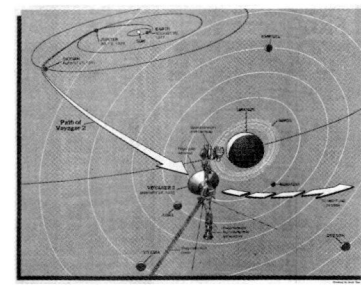

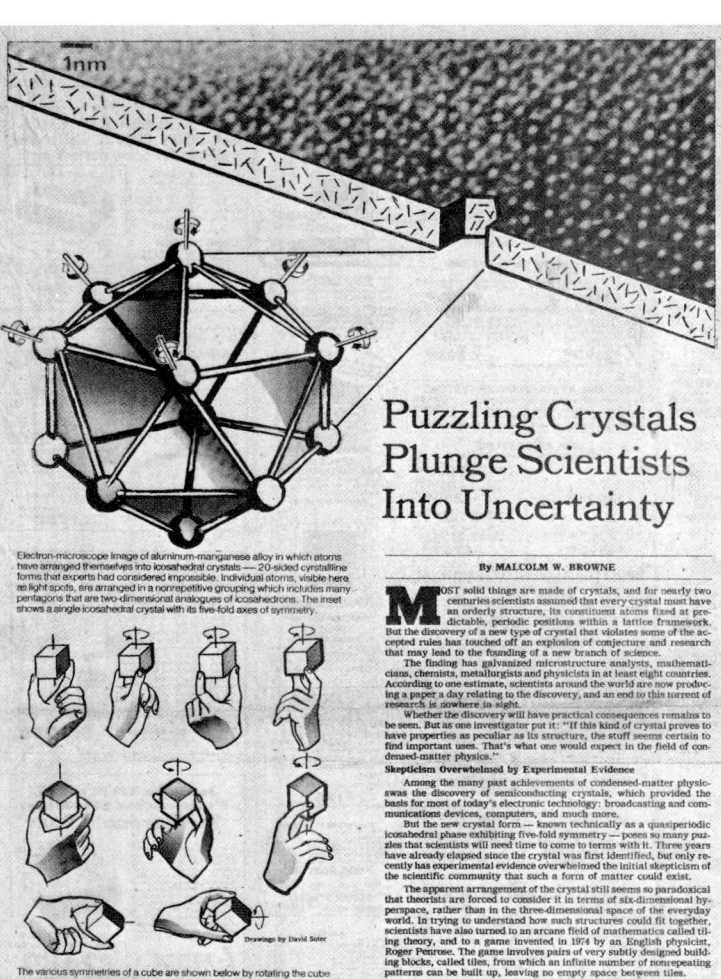

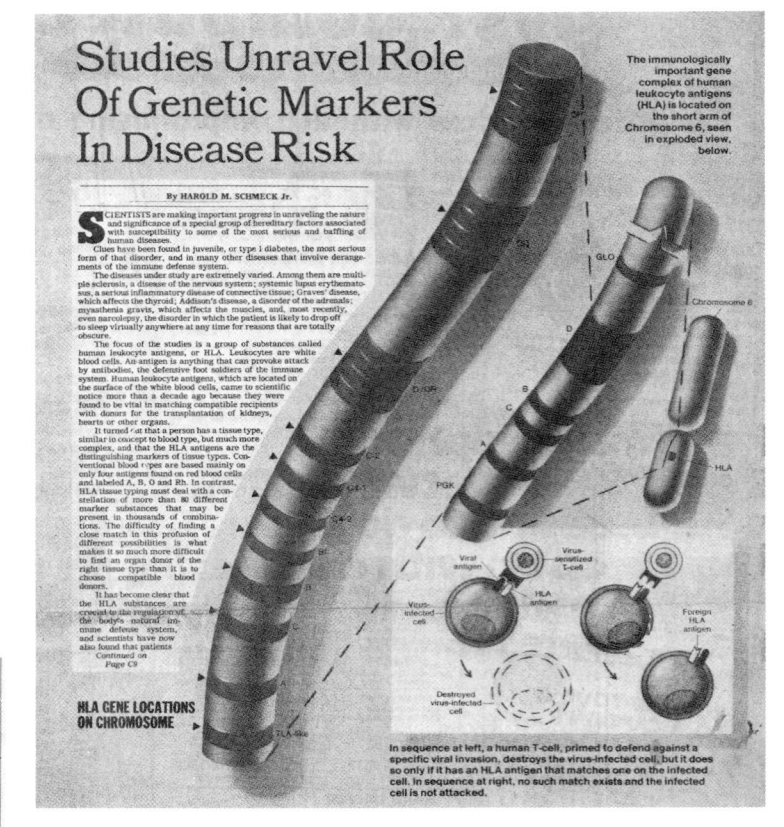

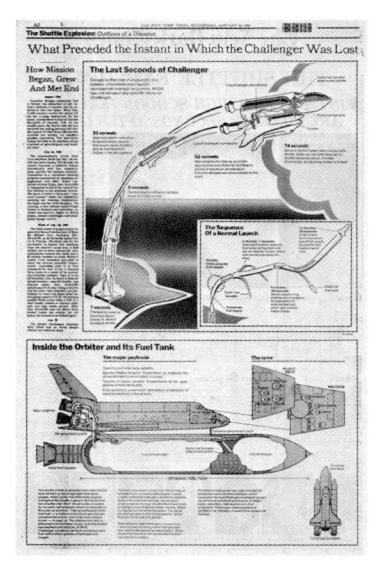

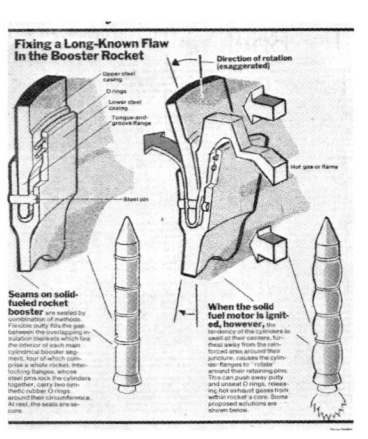

A-F THE NEW YORK TIMES
Gary Cosimini

192   The Best of Newspaper Design

17
PORTFOLIO OF WORK

A B C
D E F

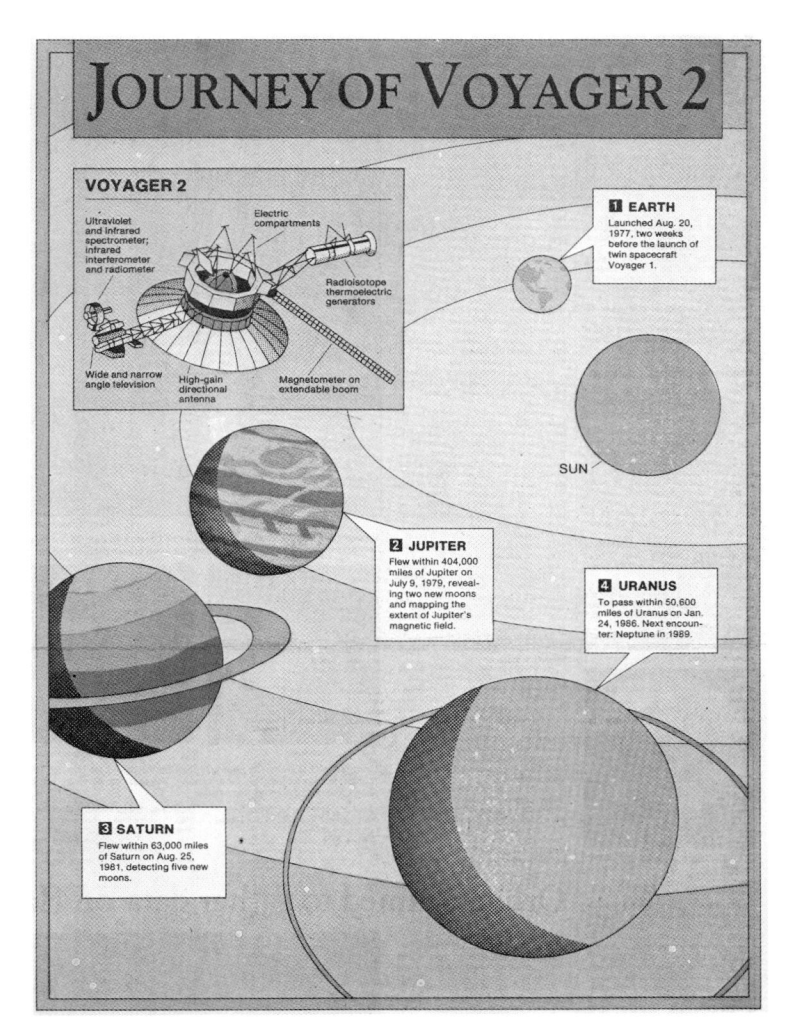

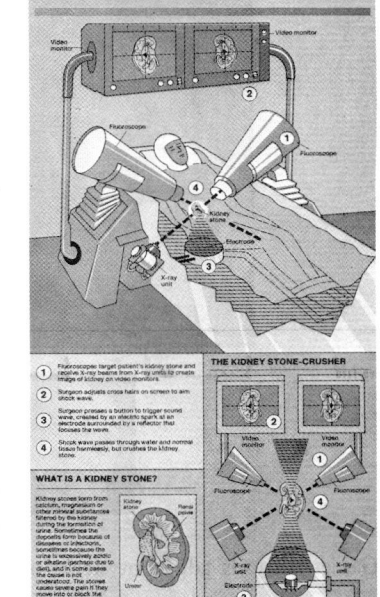

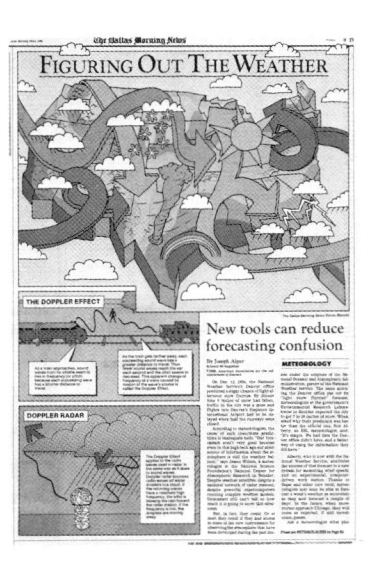

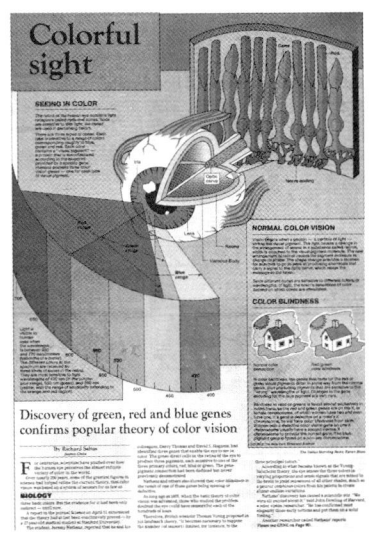

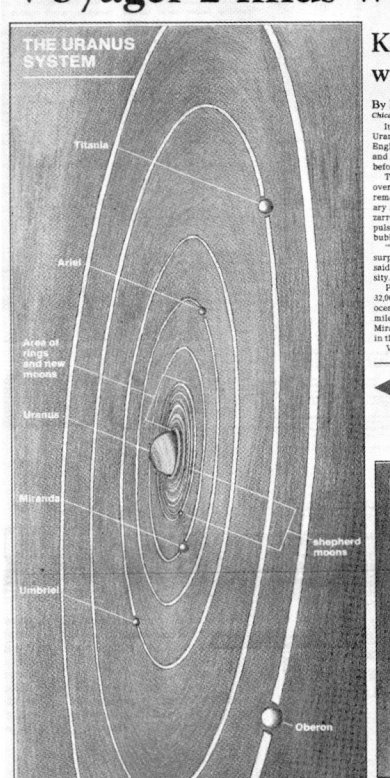

A-F THE DALLAS MORNING NEWS
Karen Blessen

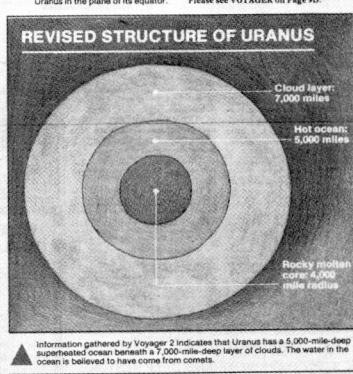

Seventh Edition 193

17

PORTFOLIO OF WORK

A	B	C
D	E	F

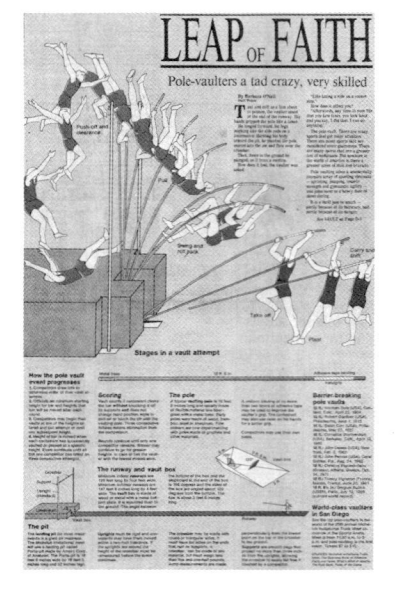

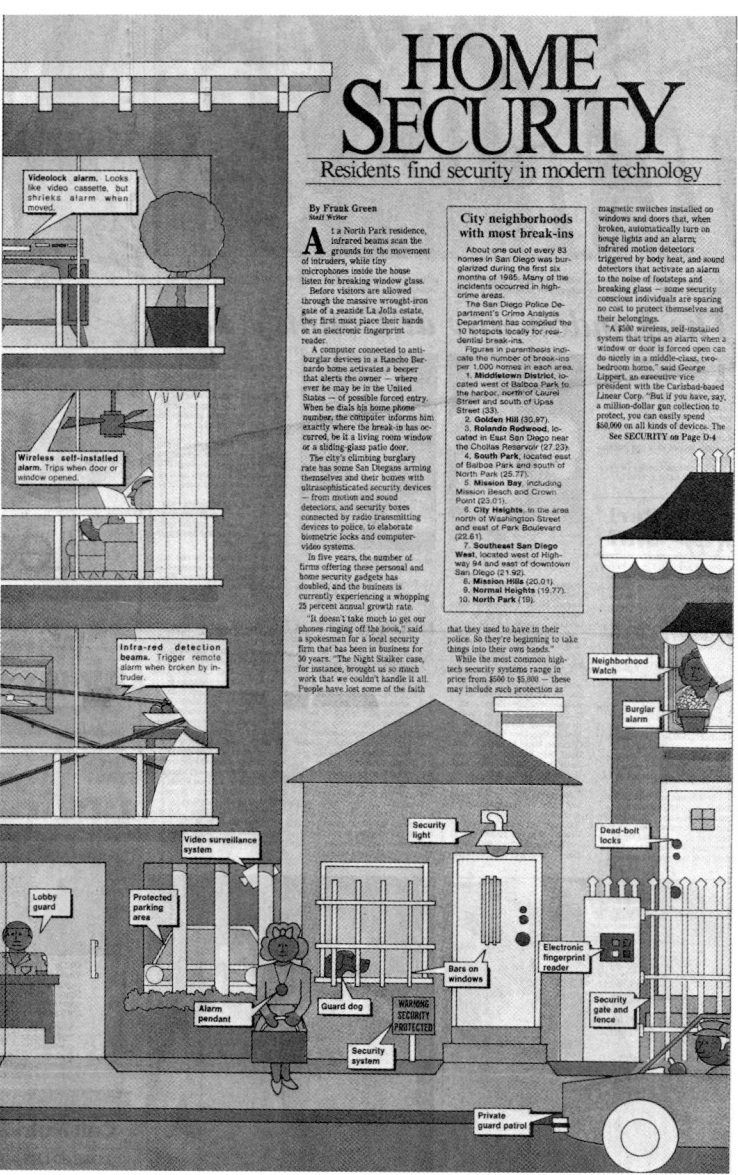

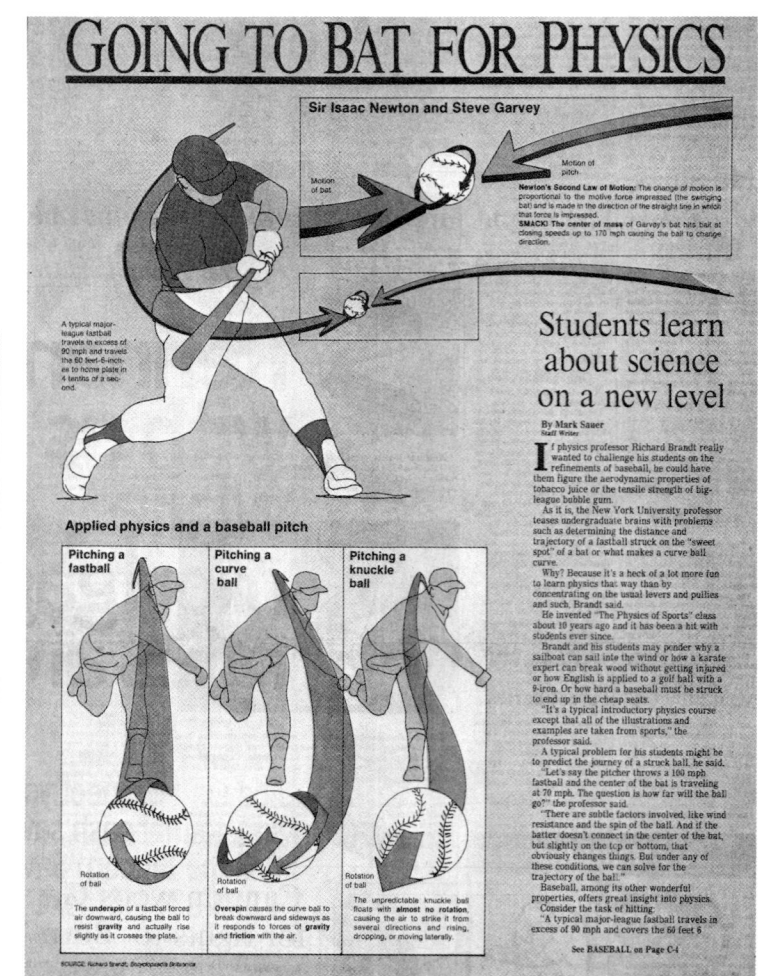

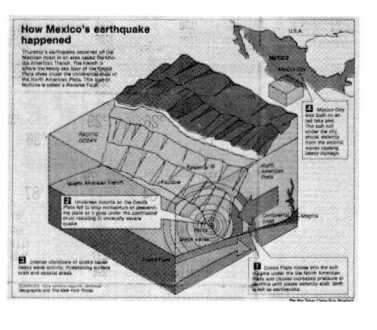

A-F THE SAN DIEGO UNION
Ken Marshall

194   The Best of Newspaper Design

17

PORTFOLIO OF WORK

A B C
D E F

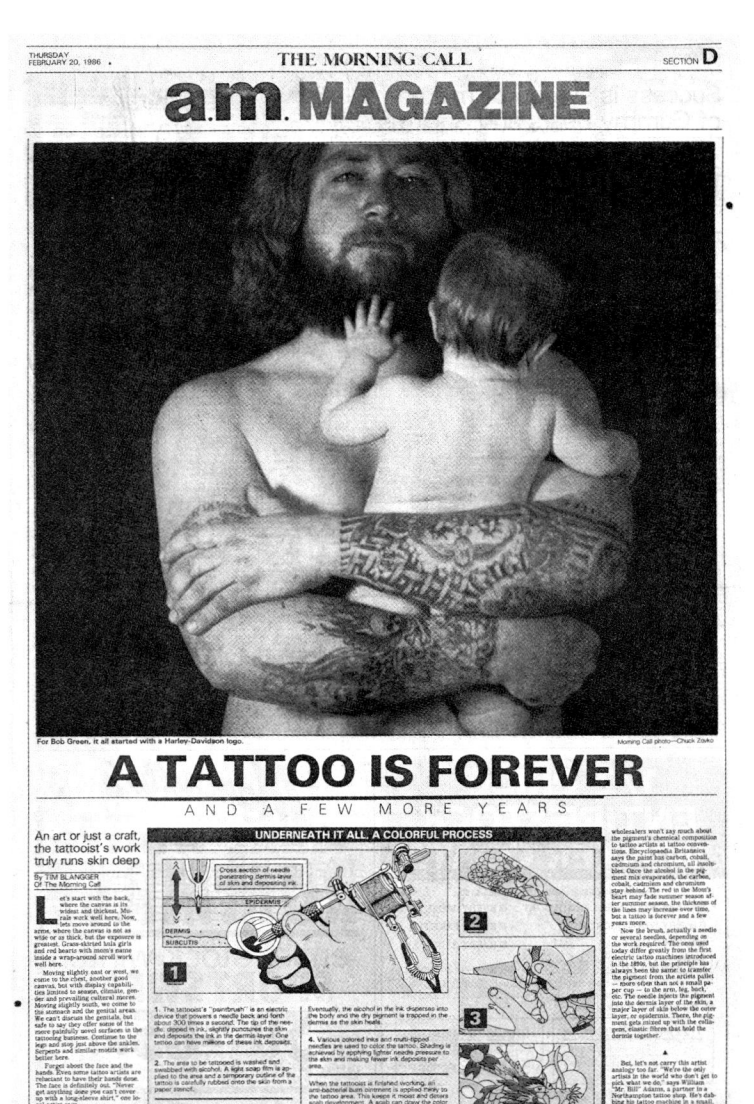

A-F THE MORNING CALL
Elaine Cunfer

Seventh Edition 195

17
PORTFOLIO OF WORK

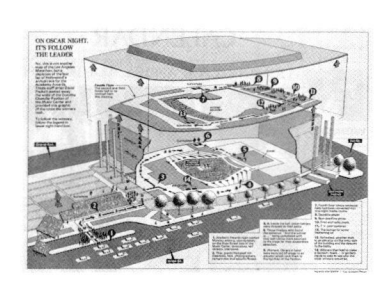

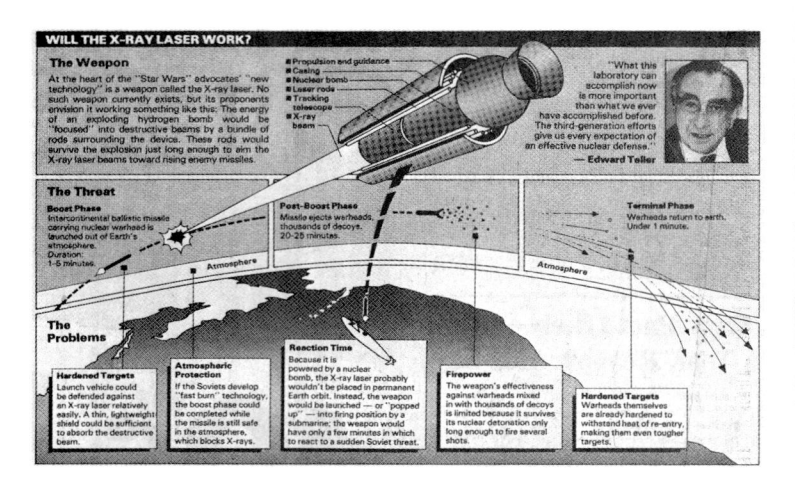

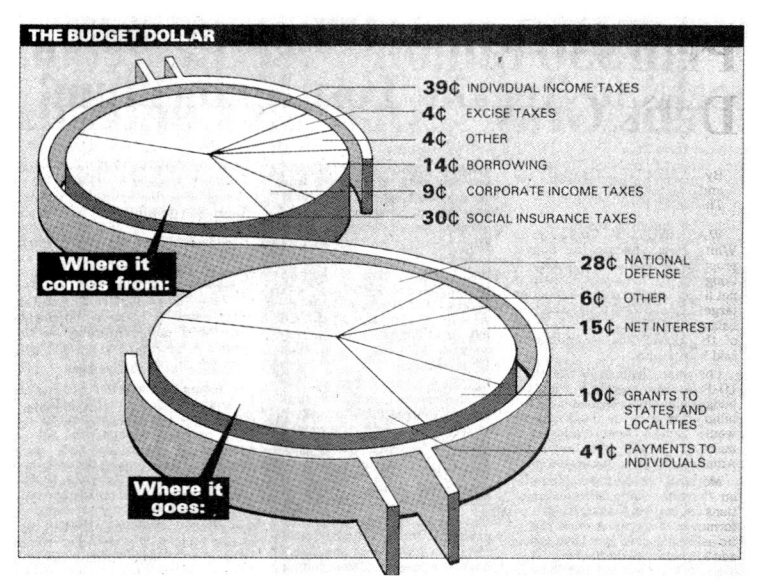

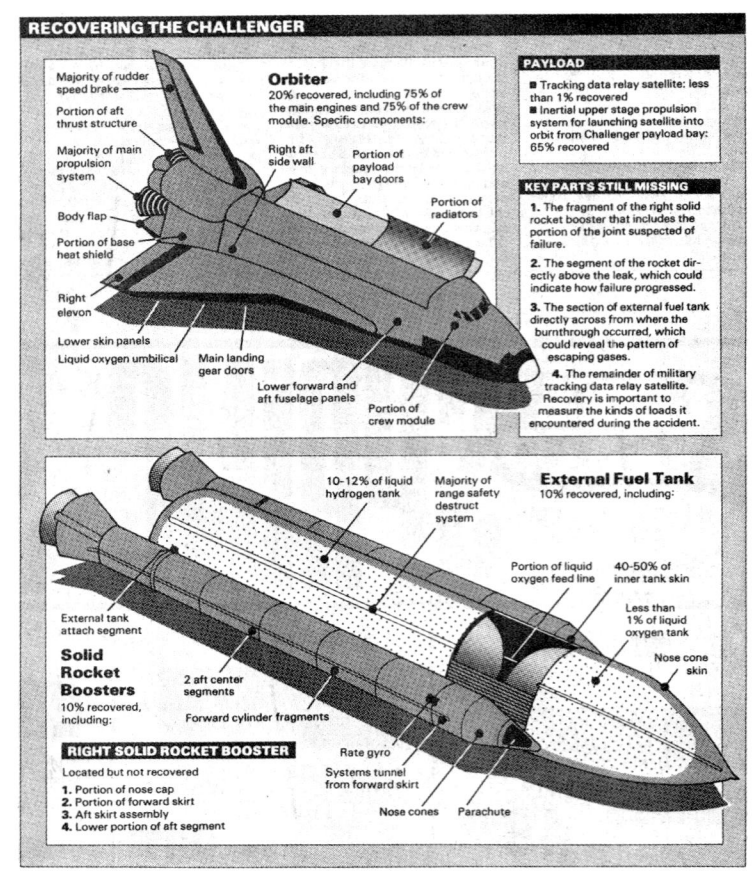

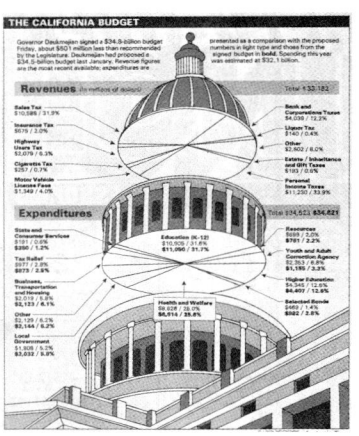

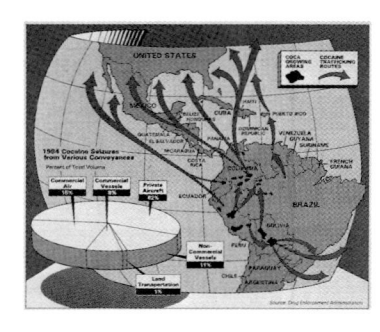

A-F LOS ANGELES TIMES
David Puckett

196 The Best of Newspaper Design

17
PORTFOLIO OF WORK

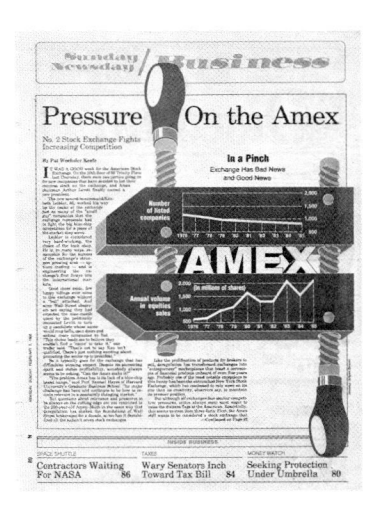

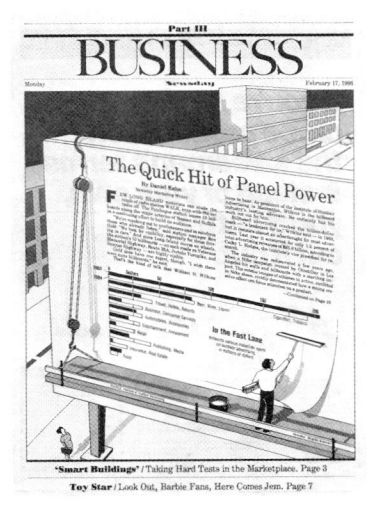

A-F NEWSDAY
Brigitte Zimmer

Seventh Edition 197

18
TYPOGRAPHY IN DESIGN

Winners were selected from full-page entries demonstrating creative use of Letter Forms • Calligraphy • Lettering.

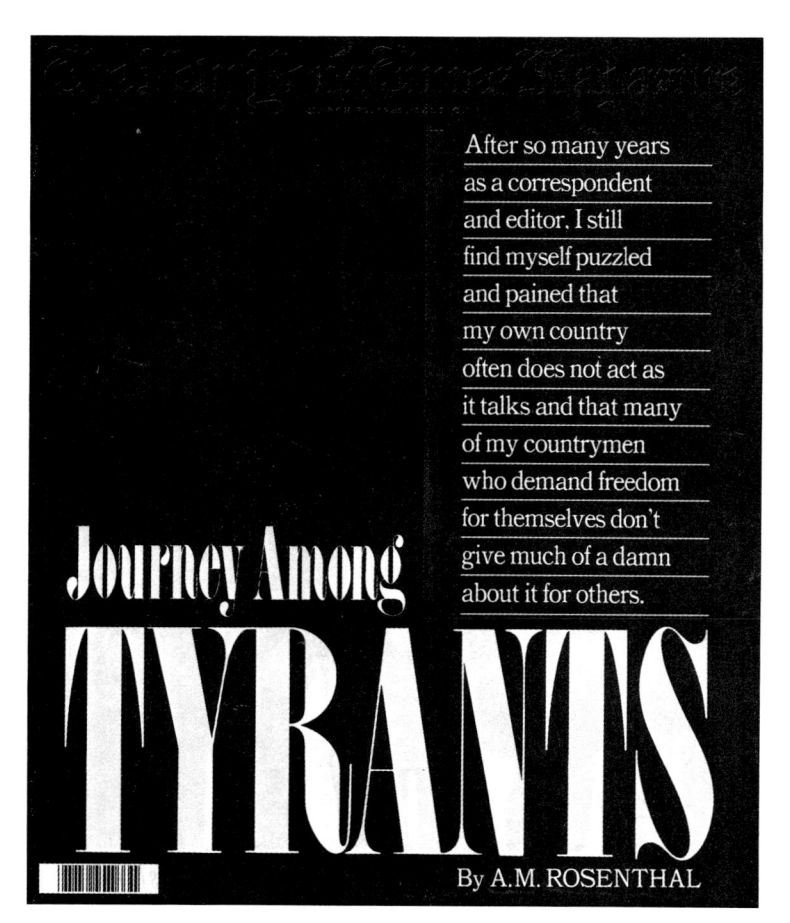

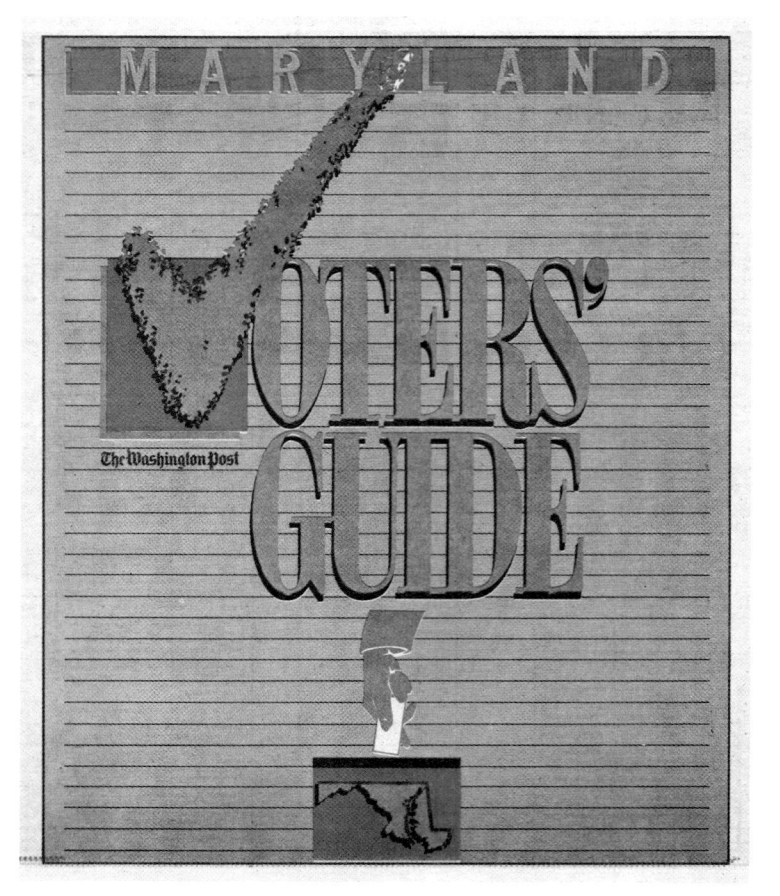

A THE WASHINGTON TIMES
Jane Palecek

B THE WASHINGTON POST
Alice Kresse

C THE NEW YORK TIMES
Ken Kendrick

D THE WASHINGTON TIMES
Alex Hunter

198   The Best of Newspaper Design

19

MISCELLANEOUS

Entries consisted of Special News • Feature Design Elements.

A-D THE SUNDAY TIMES
Peter Baistow

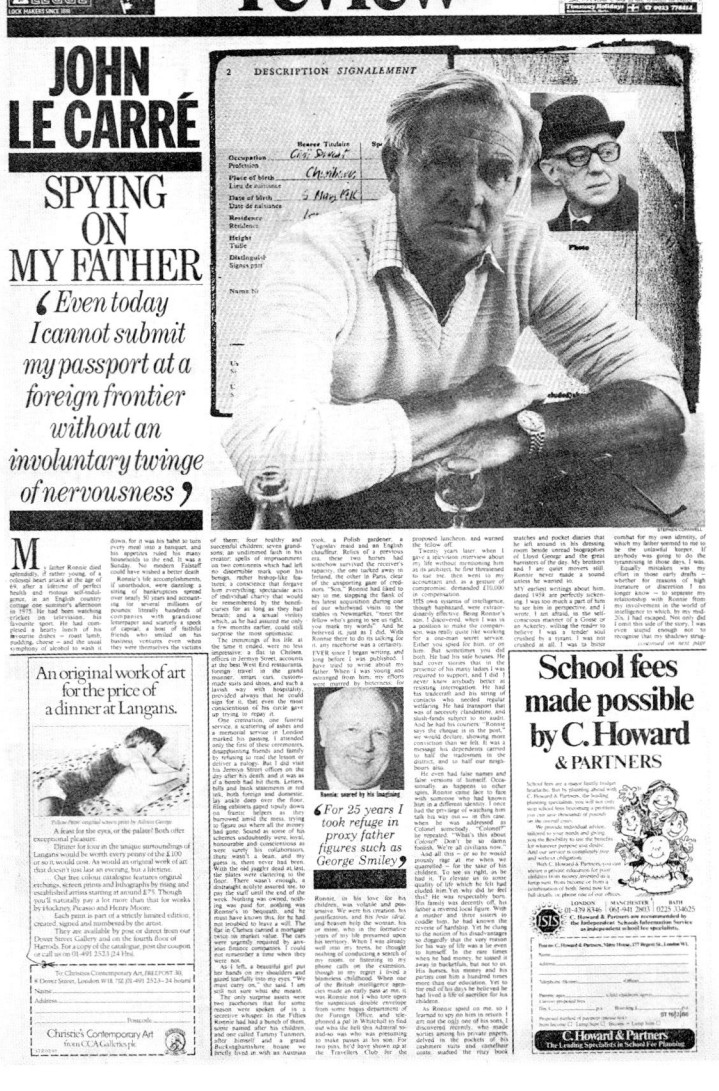

19
MISCELLANEOUS

The redesign of Novedades • Before

The redesign of Novedades • After

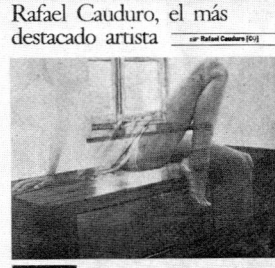

A-D NOVEDADES
Roger Black, Mario Garcia,
Claudio Rodriguez

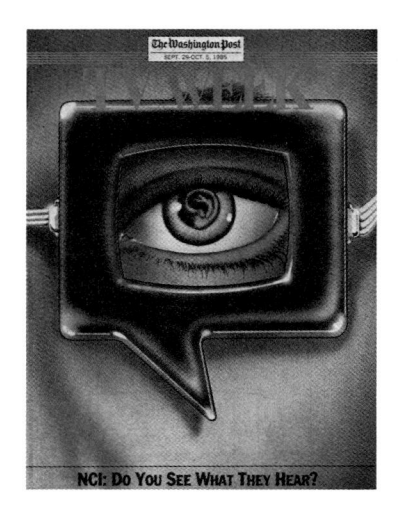

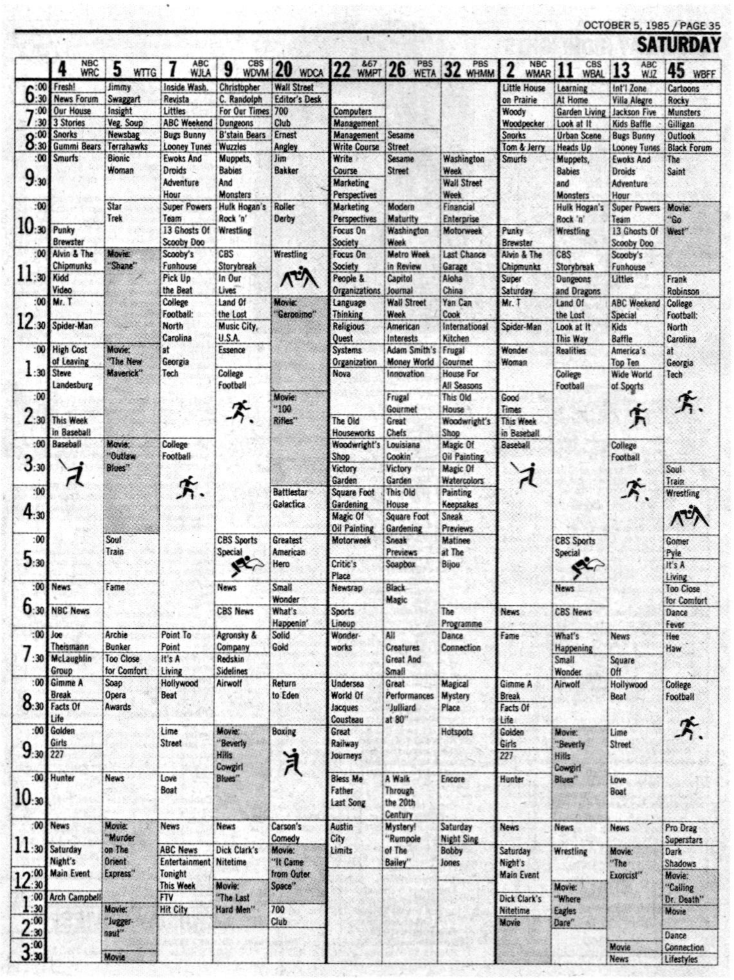

19
MISCELLANEOUS

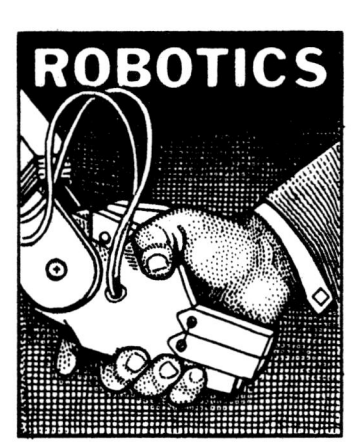

SILVER AWARD

A-C THE WASHINGTON POST
Michael E. Hill, Editor

D-I THE WALL STREET JOURNAL
Greg Leeds, Kevin Sprouls, Virginia Bubek, Jerry Litofsky, Rosemary Webber, Randy Price, Hai Knafo

202 The Best of Newspaper Design

A

A10 THE GLOBE AND MAIL, SATURDAY, DECEMBER 28, 1985

THE FEATURES PAGE

CLUES ACROSS

The brain-buster crossword

CLUES DOWN

THE GLOBE AND MAIL, SATURDAY, DECEMBER 28, 1985 A11

The ultimate challenge of 1985

Answers on page A16

A THE GLOBE AND MAIL
Frank Teskey, Eric Nelson

19
MISCELLANEOUS

A B C

A-C THE BOSTON GLOBE
Ronn Campisi

204   The Best of Newspaper Design

19
MISCELLANEOUS

A
B
C

A THE SEATTLE TIMES
Rob Kemp

B THE COURIER JOURNAL
Stephen D. Sebree

C THE LEXINGTON HERALD-LEADER
Jim Jennings, Graphics Director

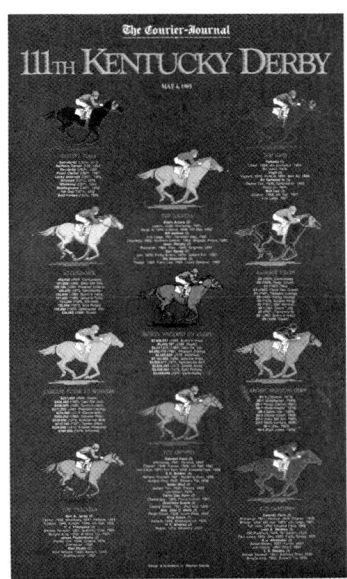

Seventh Edition   205

INDEX

Aagaard, Rolf M. 181
Aasheim, Stein P. 171
AFTENPOSTEN 102, 118, 171, 177, 181
Albano, Donna 69, 75, 84, 111, 143, 147
Aldrich, Catherine 74
Alexander, Jann 123
Alos, Rica 67
ANCHORAGE DAILY NEWS 24, 34, 47
Anderson, N. C. 112
Arisman, Marshall 143
Atkinson, Jack 137
ATLANTA WEEKLY MAGAZINE 127, 142, 145, 149
Babb, G. W. 73
Baker, Richard M. 83, 85, 86
Baistow, Peter 199
BALTIMORE SUN 69, 75, 84, 111, 115, 143, 147
Barkin, Bob 20, 185
Bartholomay, Lucy 76, 77, 78, 127
Barton, Kent 25, 130, 139
Beck, David 145
Benge, George 29, 105
BERGENS TIDENDE 94
Berglund, Erik 177
BERKELEYAN 65
Berner, Alan 178
Bernstein, Lois 168
Beu, Armin 118
Billout, Guy 127, 142, 144
Black, Roger 113, 119, 201
Blessen, Karen 187, 193
Bodkin, Tom 30, 186
Boone, Lyle 95
Booth, Ashley 118
Bosler, Cliff 30, 189
BOSTON GLOBE 63, 74, 76, 77, 78, 79, 81, 82, 83, 85, 86, 87, 104, 125, 126, 127, 128, 129, 130, 131, 133, 204
Boyles, Dwight 24
Bradford, Christy 8, 36
Braun, Marty 80
Brenneman, Susan 119, 127, 132, 133, 144, 148
Brewer, Linda 66, 76, 78
Brindley, Les 24
Bryant, Michael J. 171
Bryza, Janis 72, 73
Bubek, Virginia 202
Burgess, Donald 73, 76, 77, 78
Burnie, Ellen 124, 136
Butler, Chris 21
Byron, Don 24
Campbell, Mike 34, 47
Campisi, Ron 63, 86, 104, 125, 126, 127, 131, 204
Canale, Ed 54
Cardo, Horacio Fidel 143, 146
Carmel, Jeff 184
Carr, James 70
Carroll, Mary 169
Carroll, Mike 183
Casselman, Dierck 8, 36
Castleberry, Stephen 131
Castenada, Carlos 119, 131
Castronuovo, William 23
Cayea, John 22, 147
Chapman, Denise 129
Chapman, Gary S. 130
CHARLESTON GAZETTE 24
CHARLOTTE OBSERVER 143
Charlton, Aldona 79, 81
CHICAGO TRIBUNE 27, 28, 64, 68, 72, 73, 75, 80, 98, 110, 128, 140, 145, 183
Chiu, Joseph 127
CHRISTIAN SCIENCE MONITOR 51, 55, 67, 70, 88, 89, 92, 110, 184, 185
Christie, Jim 148
Christopher, Henry 15
CINCINNATI POST 170
Cochran, Tim 24
Cockerill, Dale 38
Colbert, George 186
Colonna, Jim 17
COLUMBUS DISPATCH 26, 131
Cone, William 151
Corbellini, Jane 73
Cosimini, Gary 192
COURIER JOURNAL 44-45, 82, 99, 100, 130, 140, 144, 188, 205
Couture, Ron 25, 103, 109
Covey, Rob 33, 41, 56, 60, 114
Cowles, David 36
Cox, Randy 25, 51, 64, 74
Crowley, Stephen 168
Cunfer, Elaine 195
Currie, Linda 65
Curtis, Richard 10, 16, 18, 27
DAGENS NYHETER 42-43
DAILY NEWS MAGAZINE 132, 171
DALLAS MORNING NEWS 29, 30, 31, 49, 68, 73, 75, 105, 156, 157, 158, 169, 187, 189, 193
DALLAS TIMES HERALD 21, 46, 65, 70, 72, 73, 82, 84, 138, 141, 142, 145, 148, 176
Daniels, Dick 141
Danzig, Mark 117, 121, 127
DAYTON DAILY NEWS 146, 148
De Seve, Peter 146, 149
DEMOCRAT AND CHRONICLE 8, 36, 184
DENVER POST 85, 86, 137, 139, 142, 146, 148
DETROIT NEWS 129, 133
Dever, Jeff 70
DiAgostino, Richard C. 115
Diaz de Villegas, Jose L. 67, 75, 76, 77, 78
Diaz de Villegas, Jose L. Jr. 119, 142, 144, 152
Dise, Allen 36, 184
Dolphens, Tom 144, 145, 153
Donohue, Nancy 68, 80
Downey-Laskowitz, Ray 30, 107
Driggs, Helen 183
Dudek, Matt 8, 36
Dudzinski, Andrzej 148
Earley, Mare 64, 72, 73
EL NORTE 169
EL NUEVO DIA 67, 75, 76, 77, 78, 119, 131, 142, 144, 152
Ellingsen, Hilde B. Bang 118
Engstrom, Paul 28
Enneson, Peter 117
Ericsson, Celeste 106
FAEDRELANDSVENNEN 101, 122
Fallsen, Tom B. 102
Farnham, David 23
Fewell, Kevin P. 27, 183
FINANCIAL POST 23, 28
FLORIDA TIMES-UNION AND JACKSONVILLE JOURNAL 98
FLORIDA TODAY 37
Frazier, Graham David 38
Fremgen, Jim 48
Froelich, Janet 132, 171
Gallagher, Bob 143
GANNETT WESTCHESTER NEWSPAPERS 70
Garcia, Francis X. 72
Garcia, Mario 113, 201
Garrison, Ben 187
Gaspard, Bill 131, 140, 141, 144, 145, 149, 167
GAZETTE 72, 170
Geiger, Ken 169
Gensheimer, Jim 163
Gerhold, Smith 183
Gilbert, Kevin T. 109
Glasgow, Dale 182, 186, 187
Goecke, John 72
Gold, John 98
Goldstrom, Robert 148, 149
Good, Michael 109
Gottlieb, Dale 132
Gradel, Marty 38, 58, 59
Green, John 21
Greenberg, Sheldon 128
Griffin, David 82, 83, 120, 137
Griffis, Lisa M. 13, 23
Griffith, Dottie 68
Hall, Michael 104, 185
Halsey, Linda 76
Hansen, John 98
Hansen, Svein 102
Harris, David 141, 148
HARTFORD COURANT 16, 25, 27, 51, 64, 74, 77, 82, 83, 143, 153, 182
Hartig, Karl 28, 182
Hawken, Bill 8
Healy, Mike 58, 59
Heller, Steve 62, 143
Hickey, John 65
Hill, Michael E. 202
Himmel, Lizzie 171
Hoey, Peter 25, 27, 64, 77, 182
Hoiland, Sven 101
Holland, Brad 128, 139, 140
Hopper, Susie Eaton 96
HOUSTON POST 39
Hulen, Stan 73
Hundley, Sam 19, 142, 147, 148
Hunt, Jane 183
Hunter, Alex 71, 198
Ireland, Jim 117, 121, 124
Iversen, Kjell 102
Jacobson, Alan 19
Jamandre, Edna 70
James, Ana 124
Jareaux, Robin 51, 55, 67, 70, 88, 89, 92, 110, 185
Jennings, Jim 205
Johannessen, Bjorn 118
Johnson, David 143
Jones, Randy 183
Jordan-Valoria, Judy 19, 186, 188
Jorgensen, Roland 102
Jost, Rick 148
Jursa, Dan 128, 140, 145
KANSAS CITY STAR 131, 140, 141, 144, 145, 149, 153, 167
Karlsson, Karen 28
Keating, John 176
Keebler, Paul 86
Keegan, Mike 84
Kelley, Bill III 174
Kemp, Rob 189, 205
Kendrick, Ken 128, 138, 140, 141, 145, 146, 148, 149, 170, 171, 198
Kent, Nancy 81, 128, 129
Knafo, Hai 202
Knueven, Mary 26
Kouba, Chris 19
Kraus, Jerelle 139, 143, 146
Kresse, Alice 198
Kundin, Andrea 36
Kunz, Anita 140
La Guardia, Diana 141
Lacava, Lucy 72
Laird, Bob 29, 187, 189
LEDGER 23
Lee, Nancy 30
Leeds, Greg 108, 202
Leen, Sarah 159
Leeson, David 156, 157, 158
Legg, Kathy 127
Lense, Ana 20, 185
Levy, Laura Lou 155
Lewis, Tim 148
LEXINGTON HERALD-LEADER 205
Linneberg, Rolf 102
Litofsky, Jerry 28, 204
Loda, Judy 63, 82, 87
Lohman, Phil 51
LOS ANGELES TIMES 25, 38, 61, 71, 73, 74, 75, 76, 77, 78, 104, 138, 184, 185, 196
Lott, Jimi 166, 169, 172

Seventh Edition 207

Lutz, Judy 170
Lyskowski, Roman 30
Mackinicki, Jim 34, 47
Macleod, John 25
Mahurin, Matt 145, 149
Manley, Marcy 29
Marr, Bill 120, 128
Marshall, Ken 107, 188, 194
Mason, Hatley Norton III 85
Massa, Robert 53, 80, 93, 106, 191
Maupin, Johnny 44, 45, 82, 99
McCracken, Steve 76
McDonald, Michael 168
McFarlane, James 188
McKinistry, Steve 57, 90, 106, 110
McPhee, Kevin 146
Mendenhall, Jim 169, 170, 173
MESA TRIBUNE 29
Meyer, Kerry 149
MIAMI HERALD 20, 25, 139, 141, 185
Mikalsen, Jan 118
Miller, David 29
Miller, Randy 86
Minister, Scott 131
Mitchell, Patricia 104
MONTGOMERY JOURNAL 13, 23, 24
MORNING CALL 195
Nacht, Merle 153
Nankivel, Neville 23
Nelson, Eric 203
Nelson, Fred 53, 56
NEW YORK TIMES 22, 25, 26, 30, 62, 66, 74, 76, 78, 79, 81, 103, 107, 109, 124, 128, 129, 136, 138, 139, 140, 141, 143, 145, 146, 147, 148, 149, 170, 171, 183, 186, 192, 198
Newman, Bob 139, 143
NEWS/SUN-SENTINEL 130
NEWSDAY 70, 132, 139, 143, 185, 197
Nicklen, Bambi 128, 134, 135

Nielsen, Liz 33, 56
Nigash, Chuck 25
NOVEDADES 72, 113, 119, 201
Nuss, Cheryl 165
O'Neill, Michael 170
Olbinski, Rafal 139
ORANGE COUNTY REGISTER 9, 17, 71, 80, 91, 112, 154, 169, 170, 173, 180, 186, 190
ORLANDO SENTINEL 14, 35, 99
Pack, John 127
Palecek, Jane 97, 198
Palmstrom, William 184
Parker, Gary 179
Parky, John 130
Pavlovich, James 133
Penberthy, Mark 84
Peskin, Dale 8, 36
PHILADELPHIA INQUIRER 120, 128, 137, 147, 148, 159, 183
Phillips, Al 143
PHOENIX GAZETTE 161
Pinnell, Brenda 24
Pitts, Ted 131, 146, 148
PLAIN DEALER MAGAZINE 127
Porter, Carol 84
PRESS DEMOCRAT 48, 169
Price, Randy 28, 202
PRINCE GEORGE'S COUNTY JOURNAL 94
PROVIDENCE JOURNAL 182
Puckett, David 104, 184, 196
Pursley, Craig 154
Quinan, Johnstone 184
Rakoncay, Frank 141
Razgaitis, Audrone 145, 149, 171
Reddy, Patrick 170
Redknapp, Terry 74, 75
Reed, Rita 170
REGISTER AND TRIBUNE 95, 187
RESTON TIMES 23
RESUME 119, 129
Reynolds, Bob 71, 186, 190

Richards, Mark 180
Riehle, Joette 8, 36
Roberts, Sharon 30, 189
Robertson, Peggy 62, 84, 87, 127, 142, 145, 149
ROCKET 148
Rodriguez, Claudio 72, 113, 119, 201
Rogers, Gary 70
Ross, Chris 30, 107
Rossi, Joe 160
Rubin, Beth 87, 142
Ryan, Greg 26, 183
Ryan, Jerry 44, 45, 99, 100
Rynearson, Mike 161
SACRAMENTO BEE 54, 70, 85, 164
Samperi, Richard 138, 140, 149, 170
SAN ANTONIO LIGHT 40
SAN DIEGO UNION 30, 107, 188, 194
SAN FRANCISCO CHRONICLE 151
SAN FRANCISCO EXAMINER 30, 32, 119, 127, 132, 133, 144, 148, 151
SAN JOSE MERCURY NEWS 26, 28, 38, 52, 58, 59, 128, 134, 135, 163, 165, 171, 175, 179
Scance, Maureen 86
Schwadron, Terry 104, 185
Schwarz, Michael 171
Schwed, Laura 70
Scwanhaisser, Mark 26
Sealy, Gerard 127
Searing, Linda 94
SEATTLE POST-INTELLIGENCER 187
SEATTLE TIMES 11, 15, 20, 33, 41, 53, 56, 57, 60, 80, 90, 93, 106, 110, 114, 162, 166, 169, 172, 178, 188, 189, 191
Sebree, Stephen D. 130, 188, 205
Seelye, Randy 48
Seibert, Dave 29
Setzer, Tom 34, 47

Shaughnessy, Janet 36
Shintaku, Howard 70, 85
Silk, Dave 187
Sims, Gayle 85
Smith Elwood 148
Smith, Jeffrey 141
Smith, Miriam 132
Smith, Rene 77
Solowan, Barbara 121, 127
Soltes, Harley 53, 162
Sprouls, Kevin 147, 150, 202
ST. PAUL PIONEER PRESS DISPATCH 96, 160
Staley, Lynn 128, 129, 130, 133
Stanczak, Ray 14
Stano, Randy 20, 185
STAVANGER AFTENBLAD 50, 86
Steiner, Peter 149
Sterngold, Nancy 74
Stulberg, Paul 23, 28
Sullivan, Patrick 167
SUNDAY TIMES 199
SUN-TATTLER 170
Sundstrom, Tommy 119, 129
Suter, David 143
Sylvia, George M. 182
Syversen, Jens Erik 102
Taylor, Chuck 33, 41, 53, 56, 57, 60
Taylor, Sheri 83
Teskey, Frank 70, 117, 121, 124, 127, 170, 203
Thomas, Jeff 38
TIMES-UNION 14
Timmons, Bonnie 139, 142, 146, 148
Todd, Mike 103
Toledo, Earl 28, 75, 183
Trapnell, Tom 61, 71, 104
Tybakken, Svein S. 122
Tyner, Susan Ballenger 67
UPSTATE MAGAZINE 171
USA TODAY 10, 16, 18, 27, 29, 182, 186, 187, 189
Van Dyke, Tom 175
Vassil, Pamela 107

Velasquez, Eric 145
Vella, Ray 70
Ventilla, Istvan 147
Vienne, Veronique 119, 127, 132, 133, 144, 148
Vincent, Kathleen 68, 75, 105
VIRGINIAN-PILOT LEDGER-STAR 19, 142, 168, 174, 186, 188
Vollath, Guenter 186
Von Tiedmann, Cylla 170
WALL STREET JOURNAL 28, 108, 147, 150, 155, 182, 202
Walsh, Matt 20, 185
Walsh, Michael 129, 133
Waltmire, Chuck 26
Warmbold, Ted 40
WASHINGTON POST 62, 70, 76, 84, 87, 123, 127, 142, 184, 198, 202
WASHINGTON TIMES 12, 15, 71, 83, 97, 109, 116, 149, 168, 198
Waters, Phil 138
Webber, Rosemary 155, 202
Wedding, George 164
Weisskopf, Kate 171
Wert, Mark 8
Whiting, Richard P. 70
Widener, Terry 141, 145
Wiederwohl, Herman 140, 144
Wigstrand, Hans 119
Williams, Elizabeth 79
Williams, Mark 99
Williamson, Michael 164
Wise, Susan 140
Withey-Culp, Deborah 65, 82, 84, 142
Wong, Gwendolyn 80, 91
Wright, Randy 48
Yalowitz, Paul 149
Yarnold, David 38, 52, 58, 59
Yeend, Richard 109
Young, Jackie 23
Zimmer, Brigitte 185, 197
Zucroff, Brad 26, 28, 52